RULE OF 24

"Sales as we knew it has been disrupted. In *Rule of 24*, the authors make the case that product evaluation, presentation and decision making cycles have been so compressed that only the nimble, adaptable, agile, fast-moving sellers set themselves up to close more deals. For those companies whose sales processes incorporates demos, you'll find the section on Guiding Principles of *Rule of 24* to be especially important. This is a sales book that provides strategic and tactical guidance that you can implement immediately. I highly recommend!"

— **Barbara Giamanco**
CEO of Social Centered Selling
Host of the Conversations with Women in Sales podcast
Author of The New Handshake: Sales Meets Social Media

"I have had the personal experience of working with Dan Conway. Dan is a true leader in his field with a passion and commitment to excellence in everything he does! His perspectives and insights will provide you with actionable steps to shorten your sales cycle and produce more revenues immediately! In this era of change... and the ever increasing rate of change, you need new tools and fresh approaches to manage your sales cycle and focus on your differentiation. Dan's expertise will provide you with immediate benefits as you explore the secrets to sales success that are truly transformative!"

— **Tom Huber**
Investor, ex-consultant at Ernst & Young, Citicorp, Fiserv and Sungard, ex-CEO/President/Board member in private equity and venture capital funded organizations.

"Bob Riefstahl's last book *Demonstrating to WIN!* became the 'IKEA' instruction manual for developing sales engagement skills. Now Riefstahl and Conway have seen how changes in technology, social, consumer-like buying behaviours, customer experience and attitudes to risk have massively disrupted B2B sales and produced the new 'superior client experience' instruction manual. *Rule of 24* is full of hard won, practical advice. If, like me, you're reading this on paper (old school), then I'd recommend at least 3 highlighter pens to highlight everything you'll want to remember and put into practice."

— **Don Carmichael**
PreSales Leader, Coach and Trainer at Winning Skills Ltd
ex-Head of PreSales Development, EMEA, SAP

"If you've ever left a sales presentation and wished for more time or more resources, you are not alone. We all wonder if there is a better way to sell with increasing pressure from our prospects to execute meetings faster. Traditional approaches are becoming a recipe for frustration, exhaustion and boring the customer. Thankfully, Bob and Dan offer a non-traditional approach in *Rule of 24* that provides tactical and practical ways for selling teams to engage more in less time with less effort. Based on their exhaustive research and field testing, this is a proven plan that works."

— **Alan Gunn**
Partner at Gunn Consulting Group

"The *Rule of 24* comes at the right time for sales organizations that have felt or are feeling a paradigm shift in the sales process. Bob does a stellar job telling stories and providing real-life examples that help define the change, explain the how and why the shift is happening, and then provide us a solution. He uses his companies research, insights from the brightest minds in how the brain works, and user stories to guide us through the how and why the sales cycle is changing.

Buyers today are more informed, connected, and prepared for the buying process than ever before and I have seen and felt, first hand, how this is impacting my organization. By building on the Demo2Win principals, learning how to do discovery on the fly, and implementing videos into the sales process to make us better sellers.

My organization partners with Bob and 2WinGlobal! and I have completed Demo2Win!, Demo2Win! Masters, and use their Bridge video platform. These tools and training have helped me to transform myself in ways that I cannot put into words. Their ability to look forward and prepare their clients for the future is second to none and "The Rule of 24" lays out their vision for the future and is a must read for all sales professionals!"

— Justin McKean
District Success Specialist, PowerSchool

"As a Digital Marketer, *Rule of 24* gave me a new perspective on the buyers journey. Understanding the way B2B organizations are now buying is vital. This allows me to meet customers where they are and provide the right content to them at every stage of their journey in order to maximize the opportunity for multiple stake holder buy in. *Rule of 24* illustrates the importance of not only how marketing engages prospects, but also the alignment and coordination that occurs with the shifts that sales engagement teams need to make once they engage the client post marketing initiatives."

— Jessica Montville, Founder at Mandarin Marketing and Communications, LLC

RULE

OF 24

DANIEL J. CONWAY   ROBERT D. RIEFSTAHL

THE FUTURE OF
B2B CLIENT ENGAGEMENT

PEACH ELEPHANT PRESS

ISBN 978-0-9951103-4-2 (PAPERBACK)
ISBN 978-0-9951103-5-9 (KINDLE)

First Printing, 2018
Peach Elephant Press
CreateNonFiction.com

ACKNOWLEDGMENTS

The authors wish to thank a number of individuals who have provided immense support for this project.

› **Chad Wilson** was a continual flow of ideas and an amazing sounding board for many aspects of this project.
› **Taunya Bunte, John Coker, Ron Kendig, Niel Powers, Jessica Montville** and former Partner **Ross Jacobsen** provided suggestions and concepts that had a significant impact on *Rule of 24* .
› **Cheyene Grow** is a "master" of video, and we appreciate all of his contributions.
› **Andrea Watson, Dan Weaver, and Jayson Bailey** turned our video automation visions into a reality. Our world-class, global facilitation and professional services team has been tremendous in helping our clients become *Rule of 24* masters.
› Professional support for this project came from our publisher, **Esbe van Heerden** and her talent pool at NonFiction, **David Steigerwald, Robert Crandall and David Kast.**

We would also like to thank our incredible 2Win! Clients as they have been amazing throughout this book writing process. It is our clients that drive us daily to continue to look ahead in the marketplace, to innovate, and in turn help you serve your clients.

Robert "Bob" Riefstahl
I would like to thank:

> my sons, **Trent and Bennett**, my sister, **Jan Kreuz** and husband **Charles** for their constant love and support.
> **Erin, Andrew,** and **Nate Renfrew** are three of the most amazing young people I know.
> **Byron Bright** has been a rock in my life since the first day I could walk.
> **Chris Chiaverina** was and always will be my most inspirational teacher.
> Close friends have been inspirational throughout this project and include **Ross Elliott, Bill Alexander, Mike Juran, Glenn Goldberg, Robert Knapp, Bill Miller, Michele Renfrew, Scott Schramme, Dave Sheldon, Bobby Knight, Mike Gordon, Rusty Bond, Craig Crescas, Eric Thurston, Scott Ellenson, Jim Hinkle** and **Mike Finley.**

Daniel "Dan" Conway
I would like to dedicate this book to my son, **McGuire Conway**. You are an incredible young man; remember to trust your instincts and takes some risks as you pursue your dreams. Your potential and opportunities are limitless.

I would also like to add a special thank you to:

> my Mother, **Nancy Conway** as your entrepreneurial spirit, strength and sacrifices have shaped my life and inspired me.
> **Tom Huber, Sue Falotico, Frank Lavelle, Joe Loughry, Shanne Noble, Cleat Simmons, Sam and Yael Bacharach, TJ Olney,** and **Ron Goodrow** for all of your support.
> My immediate family including **Kelly Conway, Amy Sheehan, Kathy Conway, Ryan Sheehan, Kevin Sheehan, John Conway** and my **close friends** thank you so much for friendships and support.

CONTENTS

FOREWORD

I was first introduced to Bob Riefstahl and 2Win! Global 15 years ago as a Sales Enablement team leader for J.D. Edwards. I witnessed an amazing transformation take place on how we executed the demo, and it led to immediate sales results. Bob had broken the code on successful demonstrations in a way I hadn't seen before, and it had a direct impact on our business. As I moved into executive roles at Oracle, SAP, P2 Energy Solutions and now, as the CEO of Personify, I have consistently witnessed the impact Bob's demo strategies and techniques have had on the sales engagement team. Until the release of this book, I didn't see the future of client engagement and client success models in front of my eyes.

Rule of 24 isn't just the future, it's today's reality. As I read this book, I was struck by the truth about how today's Business to Business (B2B) buyers are completely transforming go to market strategies in ways I couldn't have imagined a few short years ago. For example, I've personally experienced the power of using 2Win!'s techniques for personal video to advance a sale and connect with peer executives in an entirely different way.

But, *Rule of 24* is so much more than video. It is a fresh perspective in a desert of old and tired sales processes, methodologies and techniques that will energize your prospects, customers, and your entire sales engagement team. It will differentiate your products, services, and solutions from competitors before your competitors know what happened.

Enjoy your *Rule of 24* journey as it will help you achieve your strategic initiatives regardless of your industry, market or geographic reach.

— ERIC THURSTON, PRESIDENT AND CEO
PERSONIFY CORPORATION

INTRODUCTION
CHANGE HAS COME

If you've picked this book up, chances are your world is changing. The old prospect strategies aren't working like they used to; your sales process is harder and harder to follow, and you simply aren't getting as much face-to-face time as you once did. Prospects are more educated and demanding in what *they* want you to demonstrate, present, or discuss in meetings. In web meetings, they don't seem to be paying attention and then eliminate you because they didn't see or discuss something they wanted. You might feel a bit like you're losing control. At 2Win!, we reached out to thousands of business to business (B2B) sales engagement team professionals, and the data is astounding. Let's just say you're not alone!

There's a lot more demanded of you and your peers in terms of engagements. Video plays a serious role. Web tools play a serious role. In-person presentations have a totally different tone. You used to know exactly how to be effective in sales, and now you're not so sure.

Even if you're not sure exactly why you're feeling this way, or why this transition seems to be happening, there's one thing you do know: You need a solution.

Well, to that end, you really only have one option: embrace the movement. The alternative is bleak. Forrester Research forecasted that one million B2B salespeople in the United States will lose their jobs to self-service eCommerce in just five years.

LEARN FROM REAL LIFE EXAMPLES

Change is coming. We're not saying all aspects of the Rule of 24 are in play today. But as you read this book, you might recognize some of the scenarios. Others may seem like the future, but the future is coming.

At 2Win!, we've trained over fifty thousand B2B sales engagement team members around the globe. We work with half of the top four hundred software companies on six continents. We know the future is coming because, from where we're sitting, we can very clearly see its approach. Which is why we've researched, strategized, practiced, and refined the client engagement methodologies and techniques that will make you a master of the Rule of 24.

With the strategies you'll find in this book, you'll be able to finally understand why a select few of your competitors are racing ahead of you. You'll be able to catch and pass them—because you'll be riding the wave of change instead of swimming against it.

This book will provide you with an in-depth look at where you're at, where your industry is at, where your customer expectation is at, and how each of those are affected by this imminent change. Because this change is coming—whether it's upon you now, or quickly approaching, it's happening. You can wring your hands nervously, or you can recognize that this is an opportunity for you and your business to grow.

If you're choosing the latter, keep reading. That's exactly what we're here for.

ONE
RULE OF 24

A tremendous change is taking place in B2B sales organizations that is unprecedented. Prospective customers are significantly more educated, resourceful, and directive than at any other time in history. Salespeople are being forced to adapt to this new style of prospect, often against the wishes of their own organizational leadership. Traditional client engagement is no longer predominately a series of in-person meetings, presentations, and product demos, but a blend of digital and in-person events that take place over a shorter period of time. Why? Because the prospects demand it.

Does this mean B2B buyers are phasing out the importance of the customer experience? Absolutely not! It's more a matter of the customer experience is being redefined.

RULE OF 24 DEFINED

First, some background. Traditional B2B client engagements frequently consisted of a seller cultivating a buyer over a lengthy period of time to convince the buyer they needed to make a change. The buyer then assembled stakeholders to create a selection team, which would conduct an evaluation process involving multiple potential vendors. Stakeholders often included lower-level staff members, middle managers, executives, and outside consultants.

The time that would elapse between initial contact and final vendor selection and contract ranged from months to years. Each step in the process involved personal interaction between a member or members of each vendor's sales engagement team and the client's stakeholders.

Sales engagement team members included some or all of the following: business development, inside and outside sales people, account managers, pre-sale specialists, product managers, implementation specialists, client success professionals, and any other resource needed to win business—including executives.

The amount of time to complete the overall process could be further extended, depending on the number of personal interactions between multiple, potential vendor sales engagement teams and the client stakeholders. Many of these engagements required in-person meetings, including meetings between the vendors' sales engagement teams and the client stakeholders—both internal and external.

Rule of 24: The dramatic time compression driven by B2B stakeholders as they demand accelerated research, content, answers, and alignment to make a buying decision.

WHY THE PHRASE "RULE OF 24"?

In our experience working with major B2B companies across the globe, we've witnessed firsthand the rapid compression of B2B decision processes. Just four years ago, a client of ours in the Netherlands contacted us to request our assistance in helping their demo team prepare for a "finals" demo. This, as many readers know, is where three vendors are pitted against each other back-to-back-to-back, providing the stakeholders with the opportunity to review each solution in a scripted, controlled, and judged process.

Much like an Olympic diving event, each competitor must present (or in this case demo) their solution against the standards of the judges. As you might expect, the judging is almost always very close.

Our client had twenty-four days to prepare for the demo. This included reviewing the demo script, submitting questions related to the script, and conducting in-person interviews with the appropriate stakeholders.

Our engagement with them was successful. Their final demo was well received, and they were awarded the business. We were assured of more engagements in the future as their needs and opportunities dictated.

Fast-forward to four years later. Upon contacting our client about future consulting engagements, they explained that the number of major opportunities that involved twenty-four days of preparation had all but ceased. They explained that stakeholders today expect them to provide finals demos in as little as twenty-four hours, with highly abbreviated demo scripts. In some cases, they wanted demos within the hour. (For the purpose of the Rule of 24, we call that twenty-four minutes.) We began to wonder if these same stakeholders wouldn't soon want a demo in 2.4 seconds!

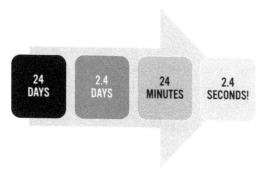

Illustration 1.1 — Compression of Buyer Expectations

This experience and the idea of compression of time for sales engagement teams to skillfully respond to the demands of stakeholders and client engagement teams ignited our quest to research and seek solutions to the Rule of 24.

BACKED BY RESEARCH

As an organization, we witnessed a trend of compressed buying cycles emerge in the form of Rule of 24 symptoms in the demo stage of a typical B2B sales process. These symptoms include more directive stakeholders, more educated stakeholders, lower patience during demo openings and product overviews, more abbreviated discoveries, and less time to prepare for a "finals" event. So we set out to see if Rule of 24 is, in fact, a reality.

In 2017 we reached out to thousands of B2B sales and pre-sales professionals via LinkedIn, as well as the thousands of professionals who had attended our B2B 2Win! workshops. The responses were geographically and culturally dispersed across all regions of the world.

When we asked B2B sales and pre-sales professionals to complete the following sentence: "Compared to 4 years ago, B2B stakeholders...," here were their responses:

› are **more directive** in what they want to see (56%)
› are **more likely to interrupt** the demonstrator to ask to see something of interest to them (48%)
› are **more educated** on product solutions prior to the demo (67%)
› **want access to information** (product videos, demos, pricing, etc.) like they experience in their consumer lives (64%)

Finish this sentence if you believe they represent today's demo reality (SELECT ALL THAT APPLY!): "Compared to 4 years ago, B2B buyers..."

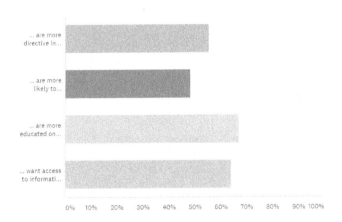

Illustration 1.2 — Research Results

When we asked about preparation time for a significant product demo or presentation compared to four years prior, the overall response was a *41 percent reduction* in time.

Suffice it to say, the evidence is compelling. Data is pouring in from experts across the globe that stakeholders are taking more and more control of the buying process, and sales engagement teams need to adapt.

SOURCES OF DISRUPTION

How is it possible that in only four years, the B2B client engagement process could change so drastically? As part of our research, we sought answers to that question. The result is a rather lengthy list of causes which, taken individually, have minor impacts on change. Combining them, however, is a bit like an earthquake shaking an ocean—with the result being a tsunami. Below is a list of what we found to be sources of disruption:

› Consumer purchasing expectations
› Technology experience
› Smaller purchases
› Shorter commitments
› Empowered research
› Generational differences
› Virtual meeting acceptance
› Cost pressures
› Time pressures
› Sun-setting perpetual product licensing
› SaaS, PaaS, Cloud

CONSUMER PURCHASING EXPECTATIONS

As consumers, most people have come to expect immediate access to information and the ability to buy almost anything at anytime and anywhere they happen to be. We can thank FANG for that. FANG is the acronym for Facebook, Amazon, Netflix, and Google. Together, their net worth is equivalent to the entirety of the Russian GDP. On Facebook, you can be in constant connection with friends, shop stores, and watch videos demonstrating products. Amazon is the largest marketplace in the world, and everything from an obscure part for a fifteen-year-old dishwasher to fresh groceries can, in some markets, be at your door in minutes. Netflix is powered by Artificial Intelligence (AI) that knows your viewing behavior better than you do. Finally, YouTube (owned by Google) is an instant source of videos for everything from sports highlights to product reviews and demos. As a B2B sales organization, the question to ask yourself is, do you really want to continue to resist the customer experience the Rule of 24 provides?

TECHNOLOGY EXPERIENCE

The gang of FANG has had a significant impact on consumer behaviors and customer experience expectations. So has the fact that the B2B stakeholder has significant technology experience outside of consumer research and purchasing. Technology permeates many aspects of our everyday work lives, and this experience has enabled the B2B stakeholder to perform many aspects of vendor research that previously needed to be provided in a document or presentation. Hoovers, Yahoo Finance, and Glassdoor are just a few examples of sites many stakeholders can leverage. If a stakeholder is considering acquiring technology, software, or apps, their own experience suggests they may have been involved in two or three similar purchases at their existing company or while employed with another company. This experience results in a stakeholder who is now much more educated and directed.

SMALLER PURCHASES

Today's B2B stakeholders rarely have appetites for large product, service, or solution rollouts. This has led to them making smaller purchases and commitments with lower risk. A software product or app, for instance, can often be swapped out for another with one month's notice. With so little to risk (in the stakeholder's mind anyway), they are much more interested in moving fast.

SHORTER COMMITMENTS

Connected to smaller purchases are shorter commitments. For example, many software companies have worked hard to transition their business to a Software as a Service (SaaS) model. In some cases, a stakeholder can cancel their subscription and put another product in place in as little as thirty days, but software companies have worked hard at engineering their products so customers won't cancel their subscriptions. (As an example, have you ever tried to switch your music service from Apple's iTunes to another service?)

EMPOWERED RESEARCH

Research on the web has never been more powerful. Search engines are more contextual and, due to AI, they're smarter as well. Reviews, videos, price comparisons, product specifications, product manuals, and product and styling configurators are all part of our empowerment. B2B supplies data for much of this research, but it is often unmanaged, outdated, and inaccurate. Nonetheless, we've come to expect our consumer empowerment in our B2B world.

GENERATIONAL DIFFERENCES

As generations continue to turn over the workforce, there is no doubt that the newer generations have customer experience and responsiveness expectations that demand Rule of 24. Why deny them? As you will learn, Rule of 24 doesn't mean you have to throw expensive human capital at this time compression. On the contrary, a combination of a skilled workforce and automation will connect these newer generations to your B2B products, services, and solutions faster and more effectively than ever before.

Not only is there a generational turnover, but it is not applied evenly. Within a given opportunity, there is often a large generational difference (with their associated technology expectations) between buyers and sellers, and between the different "roles" within the buyer. Staff, managers, and executives are more likely to be from different generations with different experiences and different expectations in the buying process.

VIRTUAL MEETING ACCEPTANCE

Virtual (web) meetings have grown as B2B stakeholders and sales engagement team members have adopted this technology. The growth in the number of stakeholders in recent times and their geographic dispersion necessitates the use of this cost-saving technology. This has led to a global acceptance of the replacement of in-person meetings, presentations, and demos with virtual. The fact that these meetings can, theoretically, happen at a moment's notice means Rule of 24 adopters must perfect this medium.

COST PRESSURES

Both stakeholders and sales engagement teams are under pressure to reduce costs. This translates into a desire for shorter, less expensive buying and selling cycles and, as stated earlier, a need to accept virtual meetings. This leads to a need for B2B sales engagement team members to become more efficient at meeting the needs of stakeholders. The use of video automation and virtual meetings are just two examples of cost-reducing moves by B2B sales engagement team members.

TIME PRESSURES

B2B stakeholders expect the process to move faster than ever before. Once asked to initiate research and purchase processes, a B2B stakeholder expects to find information quickly, connect with sales engagement team members efficiently, and gain stakeholder buy-in rapidly. This leads to time pressures on sales engagement team members and their organizations to be more responsive than ever before.

SAAS, PAAS, AND CLOUD

In the technology space, selling organizations are transitioning from a one-time perpetual license to monthly recurring licensing such as Software as a Service (SaaS). But this trend is not reserved for technology. In the B2C market, razor blades and beauty products have done the same thing, as have clothing, coffee, and even laundry detergent, turning those offerings into Products as a Service (PaaS). As a perpetually licensed product is transitioned, it opens the field up to competitive solutions. And switching from one vendor to another has never been easier for B2B stakeholders who store their data in the cloud, because they don't have to re-invest in expensive IT infrastructure. This means B2B sales engagement team members must move quickly to provide B2B stakeholders with alternative solutions.

RULE OF 24: DISRUPTIVE INNOVATION?

The term "disruption" is thrown around a lot in the business world, and it's often intermingled with the term "innovation." Harvard Business School professor and disruption expert Clayton Christensen combines the two terms into "Disruptive Innovation."

The organization that carries his name, Christensen Institute, describes it as a "process by which technology enables new entrants to provide goods and services that are less expensive and more accessible, and eventually replace, or 'disrupt,' well-established competitors." According to the Christensen Institute, for disruptive innovation to be successful, it must contain an "enabling technology" backed by an "innovative business model" that is provided by a "coherent value network." He goes on to state the following: "It's important to note that disruptive innovations are not breakthrough technologies that make good products better; rather, they are innovations that make products and services more accessible and affordable, thereby making them available to a larger population."

On the surface, and by the Christensen Institutes' definition, Rule of 24 is not a disruptive innovator. It is simply the result of a market trend that, if addressed as we describe in this book, can open organizations to new markets (such as moving down market) through innovation such as demo video automation. However, should an organization appropriately address the responsiveness demands of Rule of 24 stakeholders through organizational and sales process execution changes, they will be able to address a much larger population of B2B stakeholders. Finally, the improved consistency and quality in which a sales engagement team member's essential product, service or solution features are delivered will result in an improvement in their value network—both upstream and downstream. Thus, the full and complete implementation of Rule of 24 technologies and execution methodologies results in disruptive innovation.

RULE OF 24: WHAT DO YOU DO ABOUT IT?

As we researched the disruptive toll the Rule of 24 was taking on sales organizations, we sought solutions. Our exploration quickly shifted from isolated tactics to comprehensive strategies. While developing and testing our strategies, we remained sensitive to strategies that organizations of all types can embrace without blowing budgets, massive reorganizations, or disrupting momentum.

There are six key strategies we present throughout this book:

1. **Video and video automation** strategies that will improve prospect responsiveness, reach, and perception.
2. **Virtual meeting** strategies that will drive stakeholder engagement and effectiveness.
3. Agile and responsive strategies for **in-person** meetings, presentations, and demos.
4. Improving **teamwork** in every event that requires more than one sales engagement team member.
5. **Assessment and coaching** strategies for managers that will help you bring your entire team to Rule of 24 excellence.
6. **Organizational execution** strategies for large, mid-market, small, startup, and reseller enterprises. These strategies are the steps executives in each of those enterprises need to transform their unique sales organization to this new paradigm.

SALESPEOPLE DEMONSTRATING AND PRESENTING PRODUCTS, SERVICES, AND SOLUTIONS AGAIN?

A trend we see gaining momentum across our client base is salespeople of all types performing initial demos and presentations to stakeholders. This approach was commonplace before the year 2000 (Y2K). However, the practice stopped when products, services, and solutions became complex. These products, services, and solutions often had a large footprint, high cost, and complex implementations. But today, the practice of salespeople demonstrating and presenting products has come roaring back. Why is that? Because of the sources of disruption that created the Rule of 24 and, ultimately, the redefinition of creating a superior client experience!

The overwhelming medium of choice for sales professionals to use for these responsive demonstrations and presentations is virtual. Yet, salespeople are rarely trained in the practice of optimizing the effectiveness of the virtual medium. This is painfully evident, according to our research. Nor are they professionally trained on the proper structure and execution of product demos and presentations. For the past thirty years, that's been the job of the subject matter experts who carry titles like Solution Consultant, Sales Engineer, Pre-Sales Professional, In Service Executive, or a litany of other similar names. If you're a salesperson who demonstrates or presents your products, services, or solutions, you will find the answers to questions you may not have thought to ask throughout this book.

VIDEO AND VIDEO AUTOMATION

It is virtually impossible to address the demands of the Rule of 24 without combining new sales strategies with technology. The sheer volume of stakeholder requests and requirements, along with less seller discovery and preparation time, makes automation a necessary component of your strategy.

When we surveyed hundreds of B2B sales and pre-sales professionals, 86 percent agreed with this statement: "If I'm researching a product, and informative demo videos are available, I find they help me gain an understanding of the product and its key features." When almost nine out of ten people are asking for demo videos, well...you better provide them.

This raises three questions:

› Do you have product demo, service, or solution videos that you can put in the hands of your sales engagement team members to share with prospects?
› Are the videos of the quality that truly helps stakeholders "gain an understanding of the product and its key features?"
› Do you have a video automation tool that helps a sales engagement team member send a video, or multiple videos, to a stakeholder and monitor the consumption of those videos?

WHY NOT YOUTUBE OR A VIDEO MARKETING PLATFORM?

YouTube and video marketing platforms are engineered to be passive. That means they wait for stakeholders to come to the website, search, and find video content.

Here's an exercise: Pause your e-book reader and open a browser or the YouTube app on your device. (Okay, if you're old school, put down the book and open a browser on your laptop.) In YouTube's search bar, type the name of your company along with the word "demo" and see what returns. If you are like 98 percent of our clients, YouTube will return chaos. If the search returns any demo videos, some will be dated years back, posted by people you've never heard of, and consist of everything from one to sixty minutes in length—not the stakeholder "experience" you want! In fact, it's a bit like that nightmare many of us have had where we are suddenly in a mall with no clothes on. (Don't worry, I occasionally see a therapist.)

Marketing platforms are more controlled, but they still rely on a stakeholder to come to you, seek, search, and fill out a form (because, after all, marketing needs to show good lead conversion statistics), and the stakeholder can then consume your curated content. Statistics show that there are actually 6.8 stakeholders, on average, in every decision. If those statistics are accurate, that means each of those seven people decides which videos are of the most interest to them—and the chaos is transferred to the buying group of stakeholders. According to the CEB/Gartner website, "The biggest challenge for buying groups is not in selecting a supplier, but simply agreeing on a problem and course of action."

What B2B sales engagement team members want—what they need—is an *active* video automation platform and approach. Good B2B salespeople know the stakeholders in a selection, and they see the problem that needs to be solved. Therefore, they need control over the message. This is done through a seller's curated "playlist" of video content that is freely shared across all stakeholders. This gives B2B stakeholders what they want and need and provides a B2B sales engagement team member the ability to help a buying group move towards a decision.

In Chapter 5, we will provide you with an in-depth understanding of B2B sales-specific video-automation platforms. Chapter 6 provides you with guidelines for the types of videos your sales engagement team needs in the video automation library.

INTRODUCING PERSONAL VIDEO

Personal video has taken the traffic on the internet over by storm. Cisco, in their annual forecast of internet trends, predicts video will account for 82 percent of all IP traffic. Snapchat, Instagram, and Facebook have all embraced video because their subscribers demand it. In Chapter 7, you'll learn how B2B personal video sent through your video automation platform will help re-establish the customer experience through digital means.

CONTENT CREATION

One significant problem video content solves is the inconsistency sales engagement team members have in their ability to present their product, service, or solution in the best possible light. That's why many organizations are turning to recorded content, which is consistently and professionally presented and available for reuse at a moment's (2.4 seconds) notice.

If you're worried about the expense involved in producing this type of content across all your products, services, and solutions, we ask you to hold that thought. We will cover how you can accomplish this seemingly insurmountable task in Chapter 8.

A NEW APPROACH TO VIRTUAL MEETINGS AND PRESENTATIONS

There's no better way to talk about virtual meetings than as a love/hate relationship. You probably know of them as Skype, WebEx, Adobe Connect, GoToMeeting, Zoom, or under one of many other service provider names. The technology has revolutionized a sales engagement team member's ability to cover more prospect meetings and presentations than any other technology ever invented. But the technology is hardly the answer to effective communication. Look at these statistics from our research. We asked respondents to complete this sentence: "When I'm on the receiving end of a web demo or presentation, I find it difficult to. . ."

› avoid multi-tasking (76%)
› freely interact during the session (49%)
› connect with the presenter (44%)

I want you to take a moment to re-read the sentence with each response. It is shocking! As good as the technology has become, and as cost-effective as it is on the surface, these statistic shout that it is horribly ineffective as it is used today.

Take solace in the fact that Chapter 9 will discuss how your team can, with a few tactical shifts, take advantage of this technology when addressing Rule of 24. It's all about how sales engagement team members need to drive engagement with stakeholders on the other end of a virtual meeting.

AN AGILE AND RESPONSIVE STRATEGY FOR IN-PERSON EVENTS

Rule of 24 has amplified the cry of B2B sales engagement team members, which can be expressed as: "If only I could meet in person with my prospects, I know I could convince them that we have the best solution." The problem is, stakeholders don't want to meet in person. It's expensive and time consuming, and the meetings often don't achieve their objectives. The stakeholders have questions they want answered, and the sales engagement team members have the information they want to deliver. But rarely do the two meet.

This collision of conflicting stakeholder and sales engagement team wants and needs during in-person meetings only exacerbates the problem. Remember the statistic that 59 percent agree stakeholders are more directive in what they want to see in a demo? Our research also revealed the following: "Compared to four years ago, the amount of time I have to prepare for a significant product demo or presentation has decreased by..." and the average response was 42 percent!

So there you are—in a key, in-person presentation knowing that you have less discovery than ever before, have had less time to prepare, and you're making your presentation to more directive stakeholders. This tension needs a resolution. You need a new strategy.

In Chapter 10, we'll lay out a new approach to these critical, in-person events—such that your stakeholders will be pleased that they attended, and your sales engagement team members will have accomplished their goal of establishing differentiation and urgency.

COACHING TO THE RULE OF 24

The new approaches we recommend will require your sales engagement team managers to coach their team in new and creative ways. For example, a sudden shift from sending emails to stakeholders to sending a personal video will require coaching to master that medium. In Chapter 11, we will provide coaching recommendations your managers will need to drive their teams to new levels of performance and productivity.

TEAMWORK

As your sales engagement team embraces Rule of 24, they will find that their teamwork in key prospect events is more crucial than ever before. For example, if you have four sales engagement team members on a virtual demo, all in different locations, simply interjecting information during the session can be awkward. In Chapter 12, you'll discover some insightful approaches to the teamwork challenges your team will face.

ORGANIZATIONAL EXECUTION OF RULE OF 24

If you're in a leadership position in a B2B sales organization, executing the Rule of 24 can appear daunting. Chapter 15 will settle your concerns and simplify your execution consideration.

Our recommendations for organizational execution vary, depending upon whether you are an enterprise organization, mid-sized organization, small company, or startup. Execution starts with a self-assessment of what you have in place today for Rule of 24 adoption. From there, you can prioritize and budget. We'll discuss the common pitfalls to avoid, as well as our observations on ensuring the success of your Rule of 24 organizational execution.

Enjoy this journey to the future of B2B
client engagements!

TWO
B2B COMPLEX PURCHASES

B2B opportunities initiate in a variety of ways. Below is an illustration of the methods of initiation:

Illustration 2.1 — Opportunity Initiation

The X-Axis moves from *exploratory to directed*, whereas the Y-Axis moves from *bottom up to top down*. If an opportunity is on the left side of the diagram it means that the seller, through their own efforts, has found a way to convince the buyers to consider their product, solution, or service. This was probably done through traditional means such as prospecting, referrals, or networking.

Directed opportunities are those in which the buyer is initiating interest in the seller's product, solution, or service, by reaching out to the seller. In this case, buyers will often "direct" sellers to their needs, as they already know the problem to solve and have likely begun the process of researching solutions well before contacting the seller.

Moving to the Y-Axis, some opportunities are initiated at lower levels of an organization, such as staff members or mid-level managers (bottom up). These opportunities tend to be smaller in size and have acute needs that need to be addressed. In contrast, top down opportunities begin at the highest level of decision-making power.

Sales cycles for bottom up opportunities tend to be longer than top down, as is the case for exploratory versus directed. Let's look at each quadrant:

Top Down/Exploratory: Seller reaches high into an organization and convinces a B2B executive that their product, solution, or service will help them achieve a strategic initiative the executive is keen to address.

Top Down/Directed: B2B Executive has a specific initiative they want to achieve, metric they want to improve, or risk they want to mitigate, and they initiate an internal project to find a solution.

Bottom Up/Exploratory: Seller reaches into the lower levels of an organization through traditional means and convinces them that their products, services, or solutions will address their acute needs.

Bottom Up/Directed: Buyer, usually as part of a selection team, contacts seller with a defined list of requirements the seller must address in order to be considered and, eventually, selected.

BOTTOM UP/DIRECTED OPPORTUNITY

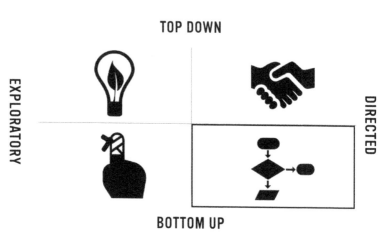

Illustration 2.2 — Bottom Up/Directed Opportunity

A traditional bottom up/directed B2B opportunity is where someone at the bottom of an organization, perhaps at the staff level, is interested in purchasing a product, service, or solution for the company. This is a request that didn't come from the executive level, but lower staff level. It is a long and complicated process, easily taking at least eight different steps of varying lengths—particularly when your product or service is a complex solution.

All successful B2B salespeople are aware that they need to go higher up in the organization with their sales process, or else their proposal will never get approved. A staff member may express their interest in implementing new processes, but they simply don't have the authority to purchase. Unless the solution attracts higher level management or executives, nothing happens.

THE 8 MAJOR STEPS OF A TRADITIONAL BOTTOM UP/ DIRECTED OPPORTUNITY FOR THE SELLER

ONE

When a lead is in this quadrant, the first thing the sales engagement team will do is contact the interested staff member and schedule a meeting with the intention of at least qualifying the opportunity. They will screen for whether the staff member is in a position of authority that allows them to make purchases. Has the staff member been granted permission to process orders?

In these situations, the staff member on the other end of the phone, email, or chat line often wants to know the price, but a good salesperson won't give out the price just yet. They will want to address the price later on in the meeting, handling the request with a response along the lines of, "Well, pricing is complex, it depends on a lot of factors, let's get into it further, so we can determine what the price is." The salesperson would prefer to give more information, to educate the stakeholder more, so they can produce a justifiable price without scaring the stakeholder off.

TWO

Assuming the stakeholder is qualified, they will move on to the next step, which will involve scheduling a meeting for an overview, demonstration, or presentation of the product or solution. When this is scheduled, the stakeholder (staff member) now has to schedule internal meetings in order to gain executive backing. This can take a considerable amount of time.

While all of this is taking place, the salesperson will need to follow up with the staff member, asking, "Hey, can we get this scheduled? Where are you in your approval process?"

THREE

Now, assuming approval from the executive level is granted, it's time to consider the budget. The next step of the buying process involves scheduling a discovery meeting. In the discovery meeting, the salesperson will typically bring in a sales or solutions engineer to ask a series of specific questions to determine the fit of the product or solution to the customer's problem or needs. We'll call this the "sales engagement team." The aim here is for the sales engagement team to get as much information as possible, so that when they do give the demonstration, it is as focused on the buyer's particular needs as possible. This is generally at least seven- to twenty-four-day process.

FOUR

After that, the main demo is scheduled. This is the main event, where all the stakeholders involved in the decision will come to an agreement together—including staff members, managers, and, potentially, the executives. The demo itself is structured around the findings from the discovery meetings.

Traditionally, the demo has a relatively predictable structure, flowing from the sales engagement team's perspective. The team will open the meeting with introductions, an agenda, a company overview, and often a solution overview prior to demonstrating their products, services, or solutions. The presentation could take an hour, or it could take three days, depending on the complexity of the offering.

FIVE

The stakeholder will then have to schedule an internal post-demo discussion to make a decision based on what they just saw and how they felt about it. They have to do this not only for the demo they just saw, but for each demo they see—from all of your competitors.

SIX

There are usually a multitude of open questions after the demo. This means the sales team will try to schedule a follow-up demo or meeting to debrief together, after which they'll schedule another meeting with the stakeholder.

SEVEN

When the prospective client company internally comes to an agreement as to which product they prefer, and ultimately what the value proposition of it is, they can get final approval and justification for moving forward with the purchase.

EIGHT

Once the vendor is selected, the executive will likely schedule a meeting with the prospective company. In some cases, due to the amount of time it has taken to get to this point, the executive might have shifted their priorities to other projects—which is a disaster for the salesperson. Assuming the executive wants to continue moving forward, this meeting begins the intense negotiations for a final agreement. This adds even more time to an already complex process.

A *RULE OF 24* BOTTOM UP/DIRECTED OPPORTUNITY

As you can see, the process of the past was arduous and time consuming. Now, thanks to a shift in buyer expectations fueled by the FANG, it begins with a staff member who, after identifying a problem, goes online and performs research. That staff member shares what they find—videos, blogs, reviews, and other content—with their manager to get their approval. The manager and staff member have already determined the price point worth targeting just by looking at information in the public domain. *All before they even reach out to your company.*

THE 5 MAJOR STEPS OF A *RULE OF 24* BOTTOM UP/ DIRECTED OPPORTUNITY FOR THE SELLER

At this point, the staff member will discuss with the executive the problem, solution, cost, and a few vendors worth considering. After the executive approves further investigation, then—and only then—via email or by filling out a form on the website, do they get in touch with the sales engagement team. If the sales engagement team is streamlined for the modern age and today's digital environment, they already have a playlist of videos that are designed for customers who are ready to buy. These videos may or may not be available to the public through services like YouTube. This means these particular videos may not be able to be consumed *unless* the stakeholder has started the sales process by reaching out to the vendor. The videos will provide an overview of the solutions and will potentially answer some of the questions the prospect asked while in correspondence with the vendor.

ONE

A sales representative will address the stakeholder directly with a personal video to provide context to the other videos, and in response to the inquiry. A personal video is one in which the seller turns on their webcam or video camera on their smart device and records an individual, personalized video to be sent to the stakeholder. They may even send a video directly responding to the buyer's questions with responses about the product's functionality.

The sales engagement team member may have a narrower set of videos to send to the stakeholder's *staff members* saying, "Here's something you can share with your manager," that really talks more about how the product is great for productivity or how it reduces risk. There might be a separate video for the *executive*, saying, "Share this with whoever needs to approve the budget." This may describe what the value proposition is for this solution.

TWO

Once the sales team has sent the videos (which can be done in minutes), they will evaluate whether the videos are being watched, how much of each video is being consumed, and if the recipients are sharing the video and other content with others. This all reveals where the customer's primary interest lies and who else is involved in the decision.

Vendors following Rule of 24 will have a demo video automation platform that will indicate which videos the buyer watched, how much of each video was watched, and whether other videos were watched, as well as the viewing histories of anyone within their buying group they shared the videos with. This information helps the seller gauge a buyer's interest and properly educates the buyers on their products, services, or solutions.

The vendor then reaches out to the buyer to schedule a meeting, generally an online meeting, which will be either a discussion or a deeper-dive demo that addresses the knowledge gaps and any new questions. Note that this may be the first meeting scheduled between the sales reps and the stakeholder—think about how much more educated the potential stakeholders are at this stage than at the first meeting in the traditional Bottom Up sales process.

THREE

From here, the stakeholders frequently organize a list of questions they want answered. The sales engagement team's job is to have a structured approach in terms of the items they are going to cover, especially areas that are competitive differentiators, unique attributes, or something the potential buyer stakeholders hadn't thought of. The sales engagement team is aware of the attractive attributes that are worth discussing and prepare accordingly.

This is the most realistic preparation for the vendor, knowing that once they are on the call, the buyer could throw any kind of question out. During the call, the buyer is in control of what they want to see and what else they want to look at. That's when the sales engagement team has to find a balance. They need to address the items they want to get covered, but also be careful to answer all the buyer's questions.

FOUR

After this online demo, the buyer and sales engagement team will arrange a meeting to discuss what they saw and cover any gaps. A final follow-up meeting is scheduled, and if the prospect has any more requirements or questions then some follow up may be required. Instead of coordinating six people all over the country—or potentially all over the world—through multiple time zones together on yet another meeting, the sales engagement team can get that additional list of items they want to cover and create a personal, custom video that addresses each of those. They send this video to each of the buyer stakeholders, and the demo video automation platform returns real-time analytics about their viewing behaviors.

FIVE

It is at this point the buyer stakeholders are in a position to make a final recommendation to the top executive. A Rule of 24 sales engagement team takes no chances on the value proposition being improperly articulated to the executive. To protect against that risk, the sales engagement team creates a personal video to the executive that clearly summarizes the value proposition and how this product, service, or solution will help the executive achieve their strategic initiatives—in the executive's terms.

In summary, a Rule of 24 Bottom Up/Directed opportunity leverages automation while, at the same time, improving the overall customer experience of the buyer stakeholders. There are (of course) variations to what we described, but the sales process is compressed, just as the buyer stakeholders want, due to free flowing information without the delays and costs of scheduling multiple, live meetings with all parties involved. In short, it's the future...it's your future.

THREE
DIGITAL SELLING & PRESENTING

To be a successful Rule of 24 sales organization, it is essential for the entire sales engagement team (including Client Success) to become masters of all mediums. Today, sales enablement training firms tend to specialize in only one or two mediums, and with age-old methodologies. At 2Win, we determined that all mediums must be addressed symbiotically.

As new mediums are innovated, we encourage our clients to embrace them, and help them with their enablement.

For example, at least one of our global clients is experimenting with offering video demos that load into a virtual reality (VR) goggle. Imagine how powerful that could be if you could give a stakeholder a 3D physical view of your product or solution! We won't cover VR in this book but, look for our blogs for more information as this, and other mediums progress.

SALES ENGAGEMENT TEAM

As discussed in Chapter 1, we often refer to our sales team members as the sales engagement team. These teams can be a combination of business development professionals, inside and outside salespeople, account managers, pre-sale specialists, product managers, implementation specialists, client success professionals, and any other resource needed to win business.

Depending on the sales organization, market segmentation, and prospect profile, the required team can vary dramatically. Market segmentation simply refers to a grouping of businesses into segments. For example, financial institutions consisting of banks, investment firms, etc. is one market segment, whereas manufacturing is another. Prospect profiles usually refer to the size of a target prospect. A B2B sales organization may have a single salesperson address all aspects of a sale to a small-profile prospect, while for an enterprise-profile prospect, the sales engagement team will consist of multiple professionals in multiple roles. B2B sales organizations often refer to enterprise deals as their largest opportunities, with them often containing long sales cycles of six months to three years.

While the size and type of teams can vary substantially, the mediums for selling and presenting your products, services, or solutions in the Rule of 24 are becoming set. In enterprise opportunities, the sales engagement team will leverage every possible medium, including demo videos, web or virtual demos and presentations, and in-person demos and presentations, depending on the goal for that stakeholder engagement.

For any market segment that involves direct contact with a stakeholder, there will be web presentations and demonstrations, along with the insemination of demo videos through a demo video automation tool. For self-service B2B transactions, demo videos are becoming critical to driving the experience of using the products, services, or solutions in to the stakeholders.

Setting aside self-service B2B prospect profiles, each sales organization, regardless of size, should have the skills necessary for building effective Rule of 24 demo video content, personal videos, virtual demos and presentations, and in-person demos and presentations. The goal is maximum responsiveness with maximum effectiveness, delivering the best possible stakeholder experience.

It is vital to have staff on board who are readily available for a situation where a stakeholder calls or chats or sends an inquiry through a social network stating, "I want to see something *now*." A Rule of 24 fulfillment of that request could involve multiple mediums—a personal video, combined with the dissemination of demo videos using a video automation tool, and an immediate virtual demo. A sales engagement team member could also telephone the stakeholder (if their number is shared) and email them (if their email is shared). You can already see the difference in customer experience between a Rule of 24 response and an old-school response.

A master of all mediums will be able to evoke engaging conversation in the direction of the stakeholder's interests and your products, services, or solutions differentiators.

Your seller will be knowledgeable enough to know which videos to send, they'll be notified the instant the videos are being consumed, and analytics will guide them to the stakeholder's interests. They'll be able to immediately initiate a virtual meeting and advance the opportunity.

These days, websites often contain a "Speak to us now!" tab or button that either floats or is positioned prominently on the webpage. This is an attempt to foster instant communication with a possible stakeholder. A member of the sales engagement team could be working from anywhere in the world and be able to respond to this kind of inquiry.

It is important in the digital selling arena to be perceived as responsive yet personalized. There is a constant need to stay in contact with potential customers, especially with such a condensed selling timeframe. By mastering all mediums and being able to connect instantly via a virtual call, a live online demo, or simply sending personalized informational videos, the sales engagement team is perceived as responsive, personalized, and top of mind with their audience.

At this point, intuition may suggest that to stay top of mind, badgering and being very "salesy" is vital. Fight this assumption. You don't want to badger in any interaction; you never want to be too pushy. That sales interaction really is a skill in itself—a matter of offering value, maintaining relevancy, and being personalized. Every time you are in contact with the stakeholder, you want the stakeholder to feel as though they are receiving valuable knowledge and insights—such as something about their business they haven't considered.

One of the largest software companies in the world has a team of four hundred Client Success Managers (CSMs). The most important role of a CSM is to make sure current customers experience ever-increasing value for their solutions—as that leads to subscription renewals. We worked with them on their agile discovery and demo techniques so that every time they contacted a customer, they were seen as a partner with the customer, exploring other possible uses for their solutions.

The CSM would initiate the conversation with questions that explored other possible use-cases for their solutions, determine the desired outcome of each of those use-cases, the impact of improving the use-cases, and the metrics that could be captured that prove the value of addressing the use-cases.

Next, they would demonstrate how their solution addresses the use-cases and reinforce the value. The result was a significant improvement in their renewals. The digital environment allows for many more opportunities to maintain this contact, especially as compared to traditional mediums. In the traditional environment before video demos, the only thing the seller typically might send to a prospect ahead of a demo would be an agenda. They *might* send out some product information, but nobody would read it.

In the digital environment, we can send a personal video introducing the team. That video might have dialogue in it like this: "Here are the people who are going to be involved in the project. Here are some vital videos we'd like you to watch ahead of time, which will allow us to make the best use of your time because you will have a good understanding from an overview perspective of how the software (or product) works." These videos are extremely valuable to busy buyers who want the information and want it quickly.

In the B2B world, there are some people on the buying side of the sales equation who are commonly referred to as stakeholders. Stakeholders have a say in the final decision of a major purchase, licensing, or change in their business. The number of people involved in these decisions has been steadily increasing over time, with research revealing that the number of stakeholders has increased to as many as six to ten individuals, on average.

In the Rule of 24, recorded video content disseminated through a video automation platform combined with virtual meetings digitally reaches all stakeholders regardless of their quantity, geographic location, or time zone.

FOUR
GUIDING PRINCIPLES OF THE RULE OF 24

In this chapter, we will discuss the guiding principles for the proper execution of Rule of 24 across all mediums. Each member of your sales engagement team will benefit by incorporating these principles in every client interaction.

The guiding principles include:

› **The 2% Factor**
› **Stakeholder Resonance**
› **Value Pyramid**
› **Bridge Demonstrating**
› **Pareto Principle**
› **Movie-View Structure**
› **Limbic Techniques**

GUIDING PRINCIPLE #1:
THE 2% FACTOR

From the Olympics to dog shows, car shows to beauty contests, marching band contests to battles of the bands—basically anything involving a panel of judges who score the contestants—the difference between first and second place will almost always average around 2 percent. For example, in the past nine Olympic Summer and Winter Games, for judged events like gymnastics or the snowboard half-pipe, the difference between the gold medal and the silver metal has averaged 2.46 percent.

Why is the gap so small, and why does this pattern exist? Based upon research, this occurrence has everything to do with biases that come into play during judging. In fact, professional judges, such as Olympic judges or dog show judges, are trained to reduce the effect of cognitive biases—but it's humanly impossible to eliminate them completely.

One key bias that skews results is known as "Systematic Errors in Decision Making," or, people using heuristics in decision making. Heuristics are simple, efficient rules that are often used to form someone's judgements and to help them make decisions. These are essentially shortcuts that involve focusing on one aspect of a complex problem and eliminating or ignoring others. Evolutionarily, heuristics allow humans to make snap decisions which could save their lives—fight or flight. We don't live in times where we are being chased by lions anymore, but our impeccable ability to make quick decisions in complex situations has remained.

Researchers Amos Tversky and Daniel Kahneman analyzed systematic bias and heuristics that serve as a mechanism for dealing with complex decisions. You might recognize Daniel Kahneman for his best-selling book *Thinking Fast and Slow*. In their research, they identified thirteen cognitive biases that come into play in an environment where an individual is forming a judgment and making a decision.

If you look at all thirteen biases and their relationship to software demos and video content, there are three that stand out. The first one is **ease of recall**. Individuals judge events with a bias toward that which is more easily recalled. Which means the more strongly your demo is associated with something stakeholders are already familiar with, the greater the impact of the bias and more it can be used in your favor. For example, if you are doing a demo, start by explaining what they're *already doing*, and then transition into how you can make it easier for them. That shows your product while including something they're familiar with. This will make your demo stand out.

The second key bias to consider is **conjunctive and disjunctive event bias**. We all tend to be biased towards overestimating the likelihood of conjunctive events, such as how a product feature could eventually lead to the achievement of an executive strategic initiative. In its simplest sense, we might demo something and say, "You can see how easy that is to accomplish, which leads to improvements in productivity, which in turn results in you being able to achieve your revenue goals."

Similarly, we all tend to *underestimate* the probability of disjunctive events. We tend to assume things will go smoothly, which is a bias you can use in your favor for any demo. If the demonstrator can create conjunctive events in the demo, in a way that flows logically, laying out the benefits on an organizational chart from the staff members up to the executives, then they are leveraging that bias. You can connect a positive aspect of the product to another area in their business using a connective structure, which means those positive assumptions will happen all throughout our presentation.

After training more than forty-four thousand people in sales engagement teams, it has become clear that very few sales teams implement the power of the conjunctive bias, which always surprises us. When you use this method for influence, you give yourself a distinct advantage over your competition.

CEB, a research and training firm that is owned by Gartner, did a substantial amount of research that, in our opinion, substantiates the power of conjunctive and disjunctive bias. One of the key concepts they address is the need for sales engagement team members to use "commercial insights," especially when talking with a key executive. According to CEB Blogs, commercial insights teach customers something new about their business. One blog further details the following three key components of a commercial insight:

> › Be credible/relevant: Demonstrate an understanding of the customer's world, substantiating claims with real-world evidence.
> › Be frame-breaking: Disrupt the customer's current logic, revealing an underappreciated aspect of the customer's environment or a flawed assumption.
> › Lead back to your unique strengths: Refer customers specifically to areas where you outperform competitors.

(See https://www.cebglobal.com/blogs/3-key-ingredients-of-commercial-insight-2/)

If you present commercial insights in a demo, as long as they are credible, relevant, and disrupt their current way of thinking, the demo will be frame-breaking. The stakeholders will accept the commercial insight and how you solve the challenge with your solution. They will then, due to disjunctive bias, naturally underestimate the potential disjunctive events.

This next bias is known as **anchor adjustment**. According to Loren Gary, the Associate Director of Leadership and Public Affairs at the Center of Public Leadership, Harvard Kennedy School, "In ambiguous situations, a trivial factor can have a profound effect on our decision if it serves as the starting point for which we make adjustments." This means that during a client engagement, a single product feature might seem insignificant to you as far as the overall solution and value. In the eyes of the stakeholders, however, that single feature has a huge impact on their perspective and can seriously affect how they judge you against your competitors.

It's all about how value is established. Let us give you an example. Our sales engagement team was trying to secure a contract for our Bridge demo video-automation solution. We were competing with a variety of other video-automation platforms. We introduced the insight that companies that share a playlist of demo videos with stakeholders before an in-person demo can reserve time during the in-person demo for presenting the key product differentiators.

Next, we demonstrated the product feature that supported this. We established our company's value—not in the feature we offered, but in our unique expertise of knowing which problem they needed to solve (more time during the in-person demos). Some of our competitors may have had the same feature, but we anchored our unique value of our expertise in the stakeholders' minds, rather than attempting to sell the value of building a playlist of videos.

Providing a statistic around a feature is another example of anchoring. When presenting a set of product, service, or solution features, you simply summarize what was just demonstrated, and then provide a statistic for which the magnitude of productivity was improved. Now, whether they accept the number or not, an anchor point was created. Even if the stakeholders decide that a 40 percent improvement in productivity is too aggressive, we can always say, "Okay, well let's say it was only half of that—you get an improvement of twenty percent in productivity. Think about how impactful that would be!"

By putting a number out there, a credible number achieved by another customer like them, you create an anchor. Now you get the benefit of the judging bias based upon that anchor. It has nothing to do with the competition at this point. Even if they're looking at your solution compared with what they already have, that anchor just created a bias over their own status quo.

These small additions to the way you present your product or service can end up being the influence you need to overcome the "2% Factor"—the difference between winning and losing. We always need to look for those little things that can add to a 2 percent (or more!) advantage over the competition, whether that's a true competitor or even just the status quo.

When presenting a product, service, or solution, you are not dealing with people who are trained in avoiding cognitive biases.

Whether this stakeholder wants to engage in twenty-four hours or 2.4 seconds, it is unlikely that they've even established criteria for their judging. That's a huge opportunity worth seizing. If you are meticulous in how you present your solution, this is an opportunity to sway their judging bias to your advantage and to make your demo memorable.

While working with an enterprise organization prospect, they had a twelve-million-dollar opportunity. They planned and practiced for an intensive, two-day, very complicated, in-person demo. Their prospect worked with a consulting firm to create a demo script containing over a hundred demo scenarios. In each of these scenarios, there was a scale from zero to five to rate how helpful our solutions would be. For instance, zero would imply that we can't fulfill their request in a demo scenario at all; we can't even modify the software to do it. A five, on the other hand, is given if the product exceeds expectations. Just based on the simple rules of a bell curve, we knew most of the scores were going to be around three. There were fourteen people judging; if we could manage to get a few 3.5s, on as many elements as possible, we knew we could land the business.

We knew the sales engagement team needed to make sure the product adhered to what the enterprise organization was requesting. We also knew that we needed to make the demo interesting, memorable, easy to recall and, of course, effective. If we did all that, we were confident we would receive enough 3.5s and win by that famous 2 percent.

Here's the way it works: If there are fourteen people, and I make this particular element more memorable and more interesting than my competitors do, ten of the people will probably still give me and my competitor a three.

However, four of the fourteen might say, "Well, that was really well done. They did better than the competitor. So I will give them a 3.5." When that happens over and over, well, that is the 2% Factor! It isn't about making every stakeholder happy—it's about impressing a few stakeholders time and time again.

During a lot of these evaluations, the customer basically comes to the conclusion that both products could work. In fact, in a lot of ways, they are very similar—so this is a common reaction. But if you apply the concepts we're talking about here, you'll manufacture a differential more often. You'll get enough judging bias that it will be much more obvious to the room that your product is the stronger option.

Even if they still see both options as strong, these strategies will provide the bias to end tiebreakers. They'll ask questions like: "How well were they able to execute?" "What are their

other customers saying?" "How well do they work together?"
These are the factors that will give your product the edge.

Another significant factor is how much conjunctive
connection you provide from your product to the strategic
initiative of the executive. In other words, whoever can connect
the foundational elements being demonstrated with the
positive impacts to the business they produce, to the executive's
strategic initiatives with the actual executive, will almost always
win the tiebreaker.

The judging process and susceptibility of biases are a factor
in real face-to-face sales, but they also come into play in the
virtual world via video demos. If you consider many Rule of
24 accelerated opportunities, like the 2.4-second situation or
the twenty-four-minute situation, the prospect has less time
to establish their criteria and their requirements. They want
information and answers, and they want to be able to see
something about your product in the moment. This means the
possibility of bias goes way up, since they become increasingly
less formal about how they are judging. Use that opportunity
to anchor on emotional and value-based wins as the demo is
conducted.

Use conjunctive bias, and connect what they say they
need to what you present—and you earn their vote.

They will generally also fall into the trap of **confirmation bias**—
seeking information that supports their opinion and ignoring
evidence that would support the contrary. Most people are
overconfident in the infallibility of their judgments—we tend
to emotionally defend our stance. In the twenty-four-minute
situation, if the first impression was strong and positive during
the demos, customers tend to defend their own judgment—

to your benefit. Often, people will be so entranced in their desire to purchase something that they might not even bother looking for additional information.

In reality, almost every product today has at least a few negative reviews. Look at any product on Amazon; even the great products still receive *some* negative feedback. A highly influenced buyer, if they already have a positive impression, will likely gloss over the "bad" reviews without thinking, placing value on the reviews they agree with.

In a case where the solution is complex, often the stakeholder will have already researched your solution. They have looked at your website or analyzed your blogs. They've looked at comparisons between you and your competitors, posted by other people. They've looked at your company, who is behind you, and checked YouTube and social media, but they still don't have enough depth of knowledge because the solution is complex. The stakeholders simply can't get all their questions answered online. Product, service, or solution complexity makes it difficult to get all the answers through online research. Eventually, somebody will say, "Let's just call them and see if they have the answers to these questions." This is the point, of course, where sales strategy along with knowledge and control over their cognitive biases come into play.

If the wind is at your back and the information and reviews are in your favor, then your product, service, or solution has an opportunity to gain distance from what would be second place—whether that's with a competitor or with the customer's status quo. You present using conjunctive bias and anchoring, enhancing that distance until confirmation bias takes over as the stakeholders defend you as their recommendation.

In the unfortunate situation that the wind isn't at your back, due to negative reviews or confirmation biases for a competitor—or even if they are just neutral—this is your opportunity to turn that around and create positive biases in your favor. At this point you simply can't afford to have a poor twenty-four-minute demo that shows feature after feature in a non-interactive session. You must focus on learning their needs and desires before either sending them demo videos that are polished and drive home your differentiation and insights, or being agile enough to establish conjunctive and anchoring bias in the moment.

At the end of the day, know this: The difference between first and second place will still end up being 2 percent.

It's not an oversimplification; it's reality. Even if you win emotionally, or even empirically by a wide margin, the prospect is still likely to come back to you and say, "You're the vendor of choice, but you should know that the voting was very close. Either product will work; we do prefer yours, but there was only a difference in the scoring of two percent." Now is the time to lean in on the biases you've established and continually negotiate from a position of value. Remember, they still want to negotiate a best price—so whether the voting was close or not, expect that type of prospect response.

GUIDING PRINCIPLE #2: STAKEHOLDER RESONANCE

My high school physics teacher, Christopher Chiaverina, was and remains the best demonstrator I have seen in my life. This guy was on par with Elon Musk and Steve Jobs. I still remember one of his classes on resonance and how it applies to us—the physical properties that apply to our life. The phenomena of resonance take place in many areas of life and in nature.

Whether it's the waves in the ocean, music, strobe lights, or a swing—all these things have resonance.

Thirty years after graduating from high school, I still reach out to Mr. C from time to time. While producing this book, I made an unusual request of him. I asked him to write a few words for me on the physical properties of resonance so I could share it with my readership. As has always been the case, he exceeded my expectations and actually applied the physical properties of resonance to emotional resonance. Here's what Mr. C had to say:

"I'm pickin' up good vibrations. She's giving me excitations."
— Good Vibrations by the Beach Boys

Fans of the Beach Boys probably don't think about a phenomenon known as resonance when they listen to one of group's signature songs. Nevertheless, resonance is all about the efficient transfer of "good vibrations," or, more formally, energy from one entity to another.

In physics, resonance is said to occur when a vibrating system or external force drives another system to vibrate with greater amplitude at specific frequencies. One has to look no farther than the playground to witness an example of resonance. When pushing a child in a swing, to get the swing to go higher each push to the swing must match the swing's natural frequency.

In the physics classroom, resonance is often illustrated by what are known as Barton's Pendulums (see figure below). When pendulum A is set into oscillation, only pendulum C, whose length matches that of A, will eventually start swinging. Once again, energy is transferred efficiently when frequencies are precisely matched.

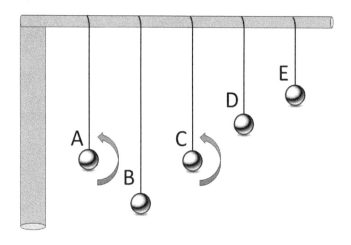

Illustration 4.1 — Barton's Pendulum

Additional examples of resonance exist in other fields such as acoustics, medicine, and psychology. Those of a certain age may remember the Memorex commercial in which Ella Fitzgerald shatters a wine glass by matching her voice to the glass's natural frequency of vibration.

In medicine, magnetic resonant imaging (MRI) uses a magnetic field and radio waves to examine organs and structures inside the body. A strong magnetic field temporarily realigns hydrogen atoms in the body. Radio waves of just the right frequency are then applied to set the aligned atoms into resonant vibrations. Behaving as tiny transmitters, the vibrating atoms produce very faint signals which are used to create cross-sectional MRI images.

The title of the above-mentioned Beach Boys' song illustrates what psychologists call emotional resonance. Emotional resonance refers to the alignment of emotions felt, and beliefs held, by two people or groups of people. Like its physical counterpart, emotional resonance allows for the efficient flow of energy, albeit psychic energy, between people rather than physical objects.

Emotional resonance dramatically increases the possibility for positive outcomes in virtually all situations involving human interactions. However, achieving resonance requires work by all involved. First and foremost, a knowledge of the feelings and desires of those concerned is requisite. Only then can connections be made and bonds formed.

When it comes to Rule of 24, resonance must be achieved in all types of interactions with stakeholders. Here are some quick examples:

› Creation and dissemination of a playlist of demo videos that match a 2.4-second encounter's request for examples of how your products, services, or solutions meet their needs.
› Personal video to the stakeholders early in the sales cycle delivered within twenty-four minutes of a meeting that clearly articulates your understanding of their needs and includes demo videos that address those needs.
› Personal video to the executive stakeholder late in the sales process that perfectly aligns your value proposition with their strategic initiative.
› Virtual meeting and demo that skillfully addresses their questions and needs, which includes conjunctive bias

evidence of the value of what you demonstrated delivers to the executive.

› Follow up personal video and demo videos within twenty-four hours of an in-person demo that addresses all unanswered questions from the in-person event.

When we are engaging with a prospect or client, we aim to create resonance with each stakeholder—mental resonance. Importantly, this isn't just resonance between you and a single stakeholder, but resonance with each stakeholder that is in the audience. A salesperson must adjust for the different types of stakeholders, whether we are discussing our value proposition to an executive in a virtual meeting, sending a personal video to a manager or performing a virtual demo to an individual contributor.

But if there are twelve stakeholders receiving this demo, how are we supposed to resonate with all of them—especially if they all have different interests? If we have staff, managers, and an executive present, how do we find resonance? How do we appeal to all parties?

Before we get to the answers of these questions, consider this illustration: If you listen to a band play one of your favorite songs and one member of the band is out of tune, your impression of the band is not going to be good. In fact, they might sound terrible to you because that one band member is out of tune (resonance). Similarly, we as sales engagement team members have to be in resonance with all the different people in the room.

It's really difficult to make everybody happy, of course—so the good news is *we don't have to make everyone happy.* We simply have to find some resonance with each group of people: staff, managers, and executives. When we are in harmony with each of them, it then allows for them to be in harmony with one another, causing agreement when they begin to evaluate the product.

GUIDING PRINCIPLE #3:
THE VALUE PYRAMID

Imagine a pyramid where the base is the staff. Generally speaking, there are more staff than there are managers; and more managers than there are executives. We call this a Value Pyramid because everybody, at every level, needs to experience some kind of value in your solution in order to get behind it. The key idea to note is that "value" is defined very differently in the mind of a staff member compared to that of a manager, and to that of an executive. Will it make their job faster or easier? Will it be less work when they do their job? Will they get out of the office on time? To a staff member, in many ways, that's value.

Illustration 4.2 — Value Pyramid

However, if I'm doing a demo and I say, "You can save four point two hours per month, per staff member, and that's actually going to equate to fifty thousand dollars over the course of the year," I'm not addressing the staff members' value. Sure, I can call out the name of the staff person as I deliver that message, but I still went out of resonance with them—I'm talking to the staff member about value that, while meaningful to their manager, isn't meaningful to them.

Managers, on the other hand, look at the impact of the features that you showed to staff. To them, value is anything you can justify that will either improve productivity or lower risk. To them, that's value; that's how you'll resonate.

Executives, of course, care most about strategic initiatives and things like the projected return on investment (ROI). This is where conjunctive bias is crucial. Your demo or presentation can connect the feature of your product, service, or solution to staff value (e.g. easy to use), to manager value (e.g. 4.2 hours per month or fifty thousand dollars per year), or to executive value (e.g. you'll achieve your goal of growing revenue 11 percent year over year). If you can resonate with *all* those groups, at different points and in different ways, you'll be setting yourself up for success.

Show the staff the product features and benefits related to them. Show the managers the summary of features and benefits in a way that provides a case for productivity improvements or risk reduction. Show the executives the summary of the productivity improvements or risk reductions that help them achieve their strategic initiatives. In that way, if we present and speak to people who are included in those different groups, we will find resonance with all those different stakeholders.

GUIDING PRINCIPLE #4:
BRIDGE DEMONSTRATING

Metaphorically speaking, your goal is to convince and guide the prospect to cross over a bridge, from their current solution (status quo) to your proposed solution. This involves working with multiple stakeholders, each with their own needs, pains, and concerns, each requiring different motivators to convince them to cross the bridge with you.

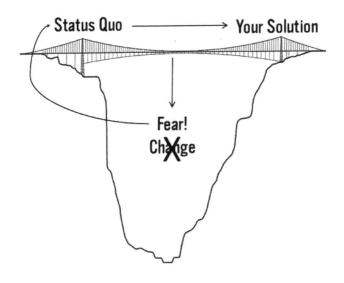

Illustration 4.3 — Bridge Demonstrating

Imagine that a collection of six stakeholders and prospects are on one side of the bridge: they're with the status quo. Remember, they probably already do some of the tasks you're proposing; they get things done—just not very efficiently. They don't like what they currently use to get the job done, and that's part of the reason they're looking at your product as an improvement.

Consider robotics in a factory. A company has people who can perform the assembly, but they're looking for ways to be more cost effective with higher quality when compared to foreign competitors. They're getting the job done today, they have the status quo, but you're offering a different way to do it by combining people with the robotics to get the work done more cost effectively with higher quality.

Look at the groups of people in this scenario—the staff, managers, and executives—and think about a bridge you cross by foot. Staff tend to be fearful of heights. They don't like change. This means we must carefully lead them across, giving them assurance and certainty the whole way. What is going to resonate with the staff in this situation? Perhaps it is not *their* job that is at risk. After all, if they are in this meeting with you, they are on the selection committee and, therefore, are probably going to be assisting and working with the robots in the factory. But it could put their friends out of work—their colleagues. So what we aim to do is carefully lead them across the bridge and reassure them that this isn't about putting people out of work. This is about protecting the business so the factory doesn't close, producing high value jobs, retraining workers with more advanced skills and making their job safer, resulting in fewer injuries in the factory.

How do we motivate them to cross the bridge in spite of their uncertainty?

People will always look to their team. The managers will want to cross when they see that their staff members are satisfied. Of course, managers will primarily cross the bridge if you're addressing their value needs, such as productivity improvements or risk reduction. But due to group dynamics, people are more likely to cross if they see other people crossing.

In general, managers are a bit more adaptable and less afraid of change; however, if they've been doing it this way for fourteen years, and it works today, why would they change it? That's when you have to provide the why—the motivation for why they'd want to make that change. Their motivations aren't going to be about what's quicker and easier; they're going to be more drawn in if they know they are being rewarded with improvements in productivity or reduction in risk. They want a clear vision as to why this bridge is even worth taking their team across.

There are only so many initiatives, especially change initiatives, that they can either afford financially or manage on their schedule over the course of a given fiscal year. This demands a clear vision as to why your initiative is more valuable than the other initiatives vying for their attention.

We are competing not just with status quo, and not just with competitors, but also with every other initiative that they're considering. Those initiatives may have nothing to do with what we're proposing—it could be a factory remodel, or expanding operations to more locations—but it is a change initiative, and they can only do so many of those. Those forces are unknown to us; all we can do is put forth our best proposition, ensuring we can systematically resonate in the best way possible with every stakeholder across the Value Pyramid, and purposely lead them across the bridge.

GUIDING PRINCIPLE #5: THE PARETO PRINCIPLE

Understanding the Pareto principle is vital to your success. Vilfredo Pareto was a 19th-century economist. He famously developed the 80/20 rule, which states that for many events, 80 percent of the effects come from 20 percent of the causes: 80 percent of most companies' revenue comes from 20 percent of their products; 80 percent of the profits in inventory come from 20 percent of the items; 80 percent of revenue comes from 20 percent of the salespeople. This principle applies in B2B, over and over again. Pareto originally derived this principle from his observations that only a vital few of the pea plants in his garden produced the majority of the peas. Concurrently, he noticed the wealthy landowners in Italy (20 percent of the population at the time) owned 80 percent of the land.

The good news for demo video content is that you only need to focus on building assets for 20 percent of your solution. Whatever you're offering, only 20 percent of it— and 20 percent of the features within it—will impact 80 percent of the stakeholder's decision. This means you only need to put attention into building content for those few features—and because of this, it becomes a very manageable amount of content.

So how does the content creation team know what makes up that crucial 20 percent of the solution and the 20 percent of the solution's features? How does that team know which aspects to feature? This is best decided as a team. Confer with your pre-sales team members, who do the demos all the time; confer with the subject matter experts and the salespeople to find out what the people are interested in when it comes to your products. Sales analytics can also indicate which are the key products in terms of potential revenue contribution. Once you've identified these key features, focus on addressing the resonance, the bias, and the Value Pyramid.

From a demo perspective, this means 20 percent of what you show in a Rule of 24 demo, whether it's twenty-four days, twenty-four hours, or 2.4 seconds, will influence 80 percent of your stakeholder's decision.

Think of the Pareto Challenge in a 2.4-second encounter. In that immediate, live event, your team member must determine the 20 percent of your products, services, or solutions that will drive the most impact with this stakeholder. So if you are in a chat window with them and they ask, "Can you show your product to me?", make sure you have staff who is available and capable of responding by asking the right questions in return. Do this, and your competition will be left in the dust!

GUIDING PRINCIPLE #6:
THE MOVIE-VIEW STRUCTURE

We have trained over forty-four thousand people across six continents. We polled the students in these demo training classes to see if they have watched one hundred or more movies throughout their lifetime. Over 99 percent of them answered affirmatively. It doesn't matter what country or culture we're in, most cultures have their own version of Hollywood. The movie industry in each culture has figured out how to get people in seats, and how to keep them there. All movies are based on an outstanding formula that has resulted in many people watching more than one hundred movies in their lifetime.

THE TRAILER

This formula starts with trailers. Trailers are short clips that highlight the best parts of the movie and that get people in theater seats. The personal video that front-ends a playlist of demo videos is your trailer. The personal video provides the context of what you are sending the potential clients and will help the sales engagement team drive the opportunity forward. Like a trailer, the personal video will capture the attention of your stakeholder, and he or she may even share it with other stakeholders. Now you're getting multiple people in the seats and anticipating your live event, be it a virtual or an in-person meeting, demo, or presentation.

ACT I

After the trailer, the structure of a typical movie is divided into three acts. Act I is the opening of the movie. This is where the writer and director conspire to create intrigue and set the stage for the remainder of the movie. Different genres use different styles within the first act. An action adventure movie, like a James Bond film, hooks you with immediate action, and then progresses to the theme song and opening credits. A romantic movie, like *Titanic*, starts with the opening credits, and then builds intrigue with an old woman who survived the sinking on a research mission to find the sunken remains.

For a demo or presentation of your products, services, or solutions, your Act I needs to create intrigue and a prediction of the value you will provide. If that's a 2.4-second opportunity, that will mean learning more about a stakeholder's wants or needs, and then showing or sending them something that satiates those desires. In a twenty-four-minute opportunity, Act I could be a playlist of demo videos for the stakeholder to review prior to your session. Alternatively, Act I could be the opening of the virtual session where you resonate with the stakeholder's key challenge.

ACT II

Act II of a movie is the body of the picture. It contains all the scenes and sub-scenes that tell the story. Producers and directors are careful to not allow a single scene to go on for too long, to assure our attention and interest is kept.

In a live demo, Act II must prove what you introduced in Act I (your prediction). Act II is a series of scenes (never more than forty-five minutes long) and sub-scene items (elements or features of the product or service), that explore the solution from the prospect's perspective. This is where you need to really engage and pull the prospect into your demo.

Think about it from the prospect's perspective. You might have a movie-view of the demo here that is only a single scene, maybe fifteen to thirty minutes long. Or, in the case of a large, complex opportunity, it could be two days long. These longer demos could contain eight or ten scenes, because you're exploring many aspects of the organization and what the products or services will do when implemented. Act II progresses from topic to topic until the demo or presentation is ready to close.

ACT III

Act III of a movie provides resolution to the story. In the case of James Bond, he's completed his mission and now is in some exotic land enjoying his success. In *Titanic*, we learn that the old woman in the research mission was actually the young girl from throughout the movie, and about the connection between her and the blue diamond necklace.

In your demo, Act III must resolve your prediction in Act I. It must conclude with the compelling reason the stakeholders should choose your products, services, or solutions.

APPLYING PARETO TO MOVIE VIEW

The Pareto Principle can (and should) be used in conjunction with the idea of a "movie view." In the case of an in-person demo, there may be a myriad of sub-scenes you need to show them; there may be two days of content, but only 20 percent of it is going to be impactful. Only 20 percent is going to influence their decision, so how can you build your content strategically? Twenty percent will require more thought, planning and time to ensure it's successful. It's wise to rehearse the scenes and set up data around them.

Pre-configure the product. If it's robotics, you might show how it works in practice—how it picks up the product and rotates it—because that is a critical aspect of the assembly process. That's part of the 20 percent. Even if you're in a 2.4-second inquiry via chat, you can bring in the Pareto Principle. In the chat, when the prospect asks a question or requests a demo, simply offer: "Why don't I send you a link to some videos that will give you an overview of the solution?"

To be able to do that, the staff in the chat window needs to be able to get enough information to know which videos to put into a playlist for the potential customer to send as a link. It would make sense, then, to have a library of these playlists to address the various situations that might typically arise. You might personalize it or customize it a little bit, but ultimately you're prepared with videos for just about any situation. But, just like a live demo, you don't want to overload the stakeholder with too many videos. Only a small fraction of what you have will be impactful and relevant, so be conservative.

EXAMPLE OF MOVIE VIEW WITH VIDEO PLAYLISTS

Think of the first video in a playlist of videos as **Act I**—an impact video. It will establish the value of the products the person is interested in. It's not going to demo the product, but it will set the stage for the impact and value that is to come. That way, if the person is a staff member and they forward it to their manager, the manager has resonance right off the bat during the first video, too.

Act II in the playlist is going to consist of the next one to three videos. These are demo videos that prove the insight and the value; they create resonance with the staff member because they demonstrate how the product functions.

Act III occurs after the sales rep is notified of the viewing and reviews the analytics of what the prospect watched, who they shared it with, etc. Based on that information, the rep can summarize the value in a personal video for the prospect. They would use their mobile or webcam and make a personal video that addresses the fact that the prospect watched the videos, and then combine it with an email or a phone call to take the next steps.

EXAMPLES OF MOVIE VIEW IN RULE OF 24 SITUATIONS

Let's say this is a twenty-four-minute opportunity; the prospect asks for a demo within the hour. The rep who received the inquiry might not be the person who conducts the demo; maybe they're going to turn it over to another resource—a salesperson or a group of sales engineers that performs these types of demos. Either way, they're going to answer in the affirmative: "We can certainly do that. Let me get a resource that'll be able to do that demo for you."

The resource might know very little at this point about what the prospect's interests are, but the rep who took the inquiry did a little bit of discovery. So that rep sets up a web presentation or a demo as **Act I**—they're going to open it. Act I is the grabber, focused on the area the prospect is interested in. For years we've called this "End of the Story First." This technique is as applicable today as it was when we invented it in 2001.

Stakeholders don't want to wait for a big buildup to what they are most interested in—your key, relevant differentiator. Instead, put those aspects first (as Act I) and you'll be resonating! The prospect will be engaged, because the product is applicable to their values. They are now going to engage in a discussion and ask some questions about what they would like to see in other areas of interest.

Act II will be a discovery into those next areas, leading to a demo specifically focused on them. This means the sales engagement team needs to be agile. When they are done with each sub-scene, they'll do some more discovery for the next area of interest and demo against that in turn.

This shouldn't be a twenty- or thirty-minute interval at the front end of the web presentation, asking the prospect a series of questions. That tends to frustrate people. Give them a grabber—an entrance into a discussion to ask some discovery questions about the next areas of interest. It's an agile exploration demo.

Act III will be a summary of the value of everything demonstrated, as well as a call to action. In this case, from the twenty-four-minute inquiry to demo, there's probably going to be a sequel. The sales engagement team member, in this case, would create a personal video that contains a summary of the value and includes the key demo videos on the topics that were discussed. The stakeholder can then share the videos with other stakeholders who might be involved in this decision.

In a twenty-four-hour opportunity, there's a little more time to perform some virtual discovery. You could do some rapid discovery, like e-discovery on the web (e.g. their LinkedIn profile). What's their company about? What are they trying to accomplish?

We can also do some email Q&A, or we might be able to have time for a brief web call. All these scenarios are about collecting more information. Perhaps they've got a punch list of things they want to see—ask them for that and they will provide it. In twenty-four hours, we've got enough time to get some—if not all—of this information out of them. The trailer I'm going to send them ahead of the demo will be an impact video. Remember the 80/20 rule; we only have 20 percent of the key content against an area. If they had ten things they wanted to see and we only have time for two of the ten, we know that those two need to be impactful. So I'll send a video with the two that are going to have the most impact ahead of time. And then the prospect comes to the opportunity quite warm because I've already established some bias.

SUMMARY

Act I sets the value with a demo grabber. Act II demos the requirements that we ascertained from the prospect—along with our differentiators, organized in scenes and sub-scenes, emphasizing those 20 percent differentiators. Act III is an agile close, which will contain the value we offer based on what we learned as we demoed, as well as what we discussed in the meeting. We'll then have a call to action, and perhaps include a sequel: a personal video that addresses any remaining questions.

GUIDING PRINCIPLE #7: THE TELL-SHOW-TELL TECHNIQUE

In the movie-view structure, each sub-scene contains a tell-show-tell sequence. The opening tell sets the context for what's to follow. When presenting to a prospect, conduct the first tell away from your mobile device, from your mouse, from your keyboard or your product—because you don't want their attention on the product, service, or solution. We want them to *listen* here, and absorb the context of what we are about to show them.

If you're performing this demo or presentation remotely, this is when you switch on your webcam. You don't want to have the product or the software screen sitting up in front of them—it will distract them from their ability to hear and retain the context. If you're in person, actually let go of the mouse, take one step to the left away from the computer, and set the context. In its simplest sense, it would sound like, "What you'll see next is how you'll be able to..." or include a scenario. A scenario-based opening tell might sound like this: "Next, I'm going to show you how you can complete your accounting month-end much faster than ever before. Here's the situation: All of your divisions have submitted their monthly financials..." Scenarios help connect the stakeholder's current reality with how your product, service, or solution will improve their situation.

Alternatively, in an opening tell, include a highlight they should watch for during the show portion of the demo. That might sound something like this: "What I want you to watch for is the moment when..."

For your demo video assets to be used throughout your B2B sales cycle, opening tells are crucial. The first few seconds need to motivate the viewer to watch the entire demo video. That's why demo videos contain a slight variation to the opening tell. Set the problem or challenge in the opening, and then provide the context for what's to follow with an opening tell much like a live demo.

When you transition into the "show" portion of the demo, focus is the key. In our first book, *Demonstrating To Win!*, we have a chapter dedicated to twenty-four "Demo Crimes." These are demo mistakes we have either made or have seen take place throughout our careers. Many of the crimes happen during the show portion of the demo. Data Dump is an example of a "show" crime. With a Data Dump, the demonstrator fails to perform a tell-show-tell, instead performing a tell-show-show-show-show-show. You get the idea! It is a dump of feature after feature that often contains phrases like, "you can also." When Data Dumping takes place, stakeholders check out. Without an opening tell in front of product, service, or solution features, the demo becomes a dump of unrelated features.

If a video demo is to be used in Rule of 24 opportunities, it is even more critical that a focused show be performed.

With video, the stakeholder doesn't just mentally check out—they actually close the video player window!

Throughout the show portion of a sub-scene, you're going to sprinkle some benefits on the audience. It might sound like this: "So, you can see how easy it was for you to find a product!"

Finally, the closing tell summarizes what they just saw and contains the most important benefit. It might sound like: "You can see how easy it is for you to close the end of the month with a complete, accurate consolidation of all your division's ledgers." This style of close sets the benefit, whether the venue for the presentation or demo is video, virtual, or in person.

To summarize, tell-show-tell is repeated in varying forms throughout a product, service, or solution demo or presentation. It is critical that this structure be followed in order to advance a Rule of 24 opportunity to the next step in the sales process.

GUIDING PRINCIPLE #8:
LIMBIC TECHNIQUES

Dr. Paul MacLean was a leading neuroscientist with published research and books from the 1960s through the 1990s. He introduced the Triune Brain theory: a neurolinguistic theory that there are three primary areas of the brain.

Those three areas include the reptilian complex, the paleomammalian complex (limbic system), and the neomammalian complex (neocortex). Conceptually, the Triune Brain theory is accepted today as behavioral tenets of people during decision-making. Of course, neuroscientists today consider it a complete oversimplification of what actually takes place in the brain, and we all agree with that. Everything is interconnected; there are a lot of subsystems functioning together. In terms of behavior, however, it's a good model for behavioral tenets, and the theory still holds true today.

The limbic system is the area of the brain that is located on both sides of the thalamus, immediately behind the cerebrum. The cerebrum supports a variety of functions, including emotion, behavior, and motivation, among others. It decides whether or not you pay attention to something. It loves sensory input, such as smell and color and movement and sounds. Just like a radar system, it's listening all the time; the limbic system just wants something to pay attention to. It's constantly communicating with the neocortex, the reptilian complex, and all the subsystems of the brain.

Compared to other areas of the brain, it processes information very slowly. Therefore, it's easily overwhelmed. For example, have you ever been in a meeting where someone couldn't stop clicking their pen? At times like that, you know something important is being discussed, but you get so annoyed you simply can't focus; you really, really want them to stop. That's your limbic system being overwhelmed. Remember the Data Dump demo crime we referred to earlier? Imagine how overwhelmed the limbic system becomes when a demonstrator shows feature after feature after feature, jumping from screen to screen to screen!

The limbic system has a desire to lock onto something; it wants to tell the neocortex, "Hey, pay attention to this and remember it." In presenting a product demo, a good opening tell is critical. Done properly, you're directing the limbic system to something this stakeholder is interested in solving or improving. The key is mapping out methods for keeping your stakeholders engaged.

Storytelling videos, props, current events, and curiosity are all very limbic. Numbers, facts, and figures are limbic—as long as there isn't an overwhelming volume of numbers. Movement is limbic, but not too much movement. You like somebody who's doing a keynote speech that doesn't stand behind the podium like a statue, but you don't want them constantly pacing across the stage. Your limbic system will start to feel anxious. "Is there a tiger in the room? Should I be worried about a tiger? What is this person nervous about?"

Using people's names is very limbic. Analogies, drawings, pictures, all these are limbic. There are ways to enhance the limbic quality of your video content, as well as in your demos and presentations. Let's say you quote an expert, saying: "Companies that implement video automation will find that their revenue growth will far exceed their competitors'." Well, okay, that's limbic—but to who? Is it limbic to the staff? No. It's limbic to the executive, because it addresses their strategic initiative. That means as a presenter, we want to call out the executive by name. "Karen, this is what Video Eye had to say."

"Our research proves that companies that use video automation in sales motions will improve their revenue"
Kelly McNamara – Video Eye

"The Bridge video automation returned our investment in just 7 months!"
Sven Dahlen – Sweden Commercial

Bridge © 2019 ZWin Globe LLC All rights reserved

The illustration on the previous page contains four limbic techniques.

The first are two quotes. Quotes from experts and customers can be very limbic. In a virtual or in-person presentation, it is important to read the quote out loud. Reading aloud is also limbic. Everybody has been taught to never read slides, but there is an exception to that rule. If you put a quote on the screen, you should read the quote word for word, because some of your stakeholders will be auditory learners (versus visual, written or kinesthetic), they'll listen to you—and for them, that's limbic.

The second limbic technique in these illustrations is the positive image that was connected to the prospect's initiatives earlier in the demo or presentation.

The third limbic is a statistic. Statistics, presented properly, are also limbic. We subconsciously anchor the stakeholders' thinking around a positive image *and* the statistic.

Finally, this illustration contains a fourth limbic: an industry expert (Video Eye).

Limbics are a powerful way to grab the attention of your audience if used responsibly. With the ever-increasing complexity of products, services, and solutions, it is all too easy to overwhelm the limbic system with too much information. Resist this temptation by treating the limbic system with the care it demands.

Throughout this book we will refer to these guiding principles. They are the foundation of success in Rule of 24 opportunities. In the chapters that follow, we will delve deep into how these guiding principles enhance your ability to perform winning presentations and demos to your stakeholders across all mediums of delivery.

FIVE
VIDEO AUTOMATION

So far, you've heard a great deal about video automation. For clarity purposes, we define video automation as a cloud-based software solution that combines personal videos with pre-recorded and cataloged video content. This can be assembled into a playlist by a sales engagement team member and sent electronically to multiple B2B buying stakeholders via email, social networking, and group conferencing tools. Stakeholder viewing history is trackable and stored for analysis by the sales engagement team and content managers.

In the simplest sense, video automation allows a sales engagement team member who has an internet-connected device to send one or multiple stakeholders a collection of videos to watch, in order to move that stakeholder through the sales process faster than without video automation.

There are a variety of specific use-cases throughout the sales process that are addressed by a video automation tool, which we will discuss at length later on. For now, consider this use-case from one of my opportunities.

Midway through the completion of research for this book, I began providing keynote speeches on the topic of Rule of 24. I received an email promoting a conference in Barcelona that brought together sales-enablement executives from all across Europe to learn and discuss the latest trends in helping sales engagement teams succeed. This was the perfect platform for us to expose the European community to our breakthrough. We even discussed the possibility of securing business for 2Win! Bridge, our video automation tool, and 2Win! training and consulting services as a successful outcome. The problem was, the lineup of speakers was already in place and the conference was only four weeks away.

Not to be deterred, I researched the board members of the association behind the conference and created a personal video that revealed the Rule of 24 insights, explained that I could be a perfect late-add to their featured speakers and, as a call to action in the personal video, requested that they watch the other videos I included in the playlist. Those videos from our video library provided highlights of speeches I had given on Rule of 24. I went on to explain in the personal video that I would contact them as soon as they watched the videos. The personal video was fifty-eight seconds in length, and the highlight reel was just over two minutes.

As part of my research, I determined how to contact four of the six board members. Two were through age-old LinkedIn connections, and two had exposed their email addresses.

Using our video automation tool, I uploaded my personal video, which I captured using a high-quality webcam (okay, it was ninety-nine dollars) and a lavalier microphone (twenty-nine dollars) connected to my laptop. Inside the tool, I created individual, personalized sharelinks (URLs) that included the name of every board member within the link. (That helps improve the chances that someone will click on the link.) Those links were then placed behind a clickable image that included a play button and their conference logo, and I waited for viewing notifications from the video automation tool.

One of the four board members clicked on the image that automatically opened a webpage and played the personal video. He watched all fifty-eight seconds of the video. He then watched 90 percent of the highlight reel.

The moment he began watching the video, the tool notified me and I immediately sent a second message to him with a link to my calendar asking him to select one of my available time slots so we could discuss the value a Rule of 24 keynote would have for their conference. He didn't schedule that meeting. However, what he did do was share my original message with the video link with all five of the other board members. Suddenly, two more board members were watching the videos from his share! You'd be right to conclude that the likelihood of someone clicking on a link or image that connects them to your videos increases dramatically if it comes from a trusted and known source.

The end of the story is that they hired me to provide that keynote speech, even though I never once spoke to them. The entire B2B transaction took place digitally—with video as the center point of the sales process.

You may not sell speeches or training services, but if you've read this far into the book, it's likely that you offer B2B products, services, or solutions to multiple stakeholders—and it can be an incredible challenge just to reach them with your key insights, messages, and value. In fact, according to Miller Heiman Group, a leading sales research firm, 86 percent of salespeople struggle with consistently delivering a relevant value proposition that gets a customer to take action. Video, on the other hand, gives a sales engagement team member the chance to craft, rehearse, and record the perfect "take" of a relevant value proposition and share it with all key stakeholders.

And here's something you may not have considered: if you send your value proposition to one of your key stakeholders, and they forward it to the top executive, you know the value proposition is being delivered exactly as you want it. If Miller Heiman is correct, and only 14 percent of salespeople can deliver an effective value proposition, what are the chances that one of your stakeholders who has no training in value propositions can deliver it correctly on your behalf? Do you really want to take that risk?

KEY COMPONENTS TO VIDEO AUTOMATION TOOLS

PLAYER

When looking at which video automation tools to use, there a few key things to consider. Video automation tools should start with the player in mind, because that's what the stakeholder uses. It should not be user or password controlled, nor should it require a mobile application. Rather, it should be a webapp that runs inside of the standard browsers (Internet Explorer, Chrome, Edge, Firefox, Safari). There are some video automation tools that embed the video into the transport mechanism, such as within an email message. In a B2B environment, that simply won't do. Corporate spam filters can flag these emails as dangerous, so they never reach the intended recipient.

Worse, this can sometimes cause "blacklisting" of the sales engagement team's company on internet servers, and they'll never be able to get through to anyone!

Illustration 5.1 — Video Player Example

The player application should have all the usual video controls—volume control, play, pause, stop, rewind, and fast-forward. It also needs to be smart enough to detect the speed of someone's internet connection, so it can automatically adjust the quality of the video to avoid annoying starting and stopping (buffering) of the video. Players should have an easy way for a stakeholder to switch between videos, find and watch related videos, contact one or multiple members of the sales engagement team, and share the videos with other stakeholders. Players are also responsible for collecting viewing history and transmitting that history back to the sales engagement team.

SHARE BUILDER

When a member of the sales engagement team decides to send videos to a stakeholder, he or she must create, at a minimum, a hyperlink that is clickable by the stakeholder. When the stakeholder clicks the link, the link automatically loads the video player and the videos included in the share. This collection of videos is called a playlist.

This backend area of the video automation platform can be a webapp that is user and password controlled. The functionality within share builders vary but, at a minimum, should include the ability to easily find video content to include in a playlist, modify titles, call to action buttons and determine how much freedom a stakeholder has with regard to loading and viewing additional videos. This gives the sales engagement team member the flexibility and control needed to create a playlist and contain the stakeholder's research to the topics being discussed.

CONTENT MANAGEMENT

This area of the webapp is also user and password controlled. One or more users of the video automation platform will be considered content managers. As such, they need the ability to load videos into the sales engagement team's content library for repeated use (as opposed to personal videos that are usually one-time use). Content managers need the ability within the webapp to index the videos with extensive titles, keywords, categories, and tags for easy search and retrieval. They also need to mark videos as "public" or "private" to avoid certain videos from being exposed to a stakeholder unless it is purposefully included in a playlist.

A content manager needs the ability to assemble standard playlists of videos and store those playlists for use by the sales engagement team.

An example of a playlist could be a product overview and two demo videos of the functionality of the product. This simplifies the job of sales engagement team members, as they don't have to always create a share list of commonly grouped videos.

ADMINISTRATION

B2B video automation tools include user validation and thus, administrative areas of the webapp are required. Administrators provision users, as well as manage and monitor user activity. Other typical administrative duties apply, such as performing white-labeling (personalizing the look of the site), enabling integrations to CRMs such as Salesforce.com, and password resets.

ANALYTICS

This area of the solution provides unique differentiation to public domain video sites like YouTube. When a stakeholder views a video, the player records all of their viewing behaviors. These behaviors include how much of each video was watched, the number of times it was watched, whether they scrubbed forward (fast-forward) in a video, if they shared a video or a playlist of videos, etc. This data is fed to the analytics engine, which answers questions such as:

> › What are our most popular videos?
> › Which videos are rarely played?
> › What is the best day of the week to send a playlist of videos to a stakeholder?
> › Did the stakeholder share the playlist of videos with someone else?
> › Did the stakeholder explore other videos? Which ones?
> › Which sales engagement team member is sending the most playlists?
> › Which sales engagement team member has the greatest open rate with stakeholders?

As you're no doubt gathering, the possibilities of what analytics can tell you is remarkable and insightful. As a sales engagement team member, you know the moment your stakeholder is engaging with your content, what they are most and least interested in, and whether or not they are sharing it with others.

Sales managers have the ability to determine which team members are successful in connecting with stakeholders and, when analyzed against sales cycle velocity and close rates, which approaches are most successful and least successful.

Content managers can analyze the stakeholder viewing completion rates for each piece of video content, which is generally indicative of the success of a video. They can also look for drop-off rates. If a video that is two minutes twenty-four seconds in length is consistently stopped between one minute twenty-three seconds and one minute thirty-four seconds, they know to analyze that specific time period for issues such as quality of content, sound, or frame problems.

Finally, administrators can analyze all statistics related to the site, content, and user activity. This helps them determine the value of the solution and, when renewal time approaches, whether they want to continue licensing the tool.

MOBILE APP

Video automation usage requires a mobile interface for both stakeholders and sales engagement team members. There is, however, no requirement for the app to be iOS (Apple) or Android (Google) resident apps. In fact, you don't want the player to *require* an app. To require a stakeholder to download an app in order to watch a video would destroy viewing rates; they'd rarely go to that effort. The video automation player should operate on any mobile browser to maintain simplicity and universal use.

There is an argument that a mobile app could be built for use by the sales engagement team members, as the app could run independent of internet coverage; however, this adds significant complexity to the overall application that simply isn't necessary. Much more can be done if the app is browser-based, and with internet coverage through mobile devices at an all-time high, simplicity outweighs the benefits of a mobile-resident app.

ARTIFICIAL INTELLIGENCE

The idea that software can learn from patterns and become more intelligent over time has taken on new energy in recent years. Within a video automation tool there is tremendous potential value in leveraging artificial intelligence (AI).

Netflix is one of AI technology's most valuable and influential companies. While it's true that they sell entertainment to consumers, they do so using very sophisticated software and video streaming algorithms, such that you can search for and watch a movie or program on any device connected to the internet at any time from anyplace.

Netflix leverages AI in a simple yet unique way that positively impacts their ability to effectively and consistently secure subscription renewals from their customers. Their AI watches your viewing characteristics and behavior, and suggests titles you might be interested in. This greatly simplifies the search for a good title and genre of movie or series.

Video automation tools can do the same thing for you and your stakeholders. For example, your company might have multiple divisions and product lines that carry with them hundreds of possible videos. AI can determine, based on your selection history, titles that are aligned with your selling motions. It could learn which videos are most frequently connected with the wins across the entire global division's sales engagement team and suggests those videos for a playlist.

For stakeholders, it would know, based on what they just watched, other videos they might find of interest. Of course, as a sales engagement team member, you may want to turn that switch off from time to time so as to not delay a decision!

Another excellent use of AI is transcription and word/phrase recognition. Consider for a moment sales engagement teams in highly regulated markets such as investments, insurance, or pharmaceuticals. In regulated markets, certain words and phrases are considered non-compliant and, as such, never allowed on company materials or correspondence.

For example, in investment markets the word "guaranteed" is allowed in very limited uses and never with commodities. Therefore, companies may like the idea of video automation, but don't want the potential liability of a sales engagement team member recording a forbidden word or phrase. AI can solve that issue. It is like your own regulatory compliance lawyer listening for and rejecting phrases. The irony is it makes videos more likely to be in compliance than a live interaction!

Video automation is in its infancy, and as the market grows and matures, innovation will develop well beyond the scope of what we've just described. However, even in its infancy, video automation can have a significant impact on your sales engagement team's ability to address the demands of the Rule of 24, competitively differentiate your offerings, and compress your sales cycles.

VIDEO AUTOMATION PLATFORM INTEGRATIONS

Most video automation platforms provide integrations or connections to other cloud-based software solutions. The most common integration is with a Customer Relationship Management (CRM) solution such as Salesforce.com. This means that if a video playlist is sent to a stakeholder, the video automation platform will record the critical information against the proper contact record within the CRM system, and record all the viewing history.

Video automation platforms also provide integrations to marketing automation platforms such as Hubspot, email platforms such as Mailchimp, and social platforms such as LinkedIn.

Integrations make the process of finding and recording information easy for sales engagement team members, as well as sharing analytics so that your organization is always well informed.

INNER WORKINGS OF VIDEO AUTOMATION PLATFORMS

There are a lot of platforms available for delivering your video, but with that comes a lot of considerations when choosing the most appropriate one for you to use. More than likely, when you look at a hosted platform, it's in the cloud. Hosted cloud solutions provide the benefit of running the platform without the need for expensive infrastructure, software maintenance, and complex video-encoding software. All those functions are managed by the video automation platform.

ENCODING

The process of video encoding is when a video source file is processed and output to a variety of formats such that no matter what computer, mobile device, or browser someone is using, the video will properly play.

Assume you pulled your iPhone out of your pocket, clicked on the camera, swiped to the video option, and recorded a quick personal video you want to send to a stakeholder to introduce yourself and set additional context for your meeting in two days. Wow, recording the video was simple! Now, how do you get it to your prospect, and how do they play the video on their Google phone?

Here's part of the problem. When an iPhone creates a video file, it records it in an Apple proprietary format that contains a .mov file extension. The file is usually too large to email as an attachment. Even if it could be emailed, the stakeholder has no interest in waiting for a large file to download. Finally, the stakeholder is using a Google phone that may or may not be able to play a .mov file. Now mix into this a stakeholder running on an ancient Windows 8 machine running an Opera browser.

All these issues are solved by a cloud-based platform that takes your large .mov file and encodes it into dozens of possible formats so that almost any browser on any device can play the video without having to download it through email.

A good platform is one that is not only going to encode in everything you'd ever want it to play on, but it's also going to place those videos on cloud-based servers that are physically located all over the world.

That way, your stakeholders receive the video from the server closest to their office, even if it's in Bucharest, and the performance is as good as it could possibly be.

HLS

HLS is a technology that intelligently identifies a stakeholder's internet connection speed. HLS technology automatically upgrades or downgrades the quality of the video based on that connection speed. Many people are familiar with this in

YouTube, where you can select the quality of the video to speed up your streaming speed.

HLS *automatically* selects the best possible video quality based upon the viewer's connection speed, which can be both good and bad. If it's a product demo, losing high-definition means losing the details of the product itself. As part of your strategy, you need to consider where, geographically, most of your stakeholders will reside.

For example, if you know that you will have a significant number of stakeholders in parts of the world that still don't support good internet speed, you may want to adjust how you record a demo video. This could include how much you want to zoom in to a software screen or a product feature. If you know that location doesn't have very good connection speed, instead, zoom into what you're showing so that a viewer without high speed internet can still properly experience your product.

ANALYTICS

Another indicator to look at when choosing a platform is the types of analytics the platform provides. We've already learned about the analytics a platform should give you. What can the platform tell you about all the people playing your videos? In a B2B selling environment, analytics are crucial. You need to know everybody to whom you sent videos, and which videos they watched. Which ones didn't they watch? Who did they share it with? What did they watch, and not watch? That means when you *do* speak to them again, you will have a really good idea of how knowledgeable and educated they are—and where their interests lie.

Analytics will also give you insight into the engagement pyramid. At the top of the pyramid are the executives, at the bottom are staff. If the only people who have watched your video are staff, then you know you probably need to send a different type of video to people in management and leadership.

GATING

Many people, as part of their video platform, use "gating" before making a video available for viewing. Gating requires the stakeholder to fill out a form or answer some questions before being allowed to view a video. In our research, we asked the following question:

"If you were required to fill out a form, how likely are you to enter the info to watch the product demo video?" In response, 41 percent of respondents said they would likely *not* fill out the form and watch the video. Another 51 percent said they *might* fill out the form. Only 7 percent of respondents said they would *definitely* fill out the form. In other words, 92 percent of respondents would be, at a minimum, skeptical about completing the gating form to review your crucial content in order to keep the sales process moving forward.

For years, marketers have been imposing gating on website visitors in order to capture their name and contact information to pass to sales as a "qualified lead." Quite often, the determining factor to gate or not to gate was whether or not marketing considered this piece of information (or video in this case) highly valuable to a possible stakeholder. The problem is, stakeholders don't like being gated, and they will *close the page* rather than provide personal information.

When the sales engagement team is trying to leverage a video automation platform to improve their productivity, they can't afford to have stakeholders elect to not watch a video or set of videos for fear of being gated. Some may argue that if a stakeholder shares the video or video playlist with another stakeholder, the video automation platform should gate this new anonymous stakeholder.

We understand the benefits to the sales engagement team member; however, if you're trying to gain broad stakeholder approval and these videos are a key element in doing so, it is crucial that all stakeholders can, and will, watch your videos. Your video automation platform will tell you your content has been shared, so as a salesperson, contact your primary stakeholder and ask them who they shared the content with.

SIX
VIDEO CATEGORIES

Video automation relies on pre-recorded videos as its content engine, much like a bookstore relies on books. In a bookstore, the on-shelf inventory is categorized and organized by subject. A primary challenge with book inventory is that, at least physically, it can only be categorized using a single approach. Fiction is in one area and non-fiction another. Within non-fiction, categories are further defined by subject matter.

Contrast a book store with a video automation platform. The catalog of videos in the tool can be stored and found by a sales engagement team member or stakeholder via unlimited search and categorization methods, making retrieval fast and easy.

There are a variety of types of B2B video that serve different purposes for the sales engagement team. Below is a summary of the types of videos used in video automation systems:

› Personal
› Explainer

› Impact
› Demo
› Tutorial
› Testimonial
› Case Study
› Recorded Video Podcast
› Recorded Webinar
› Entertainment
› 3rd Party
› Private

PERSONAL VIDEO

So far, you've read some ideas on how successful sales engagement team members leverage personal video, but personal video offers much more than a front-end message to a demo video. Many people have asked me what I mean by personal video, so here's an easy way to think about it: personal video, within the overall video spectrum, is what a voice mail is to a message. With voice mail, you wouldn't leave a three-minute message in a sales sequence, because you know the receiver wouldn't listen to the entire message and would, instead, be incredibly annoyed. The only person in my life that ever left long voice mails was my mother. "Hi Robert, it's your mom. (Like I didn't know it was her!) I was calling to see what your plans were for the New Year. Dad and I are thinking of having a party. . .(one minute later)...and I couldn't believe the car couldn't be fixed sooner...anyway..."

AUDIENCE

As implied by the name, the audience for a personal video is generally another individual or a select group of stakeholders at a single company.

INTENTION

These videos are used for setting the context of persuading a stakeholder or stakeholders to look deeper into your products, services, or solutions.

SALES PROCESS LOCATION

Personal videos can be used from the very early, business-development stage to the decision stage. Of all video types, these have the broadest use across the sales process. Consider these uses for personal videos:

› Deliver your value proposition to a top level executive even though you can't secure a meeting with them prior to the end of a quarter.
› Engage multiple stakeholders with your key insights or messages without waiting for a meeting.
› Prepare a group of stakeholders prior to a product, service, or solution demo by allowing video to address overview topics and reserving time in the demo for your key differentiators and their key decision levers.
› Address open questions from a stakeholder meeting or group demo without the need to wait until another meeting or follow-up demo can be scheduled.
› Cross sell to new divisions within your prospect's company by asking internal sponsors at your current customer to forward your share link to their colleague.

Personal videos can be a powerful weapon in your video arsenal for moving opportunities through a B2B sales process. They play a crucial role in humanizing you as a member of the sales engagement team and are necessary for providing context to additional videos you might be including in a playlist of videos to a stakeholder.

STYLING

These videos are very authentic, often with minimal graphics. Some personal-video creation tools support replacing your background with a virtual one (such as an image of your prospect's corporate headquarters). Within the video however, the focus is on the sales engagement team who is addressing the camera.

Illustration 6.1 — Personal Video Example

SHELF LIFE

Personal videos have a very short shelf life—often single use. While they may have a limited shelf life, that single view can be a crucial element in a stakeholder's review of your products, services, or solutions.

EXPLAINER VIDEO

B2B sales organizations need videos that explain, at a very high level, their broad strategy and the challenges or pains their products, services, or solutions are addressing. These videos are generally funded by marketing and produced at great expense by contracted production firms.

AUDIENCE

Explainer videos have broad appeal, likely to the entire addressable market including customers, prospects, partners, channels, and even their own employees.

INTENTION

Define the mission and vision of the company or the company's market position.

STYLING

The style can either be animated or a direct address/interview of a company executive. The trend has been toward animated videos.

Illustration 6.2 — IBM Watson Explainer Video

SHELF LIFE

Generally, the shelf life of an explainer video is on the longer end since market strategies usually don't change quickly. Explainer videos can exist for several years as long as good choices are made with wardrobe, graphics, and music.

IMPACT VIDEO

Videos that focus on impact are designed to resolve pains and, as a result, provide improvements in productivity (or reduced risk) and aggregate them into a business impact. The resulting business impact may or may not be known by the stakeholders. In these videos, the primary visual support within the video is not the products, services, or solutions, but the impact area itself. That usually translates into graphics or imagery that depicts the impact area with only quick images of the products, services, or solutions.

As discussed previously, CEB/Gartner has conducted a tremendous amount of research on the impact and success of sales engagement team members who lead with commercial insights. CEB/Gartner clients will engage with them to develop and refine their commericial insights along with the skills necessary to properly deliver them to stakeholders. These commercial insights are perfect candidates for reusable impact videos.

Corporate Visions is a global marketing and sales messaging, content, and skills training company. For many years they have been very successful at helping B2B companies create what they refer to as "Power Positions." Power Positions are created at the intersection of a B2B company's products, services, or solutions with the stakeholder's key needs where a competitor has no answer. If a Corporate Visions client created and cataloged a number of Power Positions, these would be perfect candidates for impact videos.

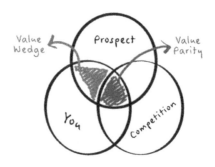

Illustration 6.3 — Copyright Corporate Visions, Inc.

AUDIENCE

Typically, impact videos are more focused toward a segment or persona, and usually they are a management or executive level audience.

INTENTION

Impact videos describe a particular challenge in the market and how your company addresses that challenge. These videos focus on a message around a topic of interest to a prospect. They don't fully define the specific impacts the products, services, or solutions can have on a company—that is done in demo videos.

STYLING

Impact videos use a live host who is a subject matter expert or departmental leader. Motion graphics and animations can also be used to visually support the concepts. The visual support is not primarily the products, services, or solutions, but the impact those have on business pain or improvements.

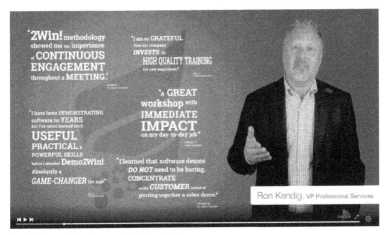

Illustration 6.4 — Impact Video Styling

SHELF LIFE

These tend to be product specific, so shelf life can be one to two years on average. These videos tend to address needs defined by market trends; as the energy in the market shifts in different directions, the messaging and approach for impact videos will need to shift as well.

DEMO VIDEOS

Unlike an impact video that relies on graphics, imagery, and key words for its primary visual support, demo videos rely on the the actual products, services, or solutions. A stakeholder watches a demo video to get a sense of using the product, service, or solution.

AUDIENCE

Demo videos are for operational stakeholders and departmental management stakeholders.

INTENTION

Demo videos provide a depth of content and specificity for how your company addresses the challenges presented in an impact video. These videos are typically used before or after meetings to introduce your prospect to your solution and help further explain topics for those who may have missed a meeting. In some instances, stakeholders will purchase from a demo video alone. However, most B2B stakeholders will still need a live demo to ask specific questions. Demo videos serve to bring focus and clarity to those live interactions.

STYLING

For a demo video, there is usually a live host to open and close the video. The live host is typically a subject matter expert from your sales engagement team. The product, service, or solution is addressed in the middle section of the video. There is usually light visual support for key messages throughout the video.

Illustration 6.5 — Demo Video Styling: Live Host

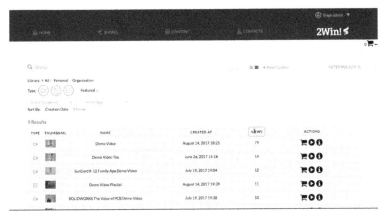

Illustration 6.6 — Demo Video Styling: Software Demo

SHELF LIFE

The shelf life of a demo video is up to a year, depending on your product development velocity. Demo videos by nature contain software screen shots, product images, or services outputs. These will go out of date as the products, services, or solutions are updated. It is important to consider maintenance for these videos—is the message timeless? Consider screenshots and images instead of live screen captures or products on camera for ease of updating.

TUTORIAL VIDEOS

Tutorial videos are, as implied, used to train customers on how to use your products, services, or solutions.

AUDIENCE

Tutorial videos are for your installed base of customers.

INTENTION

While many tutorial videos are built just to teach someone how to use a tool, we see this as a missed opportunity. In today's subscription era when adoption, expansion, and renewal are keys to profitability, we have found our clients need to rethink tutorials. B2B sales organizations are asking the viewers of tutorial videos to commit to using the product in new and different ways. This requires your client's success to have influence, and influence comes through delivering a compelling message that not only shows how to use a capability, but also why—how it applies to their day-to-day context. They need benefits.

STYLING

The styling for tutorial videos is similar to demo videos; but if volume or shelf life is a concern, go without the live host. Instead, use a PowerPoint slide (or visuals built in post-production) to introduce the speaker and support key points being made in the video.

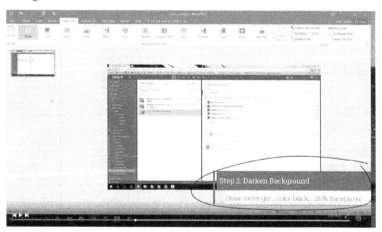

Illustration 6.7 — Tutorial Styling

SHELF LIFE

As with demo videos, the shelf life of tutorial videos depends on development velocity.

TESTIMONIAL VIDEO

These videos feature customers on camera discussing their positive experience with your products, services, or solutions. They almost always cut to images or video (commonly referred to as B-roll) of the customer's organization in action. Marketing normally funds these videos, which are often produced by outside video production firms.

AUDIENCE

These videos are for a broad base of stakeholders, but generally meant for executives and managers.

INTENTION

Testimonial videos attempt to build credibility and trust about a current customer's experience with your organization or solution.

The emphasis of these videos is on the positive experience this customer or customers have had working with your people, products, services, or solutions, but not necessarily metrics of business results they received.

STYLING

Testimonial videos use a live host who features your customers, rather than the interviewer.

Illustration 6.8 — Tutorial Styling

SHELF LIFE

Testimonial videos must constantly be monitored for customer churn and can require annual approval for re-use.

CASE STUDY

On the surface, case study videos are similar to testimonial videos, but with one key difference. The emphasis of these videos is on the tangible results customers realized after using your products, services, or solutions. These videos often start with the "before" situation and conclude with the "after" results.

AUDIENCE

Case study videos are for all stakeholders, but are generally aimed more at executives and managers.

INTENTION

These videos establish a connection between a prospect and an existing customer, which provides financial and emotional justification for making a change and entrusting your organization with that change.

STYLING

Case studies use a live host who features your customer, not the interviewer. Usually, this includes video of your customer's organization and graphic support of the business metrics they improved.

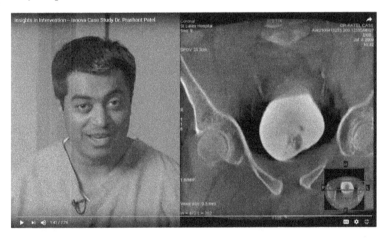

Illustration 6.9 — Case Study Styling

SHELF LIFE

Case study videos must constantly be monitored for customer churn and can require annual approval for re-use.

RECORDED VIDEO PODCAST

The term podcast was originally a portmanteau of Apple's "iPod" device and "broadcast." Video podcasts (sometimes called vodcasts) are made available by B2B companies to inform their clients of trends, ideas, and suggestions. They are often presented in subscription form and are almost always free.

AUDIENCE

Similar to impact videos, video podcasts are typically more focused toward a segment or persona, and these tend to be management or executive level.

INTENTION

Take a unique challenge, personify that challenge with a typical scenario, and show a solution to that challenge.

STYLING

Video podcasts have a live host supported by some level of visual support such as slides, graphics, or images.

Illustration 6.10 — Video Podcast Styling

SHELF LIFE

Like impact videos, these tend to address needs defined by market trends. So as the energy in the market shifts in different directions, the messaging and approach for commercial videos will need to shift as well.

RECORDED WEBINAR

Many B2B sales organizations produce live webinars for their prospects and customers. These informative events are normally thirty to sixty minutes in length. Recording those webinars has become a popular practice to entice potential viewers who were not able to attend the live event to watch the recording.

AUDIENCE

Similar to impact videos, these are typically more focused toward a segment or persona, often at management or executive level.

INTENTION

Recorded webinars provide a deep description of a particular challenge in the market and how your company addresses that challenge. This is more of a message around a topic of interest to a buyer.

STYLING

These videos typically involve a live host supported by slides and, occasionally, a live or screenshot demo of the products, services, or solutions highlighted in the webinar.

Illustration 6.11 — Recorded Webinar Styling

SHELF LIFE

The shelf life of webinars depends on the timeliness of the topic. Once topics become dated, the content manager of the video usually retires them.

ENTERTAINMENT VIDEO

B2B sales organizations occasionally produce humorous, entertainment-style videos for the amusement of their clientele and to drive traffic to their website. These videos are generally loaded to YouTube for maximum viewing and traffic.

AUDIENCE

These types of video generally have a very broad-based audience, often well beyond the target customers.

INTENTION

Use humor to attract attention to your brand.

STYLING

Video of human subjects attempting to do something that has a humorous track and outcome.

SHELF LIFE

These videos can last for years!

3RD PARTY VIDEOS

Some B2B sales organizations will catalog and make available videos by a 3rd party organization or individual. These videos range from an independent review of their products, services, or solutions to an analyst speaking on an industry trend.

AUDIENCE

Thought leaders within your prospects and customers.

INTENTION

Provide value to thought leaders and establish your brand and your people as thought leaders.

STYLING

Dependent on the third party's production.

SHELF LIFE

The shelf life of these videos varies widely, depending on their applicability and timeliness.

PRIVATE VIDEOS

These videos are created for internal use only. Your video automation system keeps them behind a curtain, and only certain individuals have access to them. They can range from test videos to internal training pieces on policies and procedures.

Owners of private videos should show diligence and caution to prevent them from being released to the public.

AUDIENCE

Internal staff

INTENTION

Procedural explanations, how-to instructions, and internal messaging.

STYLING

Live host or screen shots of a procedure that must be followed within an internal software solution.

SHELF LIFE

Shelf life varies greatly, depending on the topic.

CONCLUSIONS

While this has not been an exhaustive description of videos, you're probably gathering that the production of video requires a strategy. You and your team need to decide your priorities for video development, as well as your hosting and platform strategy for disseminating videos. Your sales engagement team needs to understand the importance of thinking strategically about the use of video and how to provide context to the videos they are sending to stakeholders with their personal video.

In the next chapter, we'll discuss what's involved in the production of personal videos by your sales engagement team members. The personal video is a critical step in establishing the effectiveness of leveraging other video categories in your Rule of 24 journey.

SEVEN
PERSONAL VIDEO

In the previous chapter, we described a variety of video categories. One category in particular deserves some dedicated thought—Personal Video. In this chapter, we will take a deep dive into how to utilize personal video as a key component in achieving Rule of 24 dominance.

Personal video can be leveraged in a multitude of ways by a sales engagement team member. It can be as simple as a "thank you" or as complex as a proposal presentation.

A CEO of one of our video platform customer companies sent a thank you video to the CEO of a new B2B client that signed a contract with their organization. The video was enthusiastically received by our client's customer, and the customer's CEO shared the personal video with everybody on his management team. That didn't just spread awareness, it built a connection and loyalty with their new client.

Personal videos are an interpersonal way of connecting with somebody regardless of the physical distance between you.

A voicemail provides a verbal message, but a video establishes a visual, personal, and human connection. It's a fantastic way to introduce yourself to all types of stakeholders in an organization, especially with people you haven't already met. It's also an effective way to introduce the additional content you are sending—by providing context to documents, proposals, or different types of videos.

Modes of interaction are changing.

Before the Rule of 24, voicemail messages and emails with attachments were the norm. Now we see, especially with Snapchat and Instagram, communication moving in the direction of video. Why is video becoming so popular? What does video do, that emails or voicemails can't do?

Research has proven that body language and facial expressions are a critical aspect of communication. And video is a way you can deliver non-verbal communication to your stakeholders. Email is great when a relationship with a client is already established, or if someone has a quick question they need answered. A personal video, however, is more likely to present itself as an opportunity to take communication to new levels of effectiveness.

We believe an examination of the science behind personal video messaging is worth exploring before discussing the methods and technology behind creating and distributing personal videos.

THE SCIENCE OF CREATING MASSIVE RAPPORT

There are subtle techniques you can employ in a personal video that generate trust; build confidence in your products, services, or solutions; convey a sense of urgency; and fill stakeholders with the emotions that lead to a purchase. Utilize these techniques, and your personal videos that establish the context for the additional information you are providing stakeholders will be much more effective. Let's examine this further.

Dr. John Bargh conducted a study on priming at New York University. Priming is a technique whereby one is exposed to stimuli that subconsciously influence their thoughts and short-term behavior. Bargh's study was made famous in the best-selling book *Blink* by Malcolm Gladwell. The following is reprinted with permission from Gladwell's book *Blink*:

> *For example, on one occasion Bargh and two colleagues at New York University, Mark Chen and Lara Burrows, staged an experiment in the hallway just down from Bargh's office. They used a group of undergraduates as subjects and gave everyone in the group one of two scrambled-sentence tests. The first was sprinkled with words like "aggressively," "bold," "rude," "bother," "disturb," "intrude," and "infringe." The second was sprinkled with words like "respect," "considerate," "appreciate," "patiently," "yield," "polite," and "courteous."*

> *In neither case were there so many similar words that the students picked up on what was going on. (Once you become conscious of being primed, of course, the priming doesn't work.) After doing the test—which takes only about five minutes—the students were instructed to walk down the hall and talk to the person running the experiment in order to get their next assignment. Whenever a student arrived at the office, however, Bargh made sure that the experimenter was busy, locked in conversation with someone else—a confederate who was standing in the hallway, blocking the doorway to the experimenter's*

office. Bargh wanted to learn whether the people who were primed with the polite words would take longer to interrupt the conversation between the experimenter and the confederate than those primed with the rude words.

He knew enough about the strange power of unconscious influence to feel that it would make a difference, but he thought the effect would be slight. Earlier, when Bargh had gone to the committee at NYU that approves human experiments, they had made him promise that he would cut off the conversation in the hall at ten minutes. "We looked at them when they said that and thought, You've got to be kidding," Bargh remembered. "The joke was that we would be measuring the difference in milliseconds. I mean, these are New Yorkers. They aren't going to just stand there. We thought maybe a few seconds, or a minute at most." But Bargh and his colleagues were wrong.

The people primed to be rude eventually interrupted—on average after about five minutes. But of the people primed to be polite, the overwhelming majority—82 percent—never interrupted at all.

If the experiment hadn't ended after ten minutes, who knows how long they would have stood in the hallway, a polite and patient smile on their faces?*

Social psychologists like Bargh have contended that stakeholders are more likely to view you and your company in a positive frame of mind if you prime them with positive phraseology. However, in his best-selling book *Thinking, Fast and Slow*, Daniel Kahneman describes how stakeholders are two to three

*From *Blink: The Power of Thinking Without Thinking* by Malcolm Gladwell, copyright © 2005. Reprinted by permission of Little, Brown and Company, an imprint of Hachette Book Group, Inc.

times more motivated to make a change to avoid a loss than they are to achieve a gain. Therefore, your competitors will likely prime a prospect with the pain they are experiencing with their current status quo. That has become a driven behavior in sales, with every sales training event a sales engagement team member has ever attended reinforcing the importance of stressing a stakeholder's pain. "Pain means change" is what we were taught.

Bargh's study and Kahneman's research are seemingly at odds with each other. Upon further examination, however, they are in perfect harmony. The examination of one of our client's real-life sales situations illustrates why:

Our client is a global software company headquartered in France. Their prospect was based in Frankfurt, Germany, so the lead sales engagement team member was located in Germany as well. The prospect's stakeholders were geographically dispersed across Europe, and our client's sales engagement team members were as well. The size of this opportunity dictated a diverse set of skills and expertise—hence, the geographic dispersion of the sales engagement team members.

Our client was a finalist in an extensive selection process against two competitors. During the sales process, our client's lead sales engagement team member learned that the prospect's senior management had already agreed to fund the project. The stakeholders were experiencing pain with their status quo. Otherwise, they wouldn't have funded the project in the first place!

At this juncture in the sales process, our client and their two competitors had been scheduled to provide a finals demo and presentation three days out. Our client decided to provide the stakeholders who attended the finals demo a personal video that introduced their company and provided context to some impact-style videos that addressed the solution's key advantages, compared to their status quo. Additionally, they wanted the personal video to provide the prospect some context to a demo video that offered a brief product overview. The overview was designed to reserve time they would need to spend presenting their key competitive differentiators during the finals live demo.

Because this prospect had already funded the project, status quo was not the main competitor. The competitors were the two other vendors that were vying for the prospect's business. Therefore, our client's personal video primed their stakeholders with positive phraseology (following Bargh's positive priming) regarding their pending change. The context they set for their impact videos stressed the improvements in the stakeholder's organization—not the avoidance of loss if they did nothing. This differentiated our client from their competitors who primed the prospect with pain and, thus, appeared condescending.

When our client created the personal video, they smiled while recording the personal video and expressed enthusiasm for the upcoming event. They were energetic about the positive impact their products, services, or solutions would have on their prospect's business.

By priming with positive word choice, visual enthusiasm, and emotional energy, they allowed themselves to be seen as a competitor who was different. They were the only vendor who was not stressing pain.

Our client's case study does not suggest that Kahneman's research is wrong. The case study does suggest that his research can't be applied to every prospect and every situation. For example, if you sell a unique product, service, or solution, and your salesperson is trying to convince the prospect to move away from their status quo, a personal video sent ahead of a demo should be primed with words that stress pain and loss avoidance along with visual and emotional cues.

In summary, a personal video is a great way to prime prospects because the priming language is reinforced with visual cues and emotions, making it more memorable. How do we do that? Next, we will explore how your personal video aligns your sales strategy with your visual and verbal expressions.

PERSONAL VIDEO COMMUNICATION ALIGNMENT

When you speak positive words, do you look at the camera or look down? Do you appear serious or joyful? These are important questions. A hard expression conflicts with a positive vocabulary. Sales strategy, emotions, language, and behavior should all be in alignment as a means of persuasion and making your on-camera appearance natural and authentic.

For example, if the strategy is to stress the positive aspects of your products, services, or solutions on the prospect's business, we teach clients that at the start of their personal video, they need to look directly at the camera and smile. We teach them to assume that the camera lens is each stakeholder's eyes and to maintain that direct eye contact throughout the video. As they introduce an idea that has a positive outcome, they get excited about it and smile. That becomes part of the priming process. They are getting their stakeholders excited about their solution, which is primed to be a respite from their pain.

On the other hand, if our client had a prospect that was deciding between their products, services, or solutions and staying with their status quo, we would have encouraged them to prime the stakeholders with business pain and/or the loss of not having their products, services, or solutions. Especially if we knew they were the only vendor the stakeholders were considering.

Corporate Visions, a California-based training and research firm, performed a study they published in a brief titled *Decide or Defer: What Type of Message Gets Executive Buyers to Purchase Now?* This study, which included 312 executive participants, supports Kahneman's findings when executives are yet to commit to a change. Corporate Vision's researchers found "executives in the study were 70 percent more willing to make a risky business decision—such as switching from their current solution to a new one—when the message framed their current situation in terms of what they stood to lose instead of what they stood to gain."

If your sales engagement team can't confirm executive backing for making a change, Corporate Visions' study proves that the personal video must set the context of the message and the included content with pain and loss aversion.

You don't always use priming to establish positives or pain and loss aversion. Instead, consider each situation and prime them with the emotions that best fit the situation. Then, develop a consistent approach to each type of situation and desired outcome.

THE 4 C'S

When creating your personal video, the four C's represent the critical elements in its production: **Connection, Context, Clarity,** and a **Call to Action**. A personal video should always begin by making a connection with the recipient. For example, use the person's name at the very start of the video. After making a connection with the recipient, your personal video provides context. The context answers the question: "Why are you sending the recipient this video?" The third key element in every personal video is clarity. For example, if your personal video is service focused, how will your service help them? Lastly, have a clear call to action—what do you want them to do once they've finished watching the video?

SCRIPTING AND TELEPROMPTING

As you become comfortable with producing personal videos that incorporate the four C's, you'll find that eye contact with the camera and proper expressions and communication become natural. The challenge for almost everyone we work with is getting to that point of comfort. Try this: Go to the Apple or Google online store and license a teleprompter app for your mobile device. They range in price from free to $25. These apps let you write your script on your computer and easily transfer it to your device. They automatically roll your script at your comfortable speaking speed, and you never lose eye contact with the stakeholder.

As comfortable as we are with creating personal videos, we still rely on a teleprompter for certain circumstances. For example, if we're trying to express our value proposition to an executive, we want to be very precise with the wording of our message. Teleprompting provides that precision with minimal time and effort. We never have to lose eye contact with the camera. We might have to do a few takes, but we will be able to read a teleprompted message that precisely articulates our value proposition.

As you progress with your ability to be conversational, natural, and authentic on camera, you may find that the only thing you need to create your video is a couple of bullet points on a sticky note next to the lens of your camera.

PERSONAL VIDEO PRODUCTION

Once you know what you want to say in your video, how do you make the video? On a scale of simple to complex, the production of a personal video is quite simple. Even though it's simple and easy to do, each element is important.

BACKGROUND

First and foremost, check what's behind you. Before you start, don't look at yourself on camera—look at what's behind you.

Is there a window that's making you look like a shadow in the shot? Is the background busy to the point where it's distracting? Be conscious of what's behind you.

GREEN SCREEN

This is simply a solidly colored green fabric or paper background. Camera technology scans green twice as often as other colors, which gives technology tools the ability to remove the background. Personal video recording tools now offer the ability to replace that green background with an image of your choice. For example, you might replace your office background with an image of your stakeholder's corporate office, as the figure below illustrates:

Illustration 7.1 — Personal Video with Background Removed

LIGHTING

The next key element of personal video production is lighting. The rule here is simple: Make sure all your lighting is in front of you. Most mobile devices deal with low light very well, so you don't need expensive studio lighting. You might consider a single box light with a diffuser, however, if you plan on sending a great number of personal videos from your place of work. Lighting must always come from the front and sides. Never have a window behind you.

MICROPHONE

Next up is your microphone. We are all for "authentic-style" videos, but your sound quality needs to be good. There's a gradient you can follow regarding your microphone. You can use whatever is built into your laptop, webcam, or mobile device, but we highly recommend you take it up a notch. Personal video shot using a mobile device or a webcam has become HD quality. Don't erode your message and HD-quality video with poor audio.

A simple and inexpensive solution can be found on Amazon. For $14 we found a lavalier microphone that sounds excellent. It plugs into a mobile device or a laptop. A step up from there is portable microphones that range from $50 to $200. You can go all the way to a pro microphone if you'd like, but we find it's unnecessary. Some of our clients prefer headphones with a boom microphone. That works great for subject matter experts on products, services, or solutions. The sound quality is excellent, and its look adds a flavor of expertise.

AMBIENT NOISE

Another consideration is the noise around you, known as ambient noise. Many people work from home, in an open office setting, or in cubicles. If your surroundings create a large amount of ambient noise, you will need a microphone that isolates sound to what's right in front of it. There are certain headsets available that are very good at canceling ambient noise.

I was on a flight from London to Denver and shot a personal video en route. I used a Jabra noise-canceling headset, and the clarity was incredible—the microphone canceled almost all the ambient noise of the aircraft.

CAMERA

When it comes to the type of camera to use, we can whole-heartedly recommend mobile devices. They have excellent cameras. But always use your mobile device in landscape mode, not portrait. When your stakeholder plays your personal video on a computer or a smartphone, it will display large black bars on either side if the video was shot using portrait mode. It plays and looks much better when it's recorded in landscape mode.

Laptops and webcams automatically record in landscape mode. If you are using a mobile device, purchase an inexpensive mount that clips to your monitor or desk and will support your phone in landscape mode while you shoot your personal video. Just make sure the angle's good—nobody likes the double-chin look!

AUTHENTICITY

We've been talking a lot about being authentic. Authenticity is great, but your videos still need to be professional quality. You're still in a business setting. If you're stumbling over your words, or you have to look off camera all the time because you can't remember what you were going to say, that's too authentic! Maintain eye contact with the camera the entire time. An occasional glance away is fine, but make sure your message is flowing. If it doesn't flow, have the discipline to do another take.

YOUR PERSONAL VIDEO SHOPPING LIST

The tools we use for creating personal videos is in constant flux. Technology advancements, new products, and new approaches drive our constant desire to be at the forefront of tools and techniques. Please visit the following link for the latest shopping list and reviews of personal video tools: http://2winglobal.com/training/r24shopping

SUMMARY

Personal video is an excellent way to prime your stakeholders in a way that's not possible using email or voice alone. These videos can be leveraged for a variety of use cases across your sales cycle. You will find that your personal videos, along with your included content, will be shared with multiple stakeholders— ensuring accurate and effective sales messaging with your Rule of 24 opportunities.

EIGHT
VIDEO CONTENT CREATION

In Chapter 6, we went into great detail regarding all the categories of video content. The categories ranged from a one-time use/short-shelf-life personal video to long-shelf-life general-use explainer videos. In Chapter 7, we focused on the strategies and creation of a single piece of content: the personal video. In this chapter, we shift our attention to the creation of other key Rule of 24 videos that are commonly used by sales engagement team members: impact, demo, personal, tutorial, testimonial, and case study videos.

We won't discuss the creation of explainer videos, video podcasts, webinars, or entertainment videos, as your marketing team and their in-house (or contracted) video professionals should be well versed in those processes. We also won't discuss 3rd party or private videos, as the former are licensed by marketing and the latter are for internal use only.

BASIC CONCEPTS

Prior to discussing the details of your Rule of 24 video content creation, it's important to have a grasp of some key concepts that apply to every piece of video you produce. These concepts apply to all the types of video that we will discuss in this chapter.

PRE-PRODUCTION

This is the process of preparing for the creation of a video. First, this process needs to determine the expected outcome of your video. Second, pre-production should answer the question: "What do I want the stakeholder to do after watching this video?" Finally, you need to determine the scope of the video. Each video should be deep enough that you prove the value of your service (or a portion thereof), but not so broad that there is confusion as to what the desired action is. The outcome of pre-production is a script that is ready to go to production.

PRODUCTION

This is the process of shooting and/or capturing the video you need, which will later be assembled into a finished product. This includes video of live host or hosts, product image capture, and software or display-screen captures.

POST-PRODUCTION

Your final video is assembled and finalized in post-production. During this process, the assets you captured in production are combined with graphics and key messaging using a post-production software tool. The outcome is a video asset that is uploaded to your video automation platform and used in your Rule of 24 sales processes.

PRODUCTION COMPARISONS

Below is a table that provides a comparison of the various video types and their corresponding production components:

Video Type	Impact	Demo	Personal	Tutorial	Testimonial	Case Study
Stakeholder Quality Expectations	High	Medium	Low	Low	Medium	High
Level of Authenticity	Low	Medium	High	High	High	Medium
Pre-Production Level of Difficulty	High	Medium	Low	Low	Medium	High
Production Level of Difficulty	High	Medium	Low	Medium	Low	High
Post-Production Level of Difficulty	High	Medium	Low	Low	Low	High
Concept to Completion	1-2 days	4 hours	10 minutes	2 hours	1 hour	Days to weeks

Illustration 8.1 — Production Comparisons

IMPACT VIDEO PRODUCTION

As we discussed, impact videos are most frequently sent to management and decision-making stakeholders. These videos express the key impacts your products, services, or solutions will have on their goals and strategic initiatives. As such, quality expectations for impact video are very high.

In contrast, their level of authenticity is low. These factors contribute to a high level of difficulty in creating these videos in pre-production, production, and post-production. As there is more thought required in planning, there will be a higher level of difficulty associated in each of the production steps. Likewise, the amount of time your team will take to span from concept to completion will, at best, be one to two days of work.

DEMO VIDEO PRODUCTION

Demo videos are usually consumed by staff level stakeholders. The stakeholders are much more focused on the facts, so their expectations of the quality of your demo video would be considered more of a medium. The stakeholders also prefer a medium level of authenticity, as it is important for them to be able to relate to the subject matter experts who are demonstrating your services.

Pre-production, production, and post–production all have a medium level of difficulty. Most of your effort in pre-production will be spent on the script and editing processes. Production will require camera shots of the product, screen captures of software, or illustrations of your services.

Finally, the post-production step must stitch the video with the product or service screen captures. It has been our experience that a team can stream through the production process of a demo video, from concept to completion, in just four hours if the process is well defined and the team is trained.

PERSONAL VIDEO PRODUCTION

Of all the video types, personal video is by far the easiest and quickest video to produce. Stakeholder quality expectations are low, yet professional. With personal video, the stakeholders are looking for a high degree of authenticity. In some cases, personal video may be your only opportunity to build a relationship, albeit one-sided, with your stakeholders. However, when compared to other video production, personal video has a low level of difficulty in every step. This is evidenced by a concept-to-completion time of typically only around ten minutes.

TUTORIAL VIDEO PRODUCTION

Tutorial videos will generally be consumed by staff level stakeholders who want to know how to use your product, service, or solution. They will rarely judge you and your organization based on your level of quality in the production of the video. What's interesting is that once your training processes are in place, you will find that your team can produce a substantial library of tutorial videos that exceed stakeholders' quality expectations.

Stakeholders want a high level of authenticity in these videos, as that provides them with confidence in your expertise and realism. Pre-production difficulty of tutorial videos is quite low, as your subject matter expert walks through how your stakeholder accomplishes a task.

Production difficulty is medium, as your subject matter expert will need to combine a voice-over of how they accomplish something with the video or screen capture of what is being accomplished. Post-production difficulty of these videos is typically quite low, especially if you can create a template that can be reused. This leads to a concept-to-completion time of only two hours.

TESTIMONIAL VIDEO PRODUCTION

On the surface, one might think stakeholders' quality expectations would be very low for a testimonial video. However, stakeholders will judge your company by how your customers talk about it. Therefore, we recommend dialing up the quality to a medium level. Because this is a testimonial, your stakeholders are expecting a very high level of authenticity. They need to believe your customers' testimonials are real.

The most challenging area in the production process of this video is the pre-production stage. It's critically important to spend the time formulating the questions you will ask your customer in order to receive the responses you desire. The actual production step is simple—decent lighting and a single camera shot works fine.

Likewise, post-production is relatively simple because you're not dealing with a large number of video assets to complete the video. Once your pre-production is in place, testimonial videos can be produced from concept to completion in as little as one hour.

CASE STUDY VIDEO PRODUCTION

Case study videos can be a real challenge. Stakeholders' quality expectations will be quite high, as will the expectations of the customer you are highlighting in the case study. Your viewers will be looking for a medium level of authenticity from your customer in the video.

The pre-production process can be an extremely difficult. Your pre-production process must be aligned with those involved in the case study to determine all the elements you want to highlight and how you want to capture the data that will be exposed throughout the video. Production difficulty can also be high since you are likely going to capture interviews, graphics, and B-roll. This then leads to a high level of difficulty for the post-production process. Good case study videos can take days to weeks to produce.

PRODUCTION PROCESS DETAILS

Over the past sixteen years we have learned that the more disciplined you are at following a well-defined production process, the more likely you are to produce compelling video assets that achieve your goals for quality, cost, and timeframe. The process steps vary widely between the different styles of video.

For example, a testimonial video doesn't require a detailed script, as compared to an impact video. You also don't want to produce every type of video asset the same way every time. Imagine how boring it would be to a stakeholder if every demo video was produced in the exact same way. However, to provide you with what you need to produce the types of video content we discussed above, here is a detailed explanation of what you should consider in all three video production process steps.

PRE-PRODUCTION

1. **Storyboard:** Determine at a high level what your video topic, the style of video (impact, demo, etc.), and your key messages are.
2. **Discovery:** Meet with the subject matter expert (SME) who will be incorporated into the video to understand the way they communicate the message that will be contained in the video.
3. **Rough draft of the script:** Work with your SME to produce a rough draft of the script to be used in the video. It is more important to pay close attention to a rough draft script in an impact video than it is with a

testimonial video. That's because impact videos rely on a live host to deliver key messages on screen, whereas a testimonial video asks a customer a question and is seeking an authentic, non-scripted response.

4. **Write "Line 1":** In the video world, the first line in a video is often called "the hook." This is where you want to convince the viewer to stick around and watch the entire video. For this reason, the proper setting of the context of the video, combined with the introducing or floating of the key benefit to the video, is needed in line 1.

5. **Write "Line 10":** Not meant to be literal on the line number, but think of "Line 10" as the last thing said in a video. It is in Line 10 that your video should provide the viewer with the final benefit and, if appropriate, a Call to Action.

6. **Internal signoff by executive producer:** This is a role in the production not necessarily dedicated to an individual. Whoever is responsible for the final production of the video should read and approve the rough draft of the script, paying particular attention to Lines 1 and 10.

7. **Technical edit:** In this edit, you need your SME to verify that the script is accurate and can be visually supported. In the case of a demo video, this means you can demo what is being said, and the viewer can see exactly what the SME is saying in the script. In an impact video, it means you can visually support your statements with graphics, statistics, or other visuals and, if value is being presented, the value is true and defensible.

8. **Structural edit:** Now it's time to edit the script for clarity and brevity. With video, the less said the more powerful and memorable the video will be. Cut out unnecessary words, phrases, and jargon. Get the script crisp!

9. **Gather visuals:** For software, this means gathering screen shots or screen captures. For products, it is product images or the product in action.

10. **Validate script fits visuals:** In this step, you need to make sure that the flow of what is in the script aligns with the visuals you gathered in Step 9. For example, with software you need to stay on a screen long enough for the viewer to absorb what's being said in the script. If the software screens switch too quickly, your demo video won't meet the goal of giving the viewer a sense of using the software. Contrast a demo video with an impact video: with an impact video, the software screen is only used for quick visual support. You want the viewer to focus on your impact message, not on how the software works. The viewer can always watch the demo video if they want that level of detail.

11. **Performance-level edit:** This is probably the most crucial step in creating an authentic and natural video. This step is performed with the on-screen talent for the video. It is crucial that the on-screen talent reads the script out loud. During this session, the editor collaborates with the on-screen talent to adjust the script to fit the talent's natural spoken language. Cues for vocal emphasis, pauses, gesturing, etc. are inserted into the script.

12. **Identification for the visual support:** This can be slides, images, graphics, or other elements of visual support. These will be inserted in the post-production process.

Crimes

Gravity
Cooks in the Kitchen
The Hot New Message
The Teeter Totter
Straddling the Line

Roles

Executive Producer
Subject Matter Expert (SME)
Demo Expert (DemoE)
Script Writer
Talent
Scripting Project Manager
Marketing Representative
Graphics Support
Presentation Expert (PrsntE)
Production Supervisor

Tools

Templates:
- Storyline Plan
- Resource Plan
- Script
- Visual Support
Screen Capture &
  Recording
Transcription Service/App
Audio Recording
Collaboration Environment

Tips & Tricks

Expert Rough Draft Options:
- Interview
- Record & Transcribe
- Author
Speaking with Punctuation
Vernacular Scripting
Bucks, Quid & Toonies
The Gift of a Word Stumble
Slow 'er Down!
Inverting
Condensing with Visuals
Performance Adjectives
W's Highlighting
Active vs. Passive Voice
Spell 'em Out

Guiding Principles

Above the Line vs. Below the Line
The 'Authentic & Proud To Share' Balance Point
Plan Down, Build Up
The Obsolescence Factor
The Resource Trap
The Short Video Rule (4 minutes) and How to Get There
Audio then Visual vs. Visual then Audio
Performance Levels Edits (PLE)
Calibrating the Message & Resources
Quality Through Iterating
Video vs. Live Tell-Show-Tells
Bands, Trio-Duets, and Solo Acts
Star Power

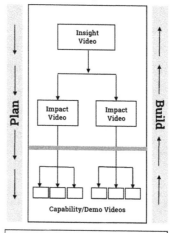

Speaking with Punctuation

Pausing - Period, Dash, Semi-Colon, Colon
Flowing - Comma String, Line Break, Bullet, Ellipse
Emphasizing - CAPS, **Bold**, Underline, 'Quotes',
  Eeellloooonnnggg-gate (elongate), Sta.cca.to (staccato)
Linked vs. Un-Linked Phrases ('&' vs. 'and')

** Insure technique used is supported by teleprompter

Storyline Meeting

Attendees:
- Scripting Project Manager
- Executive Producer (EP)
- Subject Matter Expert (SME)
- Demo Expert (DemoE)
Deliverables:
- Storyline Plan
- Resource Plan

Scripting Flow
'Below the Line' Video

DemoE Rough Draft
Line 1 Draft (Script Writer)
Signoff – EP & SME (initial)
Initial Script (Script Writer)
PLE #1 – Script Writer Only
Signoff – DemoE
PLE #2 – Writer & Talent
Screen Captures – DemoE
Signoff – EP & SME (final)
Final Edits
Talent Packet
Handoff to Production

Scripting Flow
'Above the Line' Video

PrsntE Rough Draft
Line 1 Draft (Script Writer)
Signoff – EP & SME (initial)
Graphics – Preview **
Signoff – Mktg (initial) **
Initial Script (Script Writer)
PLE #1 – Script Writer Only
Signoff – **PrsntE**
PLE #2 – Writer & Talent
Signoff – EP & SME (final)
Presentation Slides – PrsntE
Final Edits
Graphics -- Final **
Signoff – Mktg (final) **
Travel Packet to Talent
Handoff to Production

Intentions

Strong	Weak
Challenge	Inform
Convince	Educate
Excite	
Motivate	_Tone_
Prove	Confident
Reassure	Concerned
Reveal	Lighthearted

Illustration 8.2 — Video Pre-Production Scripting Plan Card

PRODUCTION

Below we will provide a comprehensive list of considerations for capturing various types of video for your content. Not all the items on the list are necessary for every type of video. For example, a demo video will be much easier to produce if you load the script into a teleprompter that is positioned in front of a camera. You don't want to do that for a case-study video, because you want the customer in the case study to speak naturally to the interviewer.

Video: There are five key considerations if your video captures require a video camera.

> *Camera:* There are many consumer-style cameras that provide automatic frame rate, resolution, white balance, and focus. However, it has been our experience that a pro-style camera with adjustable settings allows you the most flexibility in filming, and they are well worth the investment. For example, consider white balance. Vimeo defines white balance as *"the process of calibrating your camera to show colors accurately under varying light conditions. Think of it as making sure the color white is always white so that your image doesn't have blue or red tints."* If you move from a well-lit environment to a low-light environment, a professional camera allows you better control over white balance so your videos have a consistent look.

> *Teleprompter:* This brilliant piece of simple technology sits in front of your camera lens and reflects the script on a piece of glass that the camera shoots straight through without noticeable distortion. This allows your live host to look directly at the camera (and the viewer) and naturally read their performance-level edited script. It is a key piece of technology that saves you time and produces a more authentic and compelling video.

> *Background:* This can vary greatly, based on the style of video (e.g., impact vs. demo) and the need for visual support behind your live host. You may use a green

screen, which we discussed earlier. The post-production tools can remove the green background and insert a visual such as the product or a key message. This is the same process that's used to show a weather map behind the meteorologist on the evening news.

› *Framing:* This is the simple determination of how large or small you want your live host to appear in the video, and whether you want them positioned on the right, left, above, or below the frame you see within the viewfinder of the camera. This is particularly important if your background is a green screen and you intend to provide visual support behind or adjacent to your live host.

› *Lighting:* You don't need to break the bank when it comes to investing in lighting, but you should plan on purchasing some supplemental lights when shooting video of a live host or a product. White balance is much better achieved with proper lighting, and it's an easy way to substantially improve the quality of your video.

Audio: Unfortunately, we've seen (or rather heard) too many videos that used inferior microphones for capturing audio. You should assume your stakeholder is going to watch your video while traveling on public transportation like the NYC subway. With that level of background noise, your audio needs to be recorded so the playback is crisp, clear, and intelligible.

› *Microphones:* There are a variety of microphones that you can use for recording videos. If the video is interview style, such as a customer testimonial or video podcast, we use a quality lavalier (lapel) microphone. If we are in a studio with a green screen, we'll use a directional microphone that is out of the frame of the camera and mounted on a boom. Use the right tool for the job.

› *Environment:* Some videos are meant to be shot in a live office environment with activity behind the live host. If that's the case, you'll need a microphone that is highly directional to minimize background noise. Outdoor locations can require patience and extra time for production, as unpredictable noises are the norm.

› *Pace of delivery:* Slow your talent down! It is our experience that most people speak very quickly (us included) when the director says, "Action!" The production-level edit should establish the pace of the script. Stick with that pace.

› *Consistency:* Some live hosts will need coaching to put more energy into their on-screen captures. Others are simply too animated and loud. Again, stick to what you practiced in the production-level edit, and you'll capture consistent, authentic video.

Final product or screen capture.

› *Full product or screen capture:* If you are videoing a product or capturing software screens, it is important to capture as large of an image as possible. Viewers want to see detail, so make sure to deliver that in as much granularity as possible.

› *Intentional mouse movement:* If you are capturing software screens, keep the mouse as still and out of frame as possible. If you want to capture a sequence of screens that require multiple clicks, position the mouse where you would normally click, capture the screen, and then click.

> *Don't date the capture:* To preserve the timeliness of your product or screen captures, avoid capturing any date fields.

Quality considerations

> *Quality expectations of your stakeholders:* Don't over-engineer your product or software screen captures. Remember, stakeholders want authenticity in demo videos. Executives expect higher quality from impact videos. Match the quality of your videos with the expectations of your audience.

> As mentioned in the audio section, good audio is key to good video. Don't shortcut this critical element of every video.

> Using a live host to set the context of a video is best practice. As you'll learn later in this chapter, the power of "mirror neurons" is significant. If you need to get demo videos produced quickly, or your videos need to be in multiple languages, you can substitute a slide for setting context.

POST-PRODUCTION

In post-production, all the assets you created or licensed in production are taken and assembled into your final video. Post-production is, on the surface, a daunting task for most organizations, but many post-production tools have been simplified to the point of allowing laymen to be able to produce quality videos.

There is no substitute for a good editor. A professional editor can produce a video in a fraction of the time it takes someone like myself; however, there is a price to pay for that expertise. Many of our clients have trained their subject matter experts to become editors and have found that over time they become very proficient at the post-production process.

Timeline layout: Think of the post-production step of a video as a linear timeline that starts at the zero-second mark and ends at the conclusion of the video. All the assets from the production process are simply dropped onto the timeline to create the finished product. All post-production tools such as Final Cut Pro, Premier, Camtasia, and the like use a timeline approach. Along the length of the timeline are separate rows that allow the editor to insert text, music, audio, graphics, and other assets such that they are layered on the video.

Bumper: There is normally a "bumper" at the very beginning and end of a video. This term is used to describe the content that starts and ends a video, which usually consists of a company logo, full-motion graphic, and/or music. Bumpers are usually generated by marketing as part of a company's branding.

Visual Support

> *Talent:* The primary talent for a video is a live host— someone standing in front of the camera, speaking to the stakeholder. With impact videos, talent can be expanded to include people in a room who play a role in the video, as well as individuals using the product.

> *Opening tell:* Demo videos should always have talent setting the context for the video, which is what we call an "opening tell." During the opening tell, the stakeholder watching the video should be focused on the talent and the visual support. Don't have the software screen or product as a visual during the opening tell. The stakeholder needs to be able to absorb what they are about to see, prior to seeing the product service or solution. If the opening tell includes steps in a process that the stakeholder will see,

those steps can be visually supported in the bottom third of the screen or to the left of the talent using text as a visual support.

› *Key benefit:* At the beginning of a demo video, as well as at the end, the talent needs to express the key benefit the stakeholder will receive for using the product, service, or solution. It's important at the beginning to draw the stakeholder in to the video and keep them watching the video. The key benefit needs to be repeated at the end as a means of reinforcing why the stakeholder should use your service.

› *Call to action:* Often referred to as the CTA, this is also positioned at the end of the video and is often visually supported. Think of the CTA as what you want the viewer to do next. Perhaps you want them to watch the next video in the series, or you want them to click the Buy Now button. Whatever your CTA is, make sure you express it at the end of the video.

Transitions

› *Modern transitions:* Think of the transition as moving from one room to another. In a demo video, you will transition from the opening tell (where your live host sets the context for the demo) to the demo itself. You will want to insert a modern transition between those two sections in your post-production process. Modern transitions can be found in most post-production editing tools and can be seen by watching other professionally produced demo videos. On our website http://www.2winglobal.com/ you will find many examples of demo videos with modern transitions.

› *Jump cuts:* Contrasting a transition is a jump cut. A jump cut is simply an instantaneous switch between one timeline asset and another. Jump cuts look awkward if you're transitioning from one major visual asset to another, such as a live host and a product demo. However, jump cuts are frequently used to move from one statement within a testimonial video to another.

Library templates: To save significant time in the post-production process, most editors leverage templates they've created that they can easily drop into a timeline. Below are some examples of reusable templates.

› *Lower thirds:* Visualize a finished video, and divide the screen horizontally into thirds. The lowest third of the screen is usually reserved for visual support, often in the form of text. Many editors have a standard template they use for inserting text into the lower third of the screen. You should take advantage of this as well.

› *Branding:* Most B2B sales organizations use consistent branding in their videos. This includes colors, fonts, and logos. You should have templates for your branding available at a click.

› *Bumpers:* As mentioned earlier, bumpers are a form of branding and are used at both the beginning and end of videos. Like other templates, you should have bumpers available at a click.

› *Music:* If you plan to use music in your videos, we recommend using the same or similar music repeatedly. Remember, the music track must be licensed through a third-party service or be original. The volume level of the music should never distract the viewer during the video.

Rendering: Once you've completed your timeline, rendering takes all your work and produces a finished video. There are a number of considerations for your rendering process, which are listed below.

› *Resolution:* We recommend choosing the highest resolution possible. Remember that you will be using a video automation platform, and that platform will encode the video for playback on any device with any internet speed. So there is no reason to not choose a high resolution.

› *Data rate (bit rate):* At the time of this publishing, Google support for YouTube provides excellent recommendations for the proper video bit rates for each potential video resolution, which can be found at the end of this paragraph. The higher the bit rate, the larger the file size. For example, a sporting video benefits from a high bit rate, as the movement of the athletes will be very smooth. Generally speaking, high bit rates are unnecessary for most demo videos.
Google recommendations:
https://support.google.com/youtube/answer/1722171

› *Frame rate:* This option determines how many frames per second are included in your video. The YouTube support site listed above also provides recommended frame rates for videos. We generally choose a frame rate of 30 frames per second, which provides an excellent balance between clarity and file size.

› *Audio encoding bit rate:* If you desire a stereo output to your audio, we recommend a bit rate of 384 kbps. Mono output only requires 128 kbps. For example, if your video includes background music, you will want to choose a stereo bit rate for your audio. If, however, your video is a simple voiceover, there is no need to output in stereo.

SUMMARY

While all these production details may seem overwhelming, keep in mind that your production processes will vary widely between the different video types. Think of the details above as a complete menu of selections to consider as you determine your video processes. At 2Win!, we've invested heavily in simplifying the video process for our clients, and we train them on all our processes. Look for a video production partner who understands the idiosyncrasies of your video needs and is willing to invest in your organization to help you prepare your organization to address the realities of the Rule of 24.

NINE
VIRTUAL DEMONSTRATIONS

A virtual demo or presentation is the demonstration of a product or solution over an online platform such as WebEx, GoToMeeting, Zoom, or Skype for Business. Even though there are a variety of web presentation tools, the main idea is to share your screen or a presentation with a group of people. These people could all be in entirely different locations, potentially; that's the advantage. There is a myriad of reasons as to why this has become so widely adopted, but efficiency in time and location independence allows for businesses to be operating with greater levels of flexibility.

One of the biggest issues with virtual demonstrations is anonymity. Viewers are typically invisible; they're not in front of you—they can watch the presentation without being seen. There's a lack of connection and, by nature, this leads to people doing other things during the presentation. People will often be multitasking—which really means they'll be zoning out, since according to a study at Stanford, humans cannot cognitively multitask. It's a myth.

Things get worse if you have poor sound quality. If a group is assembled in a room, and they are listening to you via speakerphone, that's an incredibly weak link. When you're in a room with somebody, your voice and your presence are so much more compelling than when you sound like you're coming out of a can. It's hard to make a connection that way.

A strong demo or presentation involves connecting deeply with an audience. They understand that you understand them—you are addressing their challenges, and you know what they're trying to accomplish. You connect. In today's world, that happens because of interactivity. There is a conversation taking place. There are questions on both sides. We are listening and responding just as much as we're presenting—and this is crucial to making these connections.

If the presentation is a web presentation, it is just the presenter speaking—often uninterrupted, for at least fifteen minutes, often up to an hour. All interactivity and connection can be lost.

To increase engagement and prevent a loss of connection, put effort into the production. More effort should be put into the quality of a web presentation than in face-to-face interactions. Many people seem to think, "I'll just have a t-shirt on and a pair of shorts, and I don't need to worry about anything but an inexpensive headset and using my phone. I don't need to worry about being on camera at all, because I can do these things really quickly."

No. That's the wrong approach. The right approach is to dress appropriately for the event.

Get yourself into the mood, as if you really were in front of them. Have the correct equipment. Have a high-quality headset and microphone to ensure the audio is of the best quality possible. Use your webcam, and ask them to use their webcam. All these things are going to increase the production quality and allow for the presentation to be much more interactive.

Some people take professional calls on their webcam from their bed. It may be passable if they do not see you, but working from your bed will affect your entire demeanor and level of engagement throughout the chat. Enthusiasm is something that is contagious, so by being lazy and speaking from your bed, you may be putting your prospect to sleep. Pretend they can see you, and pay attention; your interactivity level needs to be higher than it would be if you were there in person.

If I'm in person, presenting to a group of people, I'm going to make eye contact with all the different people in the room. If somebody has a question—maybe they raise their hand, maybe they have a look on their face—I can calibrate to the situation. I can pause and ask them, "Did you have a question or a comment?" and that's pretty natural for most presenters. They read the room, they read the people; and the longer you're in front of them, the more effectively you can do this.

In a web demo, we don't have that opportunity. There is no immediate feedback. Frequently, the people on the other end of the call don't have a webcam, even today, so it becomes almost impossible to read the audience. I can't rely on the fact that nobody's saying anything to mean they don't have any questions or concerns, so I have to actually create interaction points. I have to make sure the audience is always with me. I have to drive that interactivity.

DRIVING INTERACTIVITY

With all these warnings, I can understand how virtual demonstration and presentation platforms might be perceived as a negative medium for selling. That is why establishing a connection with the audience by driving interaction is essential. The best way to do that is to truly become a master of your tools. For example, if you're using WebEx as your virtual platform, then as a presenter, you need to be a master of WebEx. You need to be able to do more than just share your screen.

For example, in WebEx there is the ability, along with many other features, to have an opening lobby. When people first log in to the meeting, it is a screen that will pop up, assembled with the appearance of your choice. Using that welcome screen, you can initiate a poll, open a chat, and provide a greeting to the audience. You can initiate immediate interactivity.

Imagine someone walking through the physical lobby of your business. If that individual were within your setting, you wouldn't ignore them; you would engage in a conversation with them. That's what this webinar "lobby" does; you greet them as soon as they come online. Generally, we use the time to chat and try to understand what the most important thing is that they want to get out of the presentation. Or we might use the space to ask where everyone is located. We're getting them used to online interaction right from the beginning. This primes and prepares them to be interactive throughout the presentation.

Illustration 9.1 — Virtual Meeting Lobby

Once everybody is online, it's time for the presenter to go on camera. As you open the presentation and begin talking to the people in the audience, make sure you look directly into the lens of the camera. That will create a feeling of eye contact with anyone watching, which we know drives engagement and interactivity. It helps them understand who you are and get comfortable listening to you. Make sure you give clear instructions here, at the outset, for how to continue interaction—whether that's through a poll, a chat box, or submitting questions.

Illustration 9.2 — Initial Meeting Interaction (chat box)

If you have slides, software, or images to present, you probably won't be using the camera. Direct all focus and attention on what you're sharing or showing; don't distract from any of that with an unnecessary live shot. But as soon as any questions come up, make sure you go back on camera to address them. In that way, you drive attention to yourself, showing them that you are there to discuss and address their needs.

Illustration 9.3 — Presenter on camera

When you first get started, create a checklist so you'll know exactly what you need to be ready for ahead of time. Remember, if you commit to consistently using these interactive tools, it will become more and more natural the more you do it.

One of the things presenters frequently do in virtual presentations is pause—which seems like a good strategy. They want to get some interactivity and make sure the audience is following them, so they pause and ask if anyone has any questions. When they don't hear anything, however, they'll say, "Let's move on," and that's where the problems arise. That technique is ineffective because the audience members don't know whether they should speak up or not. Worse, the question isn't directed at anybody.

One of the techniques to overcome quiet, anonymous attendees is to capture a roster and use that roster for individual interactivity. As people come into the "lobby," write their names down. Build a roster of who you'll be talking to. This can only work for certain audience sizes, of course, but will be incredibly helpful for interactivity if you can manage it.

If you have just demonstrated some of your solution that's directed at the staff members, for example, it helps if you know who the staff members are on the call. Once you finish demonstrating the functionality, you can check in directly with them. "So, John, I want to ask you a question about what you just saw." Pause at that point; let them get themselves together. Then ask something like: "Does that make sense, and can you see how that would be a benefit?" What we did there, quite purposefully, is start the question with the client's name. If they were multitasking, one of the ways you get them to switch tasks is to use their name first. That gets their attention, and it gives them a moment to reorient and focus on you. Then you can ask a question.

By asking them a question, you are giving them permission to speak, instead of using the common line of "Does anyone have anyone questions?" They know you are directing this question at them. The other positive aspect of this is that the other people on the call wake up a bit—they are subtly alerted to the fact that you might ask them a question next.

You would never do what we just described in a live presentation—at least not on a repetitive basis. It would be a little bit unnatural for us to always go to each member, and use their name first, but in this environment it's not, because everybody's invisible.

Always preface a question with an individual's name

MANAGING INCOMING RESPONSES

As you drive interaction, there are a few different strategies for managing those incoming responses. The first and simplest is to keep your eyes on the chat box while you present. Keep the chat window constantly open, and glance over at it from time to time. If you ask the attendees to leave responses, pay extra attention.

What if you're in the middle of your discussion? You're a solution or sales engineer in the middle of a demo, and you're pretty focused on making this work properly. You can use a partner; salespeople can be a great source of support here. They can be off camera, watching the chat box. If a question comes up that they know you should take, they can then come on camera. They introduce the question from the chat, and then you can provide a response. This, of course, requires that the salesperson doesn't bring to your attention something he knows you can't answer.

Polling, on the other hand, has its own set of strategies. If this is a larger presentation, polling is a fantastic way to get people integrated. It allows people to feel like they have a voice, to feel engaged and interactive in the presentation. In doing this, you give yourself an opportunity to ask questions, gather responses, and display the results of the poll.

A team member will definitely need to be tracking all the data. If it's that large of a presentation, not only will you probably have the salesperson involved, but you'll also want to have somebody helping you produce. If an audience member needs help connecting, perhaps they experience technical issues, you can use the chat window for that—but your producer helps them. It doesn't stop the presenter from moving forward.

Let's say you want to poll the audience after the demo segment. You can introduce it early on with something like: "We had a customer who implemented this solution; at the time, *these* were their metrics. At the end of the presentation, I'm going to conduct a poll and ask you what you think the results were at the end of their implementation." That will pique their curiosity. You introduce them to what one of the customer's concerns were, you present that section of the material, then you bring the poll up. "What do you think their improvements were? Was it A, B, C, or D?" This can be a powerful way to express the benefits of your product.

Remember: When they are voting, it's not going to be instantaneous. Be patient and wait twenty or thirty seconds for them to think about their answer. This can be quite uncomfortable the first time you do it, but it's essential to give people time to think about it and answer.

WORK WITH SMALL OPTIMIZATIONS

Small optimizations can make the virtual presentation experience much more effective. Sales engagement team members often assume the camera on their laptop is sufficient. The problem with that camera is you'll be tied to the device, including the height of the device and the location of the keyboard. Too often the laptop camera gets a chin shot, which isn't flattering. Buy a $59 Logitech webcam (USB-based), plug it in, and put it on a little tripod—or even just on top of your monitor. Get a good shot; it makes a big difference.

This may seem like common sense, but people often neglect these kinds of expenses. They'll often think, "I don't know if my company pays for that type of stuff. I can't expense it, so I'm not going to pay for it." Listen. There are times when you just need to invest in your career. Your company doesn't pay for your shoes or your shirt or your jacket, does it? Does that mean you're going to show up in a t-shirt and shorts?

Most web presentation tools also offer a whiteboard. This simply means you can use your mouse, or your touchscreen, to illustrate something to an audience. For example, if you're showing a PowerPoint, you can highlight a phrase, circle a keyword, or check something off simply by using your mouse or finger on your screen.

Why is this important? Well, remember the limbic system from Chapter 4? This is the part of the brain that loves input like movement, color, taste, and sound. In a web presentation, which is two-dimensional, you lose a lot of opportunities to get people's attention. Actions you take—like highlighting, writing on the screen, and creating illustrations as if you are using a whiteboard—bring the work to life and make it more memorable.

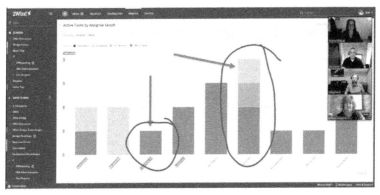

Illustration 9.4 — Illustrating using a Touchscreen

CREATING A VIRTUAL STUDIO

There are some advanced tools for conducting presentations, generally known as "virtual studios." These can be useful when you're doing a high volume of presentations. Virtual studios often contain a higher quality camera and electronic whiteboard that can transmit to the audience. If you don't want to go to that kind of expense (an electronic whiteboard with a transmitter can be expensive), you could just have a second camera, on a second laptop, directed at an actual whiteboard.

The camera that's focused on you might be a 3D-sensing camera. That's simply a webcam that contains logic and processing, which can dynamically remove whatever is behind you. What that means is, in a web presentation, you can put your slides on the screen, and make it appear that you are standing in front of the slide itself. You superimpose your slides with the webcam.

If you remove your background and you're showing some slides, there could be a point where you just stop doing that for a while. Perhaps you really want to focus their attention on the software, so all that's in front of them is the software screen. It's all about balance. You might use your headquarters or your logo as a static background. If you sell a product that's used in warehouses, as you come into the presentation, you could have a warehouse behind you. Whatever you do, make it work for your presentation.

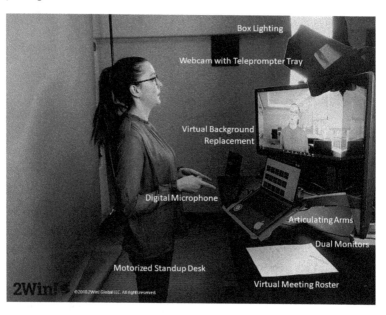

Illustration 9.5 — Virtual Studio

A virtual studio is a great investment. If you have a lot of people in a building, and they do a lot of web presentations, day in and day out, it's probably a good idea to invest in a virtual studio. It's not that expensive, and one can be made from a very small office. All it takes is a couple of box lights, a stand-up desk that's motorized to adjust for different heights, a couple of cameras, and a good quality microphone. Pair all that with a calm, neutral background, and you're set.

If you are using a 3D camera, you want a calm background. If the background is busy such as a bookshelf filled with items, it is much harder for the 3D camera to create separation. Backgrounds can be flexible, as long as they're static.

The other alternative is pop-up backgrounds. These are portable backdrops photographers use when they take portraits. If you have something busy behind you and can't change it, you can use a pop-up in the background. A professional background, like all these tools, will greatly enhance the value of the video. By contrast, if it's too produced—if there's music that sounds too extreme or graphics that are unnecessary—it can come across as a bit too slick, and you lose authenticity. Don't let this become an overproduced, expensive-looking video piece. It's just a real person, doing a real thing, in an engaging, authentic way.

CRIMES TO AVOID

There are a few common crimes or pitfalls that can happen when you're making virtual demos. The first one, and the most common one, we refer to as "change the channel." Your viewers are bored; so in their minds, they go into the realm of multitasking. Email, Snapchat, messaging, taking a phone call, having a conversation with somebody—they're just changing the channel. This can be prevented by making sure you establish a connection with the audience through interactivity.

The second crime is pretty self-explanatory: "Stop me if you have a question." They won't stop you. They simply won't, unless it's driving them absolutely crazy—and at that point, they're probably frustrated. Interactivity means that you have planned interactive points every three to five minutes. You've planned a stopping point to check in with the audience—get them to chat, ask them a question, get them to ask you a question—you're consciously driving interaction.

"Remote projector" is a concept that's all about treating your web presentation as if you're using it as a projector and you're in the room with the audience. That is *not* your medium. Make sure you use the features of your virtual meeting platform to drive interaction. Simply using your platform as a remote projector will drive your audience to multitasking.

"Camping out" is the fourth common crime. That's when you have a lengthy conversation while leaving up a busy screen. This might be a busy slide, software screen, or product screen. If you camp out, you're asking for problems—because what will invariably happen is that everyone outside of your discussion will disengage. They're either going to change the channel if you go too long, or they'll start asking questions about what's on the screen—questions which might have nothing to do with what you're talking about. This creates confusion and frustration with other stakeholders.

One way to avoid camping out is to have a "splash" slide. Use something simple, like a logo, to replace the busy screen while you're on camera. That makes it easy to direct the audience's attention away from the slide because it's a very basic slide with nothing to distract the stakeholders.

SUMMARY

When it comes to this medium, you and your team have a choice. You can either take advantage of the medium and commit to driving engagement and interactivity with your audience, or you can be a member of the herd and use the medium as a remote projector. One will lead to a differentiating remote demonstration and presentation experience, and the other will result in a multitasking, non-engaged audience that buys a better experience from your competition.

TEN
THE IN-PERSON MASTER OF 24

Who gave the best demonstration in the world? Was it Steve Jobs, when he first demoed the very first version of the iPhone? Was it Elon Musk, when he first introduced the solution to power and the elimination of greenhouse gas emissions?

Not for me. The best in-person demo I've ever seen was given by my high school physics teacher. Remember him? Christopher Chivarina. He's the one who provided a lesson on resonance in Chapter 4.

Instead of teaching physics out of a book or having you do labs like every other common teacher, "Mr. C" dared to be different. When he taught us resonance, he didn't show us Barton's pendulum.

While interesting to a bunch of physicists, he knew the demonstration of some pendulums to a group of seventeen-year-olds wouldn't pique our interest. Instead, he brought a battery-powered toy helicopter into the lab. With great anticipation, we all wondered what this crazy and fun teacher was going to demo this time. He then turned off all the incandescent lights in the room because they "glowed." He then left on the fluorescent lights, which happened to flash at sixty beats per second (60 hertz).

Now came the fun part. The helicopter took off from the table then, and Mr. C became more and more excited as he exclaimed, "Wait for it, wait for it!" He then slowed the speed of the main rotor on the helicopter until it didn't look like the rotor was moving—it appeared as though it was levitating above the table! "Look at that! The rotor is no longer moving! The rotors are in resonance with the fluorescent lights that are flashing at sixty times per second!" We were all amazed and ready to learn more about resonance.

During physics demos throughout his career, Mr. C was known to jump up on the table with excitement, take a class outside to push a car across the parking lot to demonstrate the power of inertia, and take his classes to an amusement park to experience physics in action. Mr. C is the best demonstrator I've ever seen, to this day, in my life. This great teacher put us all in resonance by appealing to everyone's learning styles and interests.

What is challenging about a demo or presentation to a business audience is that everybody is on a different resonance. You've got executives, who care about their strategic initiatives; you've got managers, who care about productivity, or risk reduction; you've got staff, who care about getting home on time. A master demonstrator can go into the audience and address the key interests for every single type of person in the room, thus bringing all stakeholders into resonance.

Masters of 24 address the needs of different people during each sales motion. Imagine an opportunity where the sales engagement team is competing for the business against their number one competitor. During the demo or presentation, the Master of 24 (master) presents a product feature, and then

addresses the staff: "So you can see that was really easy to do."
To the manager: "You know, from a productivity standpoint, if
you think about your staff and all the different improvements
I've just shown you, you can expect your metrics to improve by
eleven percent, like *this* company."

Finally, the master turns to the executive and says, "You
know, if we can do that together just like we've been able to do
with other companies, imagine what that's going to do for your
strategic initiative to..." What the master just accomplished was
resonance in the room, because she spoke to the needs of every
single person. Creating resonance in a room (virtual or in-
person) will help you differentiate against a tough competitor
more than the strength of your products, services, or solutions.

THE POWER OF "PRE-SUASION"

Before ever stepping foot in your prospect's corporate office,
you have multiple opportunities to differentiate yourself and
persuade the prospect. In previous chapters, we offered a
variety of methods for doing just that. In his book *Pre-suasion:
A Revolutionary Way to Influence and Persuade,* Robert Cialdini
discusses how to pre-suade your audience by being seen as
different, thus opening the pathways you need to convince
your prospect or customer to not just change, but select you
over your competition.

The book presents research that supports the concept
that rather than to seek to change what people think (which
is difficult), change what they *think about* by directing their
attention (easy). In his book, Cialdini cites an experiment
at Northwestern involving a side-by-side, visual, online
comparison of two sofas. One of the sofas featured comfy
cushions, and the other sturdy cushions. Of those individuals
who made selections, 58 percent chose the sofa with sturdy
cushions, while 42 percent preferred the comfy-cushioned

sofa. But when two extra sofas with sturdy cushions were added to the comparison, preference for the different and distinctive sofa with comfy cushions increased to 77 percent.

You have to be different. You need to pre-suade, in the days or hours before the event, at the start of the event, and during the event.

People like what's different. As they say, the bottom line is, "You don't just need to think different; you have to be different." At 2Win!, when we think about how, as an organization, we've trained forty thousand people on six continents, we've noticed a problem in presentations that manifests itself in a variety of sales motions: everybody opens up their presentation the same way.

They don't think differently, and they aren't different. They start the presentation with small talk, introductions, an agenda, and an overview: here's who we are, here's our company, here's our objectives today, and here's what we think you wanted to get covered. It's the same thing every time. They don't stand out.

It's not what the Rule of 24 stakeholders want. What they want is immediate answers to their questions, intriguing insights they hadn't thought of in how your product, service, or solution is unique and different than everyone else. All of that adds up to stakeholders wanting their engagements with you to be a better experience than with your competitors, because that's what gives them the confidence to select you over anyone else.

When it comes to a key in-person demo or presentation, dump the tired "Thank you for being here," corporate histories, agendas, and overviews. As you learned in Chapter 4, structure your in-person demo or presentation is like a movie that captures the stakeholders' intrigue from the outset. In other words, from the very beginning of this key engagement, you and your organization will look different—and more interesting than all of your competitors.

Today's repeating pattern of demo or presentation openings tells the stakeholders that your product, service, solutions, and company are just like everyone else they evaluate. You're a firm-cushioned sofa, and your competition offers a comfy experience.

Based on our global experience, success in key in-person demos and presentations, and all that leads up to those events, determines whether or not your team exceeds sales quota.

You or one of your sales engagement team members might do a web demo as part of the initial process, but the key event is going to be in person. You need to make sure you are different in that event and that you're pre-suading before the event.

Sending a playlist that contains a personal video and some key demo videos makes for an incredibly strong start. The stakeholders will recognize your efforts, and you'll start establishing differentiation. Use the personal video to introduce yourself, potentially your team, and key content that you believe will help pre-suade the stakeholders ahead of the in-person event. Your competition? Well, they'll send an email with a "looking forward to meeting all of you" message!

IN-PERSON DEMO OR PRESENTATION OPENING

Masters of in-person events will have the stakeholder who has served as their sponsor introduce their sales engagement team. This is structured by giving him an index card on each member of your team, and each card has the three simple elements of a neatly summarized introduction. People often wonder if a sponsor would really do that. The answer is an overwhelming "yes!" You simply need to give them an example of what you want when you ask, and they will almost always do you this "favor."

Once introductions are complete, the leader of your sales engagement team opens the demo or presentation with a limbic technique that connects your services to the strategic initiative the executive stakeholders are driving toward. This opening is brief but critical, because the best chance you have of an executive stakeholder attending an in-person demo or presentation is at the beginning of the event. Then start with the most interesting aspect of your demo. You can do this because you pre-suaded the audience with your videos.

THE JAMES BOND OPENING SUB-SCENE

Now that executive intrigue has been set, present an example of how your products, services, or solutions help achieve the executive's strategic initiative. This is your James Bond demo sub-scene. Assume your organization provides a cloud-based cyber security solution called "Blue Cube Secure." It constantly scans every possible access point to a prospect's IT infrastructure, in search of every possible nefarious intrusion.

Also, assume you've just completed your limbic opening agenda and introductions, and your prospect was pre-suaded with overview demo and key impact videos ahead of your meeting. Your James Bond demo might look something like this:

> "We thought we'd start out today's demo with a brief, thirty-five-slide company and product overview, and

then...just kidding! You've probably been through enough of those in your career. Instead, Michelle, our solution consultant, is going to demonstrate why, by the end of the demo, your stockholders can feel confident that every part of your enterprise is safe from nefarious individuals, organizations, and foreign governments."

Then, Michelle takes over the presentation and opens the demo with a black screen being projected. She steps away from the podium and laptop and delivers her opening tell.

"What you're about to see is a live graphical display of attempted intrusions into your enterprise being blocked and rejected by your new solution, Blue Cube Secure. What I want you to look for is the counter on the top left of the screen as it increments upward for every attempted incursion."

Michelle now steps back to the podium and presents the live display of a world map that shows flashes in every city where attempted incursions are traced and destroyed. The counter she mentioned is steadily increasing as she explains some of the key elements of the screen that each level of Value Pyramid would appreciate. She ends the James Bond opening by going back to a black screen and saying,

"What you just saw is a live view of attempted intrusions into our company and what happened to each of those intrusions. For those of you in IT, you will no longer waste time (*benefit*) chasing innocent attempts to access your enterprise, such as an employee who can't remember their password. This means you can focus your attention on attempts that your Blue Cube Secure solution flags as exceptions (*benefit*). For the managers, this means your staff can focus on eliminating incursions and reduce the risk of what even one incursion can cause (*manager benefit*). From an executive perspective, imagine bringing this into the next board of directors meeting as a visual aid to provide your oversight committee comfort, and confidence to the stockholders that your leadership is using the latest cybersecurity to protect their interests (*executive benefit*)."

Did you see the "so you can" progression all the way to an executive benefit? Below, we assembled the benefits of the above sub-scene for you into a "so you can" sequence:

(so you can) "no longer waste time"

(so you can) "focus your attention on...exceptions"

(so you can) "reduce the risk of incursion"

(so you can) "provide your oversight committee comfort and confidence to the stockholders."

After Michelle finishes her James Bond sub-scene, you are back at the podium to deliver a brief agenda and an opening to the first scene of the demo.

Your competition's opening? "Thank you for investing the time to host us today. Let's start with introductions... (five minutes later). Here's our agenda and what we plan on covering today. If you see anything that you'd like to add...(five minutes later). Our company has been in business for twenty-eight years. Here's a timeline of our accomplishments, here's a 'logo-land' slide of many of our customers...(ten minutes later). Blah, blah-blah, blah-blah."

Your competitor's demo starts with a product overview and the basic navigational elements of their solution. You don't have to cover that, because your videos did that for you—professionally and effectively.

I mean, in today's marketplace, it's not as if people aren't going to have researched every competitor ahead of the event. They'll know who your company is, whether you're financially viable, how many people you've got, who your key investors are, and who you've acquired. They've looked at product reviews, blogs, and websites like Glassdoor.

RULE OF 24 DISCOVERY

Let's back up from the in-person event for a moment and discuss how you gain a perspective on stakeholder priorities. In a traditional sense, it was "discovery" that took place before a key presentation.

Discovery is the process in which you get as much information out of the people you're going to present to as possible, so that you can make the presentation as focused and as meaningful as possible. The term discovery comes from the legal world regarding evidence discovery, and it's the same concept. You're really trying to figure out how to build your case. Discovery was most frequently performed in face-to-face or telephone interviews.

The problem is discovery "fatigue". Stakeholders, throughout their careers, have been through lots of these demos and presentations. Like we discussed earlier in the Rule of 24, this isn't the first time these people have bought a technology solution or a product or a service similar to yours.

Let's say you're an accounting firm trying to secure a client for auditing services. The stakeholders have been subscribing to auditing services for years. As their organization has grown, they've found the need to change auditors two times in ten years. The stakeholders are once again evaluating potential auditors, and the audit partner is coming in to present, but they want to make lots of discovery before the presentation.

The stakeholders are fatigued by another set of possible auditors, once again asking the same (or similar) discovery questions. They don't want to set the time aside to answer a bunch of questions. The stakeholders are thinking, *"These people should know our business. We sent them everything that we think they need to know, so why do they need to talk to us?"*

And so it becomes difficult to secure time with people, because they just don't want to go through this anymore. They don't want to spend the time, even though it probably would be of value. Instead, they tell the stakeholder that's leading the selection (often called the sponsor), "You talk to them on our behalf." In these circumstances, you're probably receiving very limited discovery in the form of a written document from the sponsor.

There is a huge risk in this; it's a matter of whether the information they are giving you is accurate and comprehensive, or if they've filled in the gaps themselves. The sponsor has *one* role in the company and, therefore, one perspective. That means they might not be able to understand what the others— the staff members or upper management—need from your presentation. You end up with incomplete, or even inaccurate, information. You won't have enough specificity to maximize your influence across your audience.

THE DISCOVERY GAP

"It's not necessarily that the information is unknown, it's that it's under-known."
— CHAD WILSON, VICE PRESIDENT OF CURRICULUM AND CLIENT SUCCESS, 2WIN! GLOBAL.

When Chad Wilson made that statement in a senior management meeting, I was struck by his clairvoyance. He reflected how our global facilitation team had been hearing about a significant shift in client access to discovery. Upon further investigation, Chad learned through client conversations that prospect sponsors were rarely allowing sales engagement teams unlimited discovery access to stakeholders. Instead, sponsors were funneling discovery to them and speaking on behalf of all stakeholders. Consider these two data points from our research:

Compared to four years ago, my opportunity to perform pre-demo discovery is:

Significantly Lower	10.47%
Lower	25.97%
About the Same	29.84%
Higher	25.19%
Significantly Higher	8.53%

Illustration 10.1— Pre-Demo Discovery Survey

From the data above, you would be right to conclude that discovery opportunities are about the same today as they were four years ago. Discovery is still happening, but as we learned in follow-up interviews, with fewer stakeholders and using different methods than person-to-person interviews. The problem is exacerbated by the fact that organizations like CEB/Gartner report an ever-increasing number of stakeholders in every B2B decision. Making matters worse, sales engagement teams report a 48 percent decrease in the amount of time they're given to prepare for a significant service presentation. All these facts lead to under-known information when engaging in a key client engagement like a finals presentation.

Presenters have a tendency to fill in the gaps caused by the limited discovery of the under-known with what they know from their experience working with other customers. This means a presenter often plans for an event with a lot of assumptions, and they are invariably going to have a miss. As a master, there are three primary ways of mitigating this risk; eDiscovery, sponsor discovery, and discovery on-the-fly.

eDISCOVERY

Electronic discovery, or eDiscovery, represents research a sales engagement team member can perform without any client involvement. eDiscovery research includes CRM systems, publicly available information accessed through free web sources, and cloud-based subscription services. The combination of all three data sources can provide an incredibly rich view of a potential client and their stakeholders before a significant event.

In Chapter 4 you learned about the Value Pyramid, which describes the stratification of how staff, managers, and executive stakeholders view value. Think of the outcomes of the eDiscovery as a feeder to your Value Pyramid. Here's an example:

One of our clients in Melbourne, Australia was faced with a Rule of 24 opportunity where their prospect's sponsor informed them that they were selected as a finalist in a big data, data mining selection. They were informed that they had three days to prepare for what was described as a brief demo. They were sent a document that described what they wanted to see in the demo.

Our client's salesperson immediately qualified the opportunity and assembled the team to prepare for the demo. The team began preparing by researching the company and the stakeholders involved (uncovered during qualification), using a variety of eDiscovery techniques. They searched their CRM to discern any products they had licensed in the past, prior contact history with the client and their stakeholders, and marketing materials in demo videos each stakeholder had consumed. They investigated each stakeholder's LinkedIn profile to learn more about their perspective and role. They also investigated publicly available information about the company that described their strategic initiatives. They watched videos about the prospect and their products via their website and YouTube.

All this eDiscovery was combined with the prospect's requirements document, and our client was able to quickly create a strategic initiative map that aligned product feature requests with the areas those features would impact, aligned to broad improvement strategies and their strategic initiative.

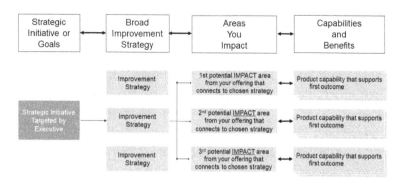

Illustration 10.2 — Strategic Initiative Map

Finally, they placed names by the impact areas so that, during the demo, they could emphasize key benefits to the right individual from the right place in the Value Pyramid.

Ahead of the demo, the salesperson sent a personal video to each stakeholder, which introduced the sales engagement team and provided context for three demo videos she wanted the prospect to watch before the live demo. These demo videos provided each stakeholder an excellent overview of each application they would see in the event, and so that time was not wasted in the live demo performing overviews. Walking into the demo, our client knew exactly what videos each stakeholder had watched. The sales engagement team was able to utilize the time well that would otherwise have been spent in overviews to perform discovery on-the-fly and fill in the gaps of their under-known information.

The event was a complete success. Our client was immediately awarded the business without the need for follow-up meetings and additional demos. It was exactly what the stakeholders were hoping for when they invited companies to compete for the project. While our client's competitors wasted time with company and product overviews and filled in the gaps of under-known information on their own, our client focused on their prospect's needs and desires, and learned the gaps using discovery on-the-fly. They showed a level of professionalism and produced an in-person demo experience that earned them the business.

DISCOVERY ON-THE-FLY

This phrase refers to performing discovery with a prospect during a live presentation or during an impromptu meeting. We recognize this is a less than an ideal situation; however, the reality of Rule of 24 is that discovery on-the-fly is inevitable. Once again, research shows that most B2B sellers have half the amount of time to prepare for a significant demo or presentation than they used to.

Stakeholders are more directive in what they want to see, and more likely to interrupt a presenter when their interests—whether known or unknown—are not being served during the demo or presentation. All these facts necessitate discovery on-the-fly. Masters know how to perform this type of discovery and use the information they learned only moments earlier in their demo or presentation. We've researched, analyzed, and perfected a formula for discovery on-the-fly. It's not as complex or as challenging as you might think.

THE "ALMOST" PERFECT FORMULA FOR DISCOVERY ON-THE-FLY

Transparently, no formula for human interactions is ever perfect—but this one is damn good! It involves active listening skills on the part of the sales engagement member. Always a good thing! It demonstrates empathy and interest in helping the stakeholder move from their current situation to their desired situation. It helps stakeholders think about what the impact would be if they moved from current to desired. It uncovers a scenario for use in creating context for a tell-show-tell sub-scene. It seeks metrics that help build the case for the value of choosing your products, services, or solutions. And finally, it gives the sales engagement team member a sense of where the person they're speaking to sits in the Value Pyramid.

Leading   Discovery On-the-Fly   Tailored
Open-Ended   Tell-Show-Tell
Question

Illustration 10.3 — Discovery-On-The-Fly

LEADING OPEN-ENDED QUESTIONS

Masters know how to ask questions that leave room for a stakeholder's answers. They do this by beginning a question with known information. We call this a leading open-ended question. For example: "Based on my research, I noticed that companies like yours typically are interested in x. What's your perspective on this?" What you've done by saying "based on my research," is established credibility with your expertise and left yourself room if they disagree.

They might respond with: "I know that most of our competitors focus on 'x'; however, we have a different perspective, and that's what makes us unique." This question revealed their true interests and uncovered under-known information. Imagine what would have happened if the demonstrator had filled in the gaps of the under-known information with a demo that focused on the wrong thing. It could lead to a disaster!

Compare these two situations: In one of them, we start off by saying, "Based on my research into your organization, and in particular, looking at your annual report, it said you're really driving toward an initiative that's trying to decrease costs across the board by leveraging automation."

In the second situation, you might say: "Companies like yours are really trying to leverage technology to drop costs across the board." The first one is more authentic and establishes credibility. The second sounds like a bullet point that marketing gave us. It sounds canned, versus authentic and conversational.

An element of competitive differentiation can be established by the way you ask questions. It's essential to exhibit to stakeholders that you've put in the work before a meeting, presentation, or demo through research. Doing so builds your credibility.

A leading open-ended question is also an opportunity to increase your credibility and expertise by incorporating an insight into your question.

We like to think of it as being athletic about how you ask questions in the moment. The prospect is *expecting* you to open your laptop, turn on a projector, share your screen, and start presenting. They are curious; they want to know what you can show them. They might ask you to "demonstrate to us these eight things." But you don't have any context for making those eight things relevant when you demonstrate them if you have under-known information.

Let's say the stakeholders have invited you and your team to their offices to address a list of eight items of interest. You're discussing item number four on their list, and there are six ways your solution can address the needs of that item. Do you demo all six ways? Or do you try to find out which two ways are going to be the most relevant, and let those be the two that are explored in the demo?

It's going to be more beneficial, for them, if you can promptly get straight to the answer and make it look simple and easy to implement. It also gives you more time to present the other topics, and it makes your service look less complicated. Therefore, you need to understand and build context around item four by asking them a few questions. So you need to be agile, or athletic, about how you do that.

When you get to item four, you're going to ask a leading open-ended question about the item. Compare these two questions about forecasting inventory for a wholesaler:

1. "Tell me what forecasting methods you prefer." (*Open-ended*)
2. "It has been our experience that for organizations like yours, you prefer simple averaging for many products, but exponential smoothing for select, higher volatility products. What is your opinion on this?" (*Leading open-ended*)

Many of us have been trained to use the approach of question one. Be as open-ended as possible. The problem is, today's stakeholders want *your* opinion. They want to know you have an opinion and position. Part of what they are buying is your expertise.

Additionally, in the past, you had time to build a relationship with stakeholders, which built trust and comfort. With today's Rule of 24 stakeholders, you don't have time, and they don't have the patience for lengthy relationship building. Pure open-ended questions place a stakeholder in an uncomfortable position. The stakeholders don't know if they should open up and tell you everything they know—leaving themselves exposed to what they don't know.

In contrast, the expertise built into the leading open-ended question above creates credibility and trust. Stakeholders will appreciate the fact that you have an opinion and will answer your leading open-ended question thoughtfully. Your leading open-ended questions drive toward your service strengths; which, taken as a whole, is where your advantages lie.

Let's take specific questions that attempt to expose pains. Open-ended questions about pain lead to personal vulnerabilities. Therefore, use a leading open-ended question approach to allay those fears.

It's a little bit like basketball: you've practiced for months, you know what you need to do, and you know the rules of the game, but you still have to be in the moment, looking for openings, doing all the things you need to do to score. It's never going to be the same. It's fluid, and it's moving; you have set plays, but you also you have to adapt. It's the same thing with discovery on-the-fly; you're going into the offense with a plan, but you also know the plan needs to be adaptable.

Another example can be found in late night talk shows. The host has a list of questions, but he has to be very quick on her feet, because she doesn't really know how the guest is going to answer. They need to be able to go off script.

This skill becomes especially important when we need to understand our prospect's needs. For example, let's say I'm the sales engineer, and I've been talking to the salesperson to prepare for my demo. The salesperson informed me that one of the key stakeholders found a certain topic important to them, but I don't really know why. For example, the warehouse manager really wanted to improve productivity.

On the surface, the "why" was obvious. But I really don't understand, from *her* perspective, why it's so vital. I tried to learn that information before the demo through traditional discovery, but because it was a Rule of 24 opportunity, there simply wasn't time to interview her. When I got to that topic in the demo, I turned to the warehouse manager and explored the issue with her, together, before I presented the solution to the warehouse team.

I'm not spending the first thirty minutes of the demo asking all these questions. I interspersed our discovery on-the-fly questions throughout the presentation, then demonstrated responsively to the information learned; that's being athletic.

When you perform discovery on-the-fly and responsively demonstrate, you get on firmer and firmer ground, and that helps ensure your future questions are relevant. You keep the questions contained in the topic around what you are about to demo or present a solution against. You could probably expand your questioning and the conversation, and go into a variety of other topics, but if they're not relevant to what you want to demo next, they're not productive.

The skill here is all about keeping your leading open-ended questions narrow and being able to know when to stop the questioning and do the demo. We call this "narrowing."

Rule of 24 stakeholders will get frustrated if you spend too much time asking broad, open-ended questions that lead to multiple topics in unrelated areas. And you will be frustrated, since the value of your solution will be lost in a sea of possibilities—making your presentation unmemorable.

You might be wondering, "How do I build a library of insightful leading open-ended questions?" The answer lies in your experience and expertise. You already know the problems your services solve, so draw on that for the front end of your leading open-ended questions.

For example, if I were presenting a solution that conserves energy in a commercial building, a leading open-ended question could be created out of one of many methods you offer that help accomplish that goal. "Many of our clients have found that intelligent, interconnected, zone-based thermostats that detect if someone is in a room help save as much as eleven percent of the total energy consumption of the building. I'm curious, what are your current strategies in new construction for temperature control and energy conservation?"

The "leading" portion of this question is actually a statement that is derived from a key feature of the solution and turned into key-value benefit of the results from this feature. The statement was derived from a case study of an existing customer. The individual asking this leading open-ended question simply took that insight and placed it at the front end of their open-ended question. Doing so results in a confident, expertise-laden narrowing question that leaves room for the stakeholder to express their opinion, and will help you build context for this portion of your demo or presentation.

REFLECTING, PARAPHRASING & EXTENDING

After starting an investigation with the leading open-ended question, you'll want to reflect, paraphrase, or extend their response to further explore the topic. A pure reflection of their response is useful for showing your stakeholder that you heard her, and it helps you remember what she said. This is particularly useful when you don't quite understand their response and need a mental pause after reflection to request clarification.

Paraphrasing provides all the benefits of reflecting while adding the benefit of demonstrating that you are thinking and reasoning with their response. Extending your paraphrase shows that you are thinking, reasoning, and applying what you heard to what she needs in the future.

Let's use the leading open-ended question from above to illustrate reflecting paraphrasing and extending:

> **You:** "Many of our clients have found that intelligent, interconnected, zone-based thermostats that detect if occupants are in a room help save as much as eleven percent of the total energy consumption of the building. I'm curious, what are your current strategies in new construction for temperature control and energy conservation?"

> **Stakeholder:** "Today, we use zone-based thermostats that are centrally controlled, but that system doesn't detect occupants like you're describing."

> **You (*reflect*):** "Got it. Today, you only use zone-based thermostats that are managed centrally, and they don't have the capability of detecting occupants."
> (versus)

> **You (*paraphrase*):** "I understand. If I hear you correctly, whether a room is occupied or not, the temperature always remains the same—so you're potentially cooling or heating an unoccupied room."

> **You (*extend*):** "I understand. If I hear you correctly, whether a room is occupied or not, the temperature always remains the same—so you're potentially cooling or heating an unoccupied room. So it stands to reason that a system

that detects occupants could save a substantial amount of energy."

EXPLORING THEIR RESPONSE

Your responsive demo or presentation will be effectively positioned if you can skillfully explore their response to your leading open-ended question. Paraphrasing and extending are skills you need to master during discovery on-the-fly. There are five elements you need to be able to explore while performing discovery on-the-fly. These elements are:

1. Current: How are they accomplishing something today?
2. Desired: How do they envision improving on what they do today?
3. Impact: What would the impact be if they moved from current to desired?
4. Scenario: Can they describe a scenario that you could use in your demo or presentation that illustrates current and desired?
5. Metrics: If they were able to successfully move from current to desired, and it had the intended impact, how they would measure the improvement?

To illustrate how exploring a question using our narrowing approach provides a perfect platform for you to responsively demo, let's expand the leading open-ended question from earlier. This time, we will put in parentheses the skills and elements that will help you with your responsive demo or presentation:

You: "Many of our clients have found that intelligent, interconnected, zone-based thermostats that detect if occupants are in a room help save as much as eleven percent of the total energy consumption of the building. (insight) I'm curious, what are your current strategies in new construction for temperature control and energy conservation? (*current*)"

Stakeholder: "Today, we use zone-based thermostats that are centrally controlled, but that system doesn't detect occupants like you're describing."

You: "I understand. If I hear you correctly, whether a room is occupied or not, the temperature always remains the same—so you're potentially cooling or heating an unoccupied room (paraphrase). So it stands to reason that a system that detects occupants could save a substantial amount of energy (*extend*)."

Stakeholder: "Makes sense. I just haven't seen anything like that so far."

You: "So you can envision moving your smart system like this to save energy? (*desired*)"

Stakeholder: "Depending on the cost, sure."

You: "Okay. If the system is in place, walk me through a scenario of what building management does to control the temperature of the zones on a floor of a commercial building using your current methods, versus how you might see this working in the future. (*scenario*)"

Stakeholder: "Well, today, unless the building manager somehow knew the zone was going to be occupied, they simply don't bother to close off that zone. Realistically speaking, that's not practical unless somebody contacted them to let them know. Going forward, using what you are describing, I could envision a fully automated hands-off approach to that type of energy conservation."

You: "How would you measure the impact of a fully automated environmental control system? (*metrics*)"

Stakeholder: "I suppose in its simplest sense, we could measure what energy consumption is in this building compared to other structures in the portfolio. However, no two buildings are the same, and weather varies from one year to the next, so I'm open to ideas."

You: "What if your new system could dynamically calculate the energy savings when a zone is shut down due to vacancy? Can you see how that might provide an accurate picture of your energy and cost savings" (*insightful metrics*)"

Stakeholder: "Sure. Can you show me that?"

As you can see, through this line of questioning you have everything you need to responsively demo or present your solution immediately following this discovery on-the-fly.

TERMINOLOGY & THE IMPORTANCE OF LANGUAGE

Stakeholders will naturally use their own terminology as they explain something. You can count on that. They'll refer to terminology that's common within their industry, or even just specific to their company. This is yet another reason why discovery on-the-fly in your demo is so valuable: that terminology will be fresh in your mind and will improve your resonance. Learn to recall the terms quickly, without having to refer to your notes, by using their terms in your paraphrasing and extending reflections. Now they'll see you as a good listener, connected to what they do. If you make any mistakes, they'll be kind about correcting you—they won't hold it against you.

STAKEHOLDER RESPONSES – PROCESS OR PERFORMANCE

Process-oriented responses focus exclusively on the task and how it's accomplished. Performance-oriented responses come from stakeholders who articulate how the solution you are exploring would improve the performance of their job, department, or organization, or how you might reduce their risk.

As you examine the stakeholder responses to the funneling questions above, ask yourself this question: *Were her responses process-oriented or performance-oriented?* If you answered process-oriented, you're correct!

Your ability to discern a process response versus a performance response will be essential in your responsive demo or presentation. A stakeholder with a process response will be focused on the steps you take in your demo. Generally speaking, process-oriented individuals are members of the staff and at the base of the Value Pyramid.

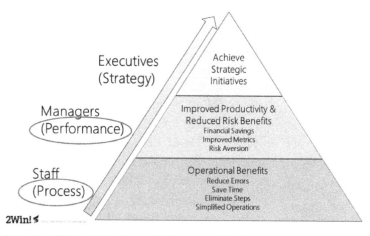

Illustration 10.4 — Value Pyramid: Process vs. Performance

Process-oriented individuals will also absorb operational-style benefit statements in the closing tell of your sub-scene. Below is a list of examples of operational-style benefit statements that resonate with staff:

› You can see how **easy**...
› You can see how **completely automated**...
› This will save you **time**...
› You can see how **fast**...
› What I showed you will **reduce errors**...
› This will **reduce frustration**...

Performance-oriented individuals are frequently in the ranks of management. These stakeholders can be found at the second level of the Value Pyramid. They appreciate being able to follow your flow during the demo or presentation. But to resonate with them in your closing tell, your benefit statements need to go beyond operational benefits. After directing your operational benefit to a staff-level stakeholder, you should turn to the performance-oriented stakeholder and complete their benefit statement using the conjunctive phrase "so you can" and deliver a benefit that articulates improved productivity or reduced risk. Below is a list of examples of operational benefits followed by improved productivity or reduced-risk benefits using the conjunctive phrase "so you can":

› You can see how **easy**...so you can improve the **efficiency** of your entire staff.
› You can see how c**ompletely automated**...so you can **improve your square foot to dollar expense ratio**.
› This will **save you time**...so you can have your building managers **reduce building costs** in other areas.
› You can see how **fast**...so you can **squeeze every dollar of savings** from your energy expense.
› What I showed you will **reduce errors**...thus **reducing the risk of non-renewals**.
› This will **reduce frustration**...and **reduce staff turnover.**

RESPONSIVE DEMONSTRATING & PRESENTING

Throughout this chapter, we've been referencing "responsive demonstrating" or "responsive presenting." The Merriam-Webster (MW) dictionary provides the following example in their definition of the adverb "responsive":

"Quick to respond or react appropriately or sympathetically: sensitive."

MW's definition of "responsive" fits perfectly into our description of responsive demonstrating and presenting. With this in mind, consider this definition of responsive demonstrating and presenting:

"A demonstrator or presenter who is quick to respond or react appropriately or sympathetically by demonstrating or presenting the information they received moments ago from a stakeholder."

With responsive demonstrating and presenting, you're bringing the audience in as a participant using their name, terminology, current desires and pains, impacts, and metrics. If, however, you spent forty-five minutes gathering all that information before you begin demonstrating or presenting, it becomes almost impossible to effectively and accurately address that large chunk of information.

In a responsive mode, you present against the smaller set of information. After demonstrating one, two, or three short sub-scenes against the information you have just uncovered, perform more discovery on-the-fly, gathering additional terminology, current desires and pains, impacts, and metrics. With this new small set of information, you responsively present one, two, or three more sub-scenes. It's a simple "rinse and repeat" cycle of discovery on-the-fly and responsive demonstrating.

We are not suggesting that your sales engagement team should stop attempting to perform traditional discovery ahead of their demos or presentations. On the contrary, we strongly encourage this practice to continue whenever possible. However, when a Rule of 24 prospect refuses your requests for traditional discovery well ahead of the demo, you have three choices:

1. Rely on eDiscovery and/or limited discovery and risk demonstrating or presenting against under-known information.

2. Leverage eDiscovery, limited discovery, discovery on-the-fly, and responsive demonstration presenting.
3. Walk away from a Rule of 24 prospect.

We believe Option #1 has the most inherent risk. In speaking with our clients in over forty-four countries, we have learned of too many instances when betting on under-known information led to a presentation that became overly complex, as all options had to be presented, and presentations that were poorly received by the stakeholders because the sales engagement team bet on the wrong choices.

Option #3 is certainly a valid choice, particularly if the sales engagement team believes a decision for a competitor has already been made, or they are unable to properly qualify the opportunity.

Today's Rule of 24 sales engagement team embraces Option #2, which uses their ability and skill to combine the eDiscovery, partial discovery, and discovery on-the-fly, with a responsive demo or presentation.

Assume you're in a responsive demo sub-scene to the discovery on-the-fly questions from earlier. These questions uncovered the prospect's interest in your system's ability to automatically shut down airflow to an unoccupied zone. You have two stakeholders in the demo who are keenly interested in this area of your solution.

James is a staff member who is responsible for being on-site in a commercial building and adjusting zone thermostats. Monica is a regional manager for commercial properties in the area and is responsible for overall cost control. You have just completed the demo of your system, which detects an unoccupied room and adjusts the zone accordingly.

You're now ready to present the closing tell benefits to that sub-scene. You step away from your laptop, look at James, and say, "You can see how completely automated your new environmental control system will be, twenty-four hours a day—which provides building managers like yourself the time to be proactive on driving other efficiencies throughout a property."

This was the process-oriented benefit statement. You then turn to Monica and say, "Monica, this building automation will improve energy efficiency so you can achieve energy savings of eleven percent—like Sierra Properties was able to do. Imagine the cost savings if you implement this solution in all the properties in your region." You walk over to the white board and engage Monica in the math of the savings across sixteen properties and two million square feet of space.

DELIVERING VALUE AND RISK REDUCTION IN YOUR DEMO OR PRESENTATION

Now that we have established that managers care most about productivity improvements across their teams and reduction in business risk, we will turn your attention to the timing of the delivery of those benefits. Some so-called pundits have argued that the beginning of each scene of a demo should begin with the delivery of value or reduction in risk. We completely disagree.

You simply haven't earned the right to present those critical benefits in the beginning. You earn that right by **proving the value** or risk reduction with the sub-scenes of your demo or presentation.

After working with tens of thousands of sales engagement team professionals, we advocate that you "*prepare*" the managers for the value or risk reduction at the start of your scene. This can be done by using a variety of limbic techniques that capture the attention of the managers and pique their curiosity for the results that you will deliver at the end of the scene.

We have found there are five highly effective limbic scene openings that provide a platform for delivering value and risk reduction at the end of the scene and, most importantly, make the information memorable. Those scene-opening styles are:

› Illustrative analogy
› Customer case study
› eDiscovery findings
› Industry expert
› Curiosity

Each scene-opening style can stand alone or be used in combination with others. These limbic scene openings are the perfect way to set up the delivery of your productivity improvement or risk reduction benefits at the close of the scene. Virtual and in-person demo and presentation methods benefit from these techniques, and any of them can be used in either venue.

ILLUSTRATIVE ANALOGY

From a degree of difficulty perspective, many of our clients find this limbic scene opening to be the most challenging. Many sales engagement team members consider this style of scene opening to be high risk, but high reward. Illustrative analogies must make a solid connection between the analogy and the prospect within sixty seconds of the introduction of the analogy. It involves starting your scene with a story, supported by other limbics such as images on a slide, a drawing on a white board, use of props, and even humor. These stories are most memorable when they describe something far from what you are selling.

For example, if a scene is introducing your automated detection of human activity for your zone-based environmental control, your limbic opening will be best remembered if your illustrative analogy is not related to technology or heating and air conditioning. However, an illustrative analogy that is initially unrelated—but ultimately connected to the prospect's goals for this area of your presentation—is highly effective.

In this example, assume you are demonstrating your automated detection of human activity for your zone-based environmental control system. You begin the presentation for this section of the demo with a slide that includes a full-screen image of a beautiful beachside resort.

Illustration 10.5 — Illustrative analogy - Beachside resort

You walk in front of the room and go from your logo slide to this full-screen image, and you say this: "Last winter I had the opportunity to go to Bali and stay at this all-inclusive resort. I'll tell you right now, the resort was as incredible as this picture! It was not only beautiful, but the service was amazing, the food was outstanding, and the entertainment was top-notch. What was equally incredible was that they delivered that experience for less money than a regular luxury beach hotel.

This resort in Bali reminds me a lot of the experience you want to deliver from an environmental perspective to your tenants, and actually save money along the way. In this section of the presentation, we're going to show you how you can deliver a Bali experience in every zone of every building you manage—while saving a significant amount in energy costs. You'll also see how you'll receive a return on investment in just two years, like two of our customers that I will highlight at the end of this section of the presentation."

At the end of this scene, you'll return to your opening analogy with images and connect it with what you learned during your discovery on-the-fly and responsive demo. But you won't do that by having a slide filled with words and numbers. If you do that, you'll flood a manager stakeholder's limbic system with too much information, and they'll get nothing out of the close of your scene. Instead, you'll present the results in a slide more like this:

"We experienced an 11% reduction in energy use in the first 30 days!"
Sandra Anatoli – Seven Continents

"Tenant reaction was overwhelmingly positive."
Sven Dahlen – Sweden Commercial

Illustration 10.6 — Illustrative analogy – closing slide

With the slide above, you would use humor and engaging contrasting images to create separation between their situation today and your solution going forward. The slide would build with the images first, then with a click, the first quote would appear. You would read the first quote to them (from Alex) and comment on how the responsive demo is connected to this quote. With a second click, the quote from Sven would appear. And you would once again connect it to what you just provided in the responsive demo.

Quotes like this are an excellent way to show benefits to the manager stakeholders in the form of evidence. Variations on this slide could include actual cost savings, ROI calculations, or evidence of risk reduction. Another variation would be to simply display the images side by side in a larger format and present the evidence of cost savings or return on investment on a white board or flipchart. A video of a customer testimonial could also be used instead of the quotes. Closing with your analogy can be important in a responsive demo.

You learn so much about the potential client's key interests during a responsive demo that having the flexibility to adjust your close and present the value on the white board provides a truly tailored experience for the stakeholders.

CUSTOMER CASE STUDY

The second scene style is the use of a customer case study. This style opens with information about one of your existing customers that was able to achieve results in areas similar to what your prospect is seeking. Your eDiscovery and other pre-meeting discovery provided you with enough background to know that this particular case study would be relevant. With case studies, relevance is crucial.

If your prospect can't see themselves in your case study, this opening and closing will be considerably less effective.

Before working with us, our clients would often make the mistake of thinking a case study opening included the distribution of a detailed case study document to the stakeholders. Don't make that mistake. If you provide a handout at the opening of this portion of the demo, the stakeholders won't know if they should read it now or pay attention to you.

That forces you to say something like: "I'm passing out this case study, but please don't read it now." This begs the question, why hand it out in the first place? If you have a detailed case that is documented, let the stakeholders know you'll provide them a copy of the case study at the end of the presentation.

This opening can be accomplished with either slides or a white board for visual support. The opening sets the productivity or risk reduction goal, and the closing provides the case study evidence of goal achievement. The illustration below provides a slide example of a case study opening:

Synergy International

Reduce zone temperature requests
- 230 ... ???

Reduce energy per square meter
- € 0.21 ... ???

ROI
- xx months???

Illustration 10.7 — Case Study Opening Slide

With this opening, you are establishing the criteria to the manager stakeholders of the productivity improvements and the value your case study (and your solution) supports. The slide builds, but you are not giving away the results until the presentation is complete. (More on the use of curiosity later in this chapter.)

The presentation opens as it normally should with a James Bond sub-scene, progresses to discovery on-the-fly and responsive demonstrating, and concludes with a reveal of the results of the case study. The concluding slide would look something like this:

Synergy International

Reduce zone temperature requests
- 230 ... 22

Reduce energy per square meter
- € 0.21 ... € 0.17

ROI
- 22 months

Illustration 10.8 — Case Study Closing Slide

During the conclusion, you would turn to the manager stakeholders and discuss the results of, in this case, Synergy International. You would relate those results to your prospect's organization as evidence of the value your solution provides.

As mentioned earlier, this same approach can be performed using a white board or flipchart. Doing so introduces one additional limbic technique—the perception that you are so well prepared, you can articulate these results at a moment's notice. This is very impressive to manager stakeholders.

It also gives you the flexibility of adding, replacing, or eliminating a case study metric if you determine through your responsive demo that it is no longer applicable.

In a virtual demo or presentation, use of an electronic pen and digital white board is very limbic and impactful with every stakeholder.

You can also use pre-suasion as another variation of the presentation of a case study. This can be accomplished through your video automation platform, if your marketing department has created a video that highlights the case study. You send the case study video along with a personal video to the stakeholders ahead of the in-person or virtual event, and then alter your presentation to account for their viewing history.

DISCOVERY FINDINGS

This opening is usually combined with key information your sales engagement team learned through traditional formal discovery, and it can be combined with discovery on-the-fly by using your white board. As your discovery on-the-fly exposes opportunities for productivity improvements or risk reduction, you list them on the white board. At the conclusion of that portion of the responsive demo, you interact with the manager stakeholders to estimate and record potential results.

If you know the productivity improvements or risk reductions they seek ahead of the in-person event, you can formalize that on a slide or interactively reflect that information on the white board. At the conclusion of that section of the demo, return to their goals and document the potential results.

INDUSTRY EXPERT

This style of opening and closing leverages an industry expert the prospect respects. In the opening, the bar is set by the industry expert as to what an "industry leader" or "best practice" organization should seek. This style of opening would be done with the slide that includes an image of the industry expert or their logo. The scene would conclude by revisiting the first slide and discussing the results of what you just demonstrated.

CURIOSITY

This is an incredibly effective limbic technique, as humans are naturally curious. Curiosity can be combined with any of the styles we've discussed so far. This technique typically involves piquing a stakeholder's curiosity by waiting until the end of the scene to reveal the results.

Illustrative analogies naturally contain curiosity.

As you begin this style of scene opening, the stakeholders are curious as to what the slide and analogy have to do with your demo or presentation. The challenge with curiosity is that it can be a fleeting emotion. For that reason, we want you to make a connection between your illustrative analogy and its relevance to the stakeholders within sixty seconds.

When opening with the customer case study, we want you to release each stakeholder's curiosity after presenting the opening slide or completing the white board illustration. You do this by telling the stakeholders, "At the end of this section of the presentation, we will present you with the results."

ANCHORING

Daniel Kahneman, the bestselling author of *Thinking, Fast and Slow*, describes in his book a concept called "anchoring."

According to Kahneman, anchoring occurs when people consider a particular value for an unknown quantity before estimating that quantity. In other words, they have anchored in their minds—either because you anchored it there or they got in there ahead of time—a quantity of something before you actually present a quantity.

Here's an excerpt from his book:

> *"Visitors at the San Francisco Exploratorium were asked the following two questions. First: Is the height of the tallest redwood more or less than 1,200 feet? Second: What is your best guess about the height of the tallest redwood? For other participants, the question used a low anchor: If the height of the tallest redwood is at least 180 feet, what is your best guess about its height? The difference between the two anchors was 1,020 feet, meaning that (as expected) the two groups produced very different estimates. The ones primed with 1,200 feet as an anchor guessed, on average, 844 feet. The ones that had an anchor of 180 feet gave an average estimate of 282 feet. That's an incredible shift in perspective!"*

USE OF ANCHORING IN YOUR LIMBIC OPENINGS

During an in-person (or virtual) demo or presentation you can combine anchoring with curiosity, which results in a highly effective, value-based limbic opening to your presentation.

For example, assume you are trying to convince a food wholesaler in Europe to purchase a fleet of long-haul, self-driving trucks. A research firm predicts that in five years the overall cost savings will be 38 percent over a traditional, driver-based fleet. You want to use that statistic to compel the stakeholders to choose your proposed fleet over status quo. Before showing the slide with the chart that shows the cost savings, you anchor them with this question (which I'd recommend putting on a slide):

In five years, adoption will grow by (choose one):

›   20%
›   40%
›   60%
›   80%

Take the time to get answers from the audience. What you're doing is anchoring the audience with 20 percent if they insist on thinking conservatively, or 80 percent if they think you're going to go big in your number. In reality, the figure will be 300 percent! It will be on the next slide, it will be very large, and the typeface will grow.

Anchoring is also how you can bring out your value statements. In this case, anchor your value from a customer that you know overachieved. Next, admit to the prospect that their circumstances provided a perfect opportunity to overachieve, but ask her what *she* thinks *she* could achieve. Her number will be lower, but skewed to the overachieving customer.

Now, instead of throwing a pebble into the water, you've thrown a boulder. You've disrupted what your prospect has been thinking.

In the example above, you're purposefully disrupting resonance, then reestablishing it with the manager and executive stakeholders from your Value Pyramid.

QUESTION AND OBJECTING HANDLING – FISH ON!

There is a hobby in the United States and in other parts of the world called "deep sea fishing." Those who take it seriously call it "sport fishing." If you've never had the opportunity to experience this adventure, let us explain. If you have the resources and live in certain coastal areas, you can purchase a sport fishing boat like the one pictured below.

Illustration 10.9 — Sport Fishing Boat

As you might guess, a boat like this is very expensive—out of reach for most of us. So, instead of buying a boat like this, you can charter (rent) one on a daily basis. The charter comes with a professional sport fishing captain and all the gear you need to have a great time. If you were to pay for this charter yourself, you'd pay around twelve hundred dollars in Key West, Florida.

On your own, that's still expensive. So, you gather a group of friends from all over the country and everyone flies to Key West for a long weekend on the island and a day of sport fishing. If there are four of you, the per-person price is down to three hundred dollars. That's just what we did, and here's how it panned out:

Everyone arrives safely the day before the charter and checks into the same hotel. It's time to go out and have some fun before the big day! Well, that went on until one o'clock in the morning, and everyone has to be on the dock, ready to go by sunrise. Ouch!

Illustration 10.10 — The Next Morning!

Needless to say, we get a slow start, but we rally and make it to the dock on time because we all remember the charter captain telling us on the telephone, "We've been catching so many fish I thought we'd sink the boat!"

The captain gives us instructions before we leave the dock. One important instruction is, "When I yell '*fish on*!' you all need to be ready. Make sure you know who gets the first turn at pulling in the first fish. That person will grab the rod that has the fish on it and reel in the slack on the fishing line. Everyone else, grab every (fishing) rod that doesn't have a fish on it and reel them in as fast as possible, so the fishing lines on the rods don't tangle behind the boat. Got it?" And we all reply, "Yes sir!" We all have a brief meeting and agree that Christine will be the first person to reel in a fish.

As we leave the shore, pounding through the waves, we all regret the fun we had the night before. It is now noon, and the captain hasn't said "Fish On!" once. Good news, though—the beer is cold, and we all enjoy one as it takes the edge off the night before.

We are all relaxed, and two people are taking a nap when the captain yells, "*fish on!*" We all jump into action and assume our agreed-upon roles.

Christine removes the slack in the line that has the fish on it, and the rest of us grab all the fishing rods with no fish and quickly reel them in so the fish Christine has doesn't swim across the lines and create a massive tangle. It takes Christine forty-five minutes of fighting the fish, but she reels in a beautiful tuna that we enjoy for dinner ater that evening.

Illustration 10.11 —— The Big Tuna!

In many ways, this story reminds us of handling questions and objections that can surprise you during your live events. If you agree on roles and you know what to do ahead of time, you will be successful at these crucial moments in your demonstrations and presentations. If you don't, it's "Fish *off!*"

QUESTION AND OBJECTION HANDLING PROCESS

What the captain was doing during his orientation in our sport-fishing story was providing the group of friends a proven process that would help them catch a fish and avoid problems with tangled fishing lines. The same holds true when you're in a live event, and suddenly you're interrupted by a question or objection. Our experience is that the overwhelming tendency is to only focus on immediately answering the question or objection. In other words, the sales professional is focused on the rod with the fish attached to it and not aware of how all the other fishing lines are about to get tangled.

We've developed the Fish On framework to solve this problem for you. Masters know how to use this framework to achieve desired outcomes for almost any question or objection stakeholders may pose.

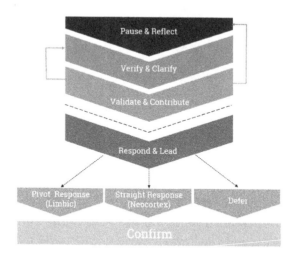

Illustration 10.12 — Fish On Framework

With some conscious, purposeful practice, the steps in the framework will allow you to flow through the process and deliver confident, well-received responses to all types of questions and objections, regardless of the level of difficulty.

PAUSE & REFLECT

Whenever most sales engagement team members are involved in a high-stakes and high-pressure situation, there's a natural tendency to have a physical response—particularly when you're surprised or confused by the question or objection. It is during these moments that our reptilian brain, which controls adrenaline, among other things, kicks in. With adrenaline in your system, you will tend to provide a response as quickly as possible.

You don't want to respond like that. Immediate, rapid responses are the result of poor listening skills, and often results in cutting off a stakeholder's question, as well as answering the wrong question. Pausing and reflecting gives you a chance to get out of that physical place, so give yourself a moment by pausing before you take the next step. Wait two seconds.

An immense amount of processing takes place in the human brain in two seconds. During that pause, silently reflect on what the stakeholder asked or said. Think about what they *actually* said, and not how the words made you feel. Two seconds will feel like an eternity, but it really isn't. To the stakeholders, you will simply appear thoughtful. And guess what? Silently reflecting is being thoughtful!

VERIFY AND CLARIFY

In this step you're trying to determine the real question or concern that's being voiced by the stakeholder. As experienced professionals, you've no doubt been in situations where somebody expresses a concern (objection), but after you discuss it, you realize their actual concern is something completely different.

"Verify and clarify" is about seeing that there may be deeper thoughts underneath the initial question or objection. Don't get caught in a literal question trap. A stakeholder might just be a verbal processor, and they're trying to express themselves but aren't articulating the real question. In other instances, the literal question they ask has a deeper underlying concern that they simply are not expressing. It is your job to determine the root question or objection, and this step helps you accomplish that. Below are a couple of examples of verifying and clarifying statements:

> "What I think I hear you saying is...Do I understand you correctly?" Reflect to the stakeholder that you heard them clearly, because when they hear it back they get the chance to clarify their thoughts. They might say, "Not exactly. . . What I meant to say was. . ."

> "That depends...What are you trying to accomplish?" With this example, you're talking to them about the impact of their question or objection. This is good when being asked or challenged about how your products, services, or solutions do something compared to how they do it today.

The stakeholder might ask, "Do you do such and such? Because our current system does such and such," and you respond with, "Well, that depends, what are you trying to accomplish?" Your question helps change the conversation from a Yes/No response to a more Consultative/Conversational response—and that is the only way you'll get to the root cause of the question or concern.

VALIDATE AND CONTRIBUTE

This step is all about you expressing empathy for their question or concern. By validating their concern, you put the stakeholder at ease—particularly if it is a sensitive issue. The validation might sound like this: "I can appreciate why you're asking that, because many of our successful clients asked that same question." Professional empathy opens a pathway to your response.

When you contribute, you provide your perspective and narrow the discussion. In the following statement and question, I'm contributing the real root of the concern other clients have, as I suspect it is the same with this stakeholder. "As we discussed this concern with our current clients further, we learned that... Is that the same for you?"

This step may loop you back to the verify and clarify step as you continue to uncover the real question or concern. Let it naturally flow there. The two minutes you take in these stages will save you ten minutes if you make an incorrect assumption—or worse, save you from losing the opportunity.

RESPOND AND LEAD

Once you finally understand the root question or concern, you respond. Before we train people on the Fish On! process, many think there is only a straight response that directly answers the question or concern. However, we find that masters make one of three choices for the type of response they provide: straight response, pivot response, or they defer.

Straight Response — As the name implies, this is a direct response. Give this response if you know the answer and you believe it will be well received. However, try this adjustment when using this type of response: incorporate what you learned in the Verify & Clarify stage so that you reflect back the way the stakeholder is thinking about the root cause of their question or concern. Incorporate the terminology they used during the prior stages. Using their terminology further honors their question or concern and makes your response easier for the neocortex complex of the stakeholder's brain to remember. If you don't respond from the stakeholder's context, you've dishonored the validation process and made it more difficult to remember.

Pivot Response — This response is about changing someone's perspective. It's less common than a straight response, but can be very effective.

This response is perhaps better described with an example from one of our clients. This client licenses a type of nurse scheduling software solution for hospitals that saves hospitals millions of dollars per year in staffing expenses. With such a strong return on investment, they price their solution accordingly. So, as you might guess, they regularly face a price objection.

The salesperson can't radically change the price. That would undermine their organization's position in the market. The straight answer to the objection is, "We offer such a strong return on investment that we believe the price we are requesting is fair." That response fell flat whenever they used it. Here's what they decided to do after learning about this style of response:

"I respect your position on our price. Many of our successful clients felt the same way when they signed up for our solution; however, they believed the return on investment was strong enough to justify the expense. It sounds like you feel differently." The executive stakeholder responded by stating that she understood why some hospitals might pay the high price for their solution but she simply didn't have the discretionary spending to afford the solution.

From here, the salesperson pivoted the response with the following: "Our discussion on pricing reminds me of a decision I had to make for my daughter. She was an excellent gymnast, but she broke both of her wrists in a terrible accident on the vault. She was devastated, as she had dreams of competing in the NCAA and potentially the Olympics. I live in rural Georgia, and the local orthopedist told us that she would heal, but she'd need to give up the sport. We decided to get a second opinion, and we drove ninety minutes to Atlanta to a well-known specialist. He told her that she would be able to compete again, but she'd need to go to physical therapy at a specialty clinic in Atlanta twice a week for six months to fully recover.

"We had a difficult decision to make, much like you do. The time and expense to drive to Atlanta and complete her rehabilitation were tremendous, but to me, it was worth it. Today she is a gymnast at the University of Georgia. I heard you on the challenge of finding the discretionary funds to put behind this initiative, but like my daughter's situation, once you're saving tens of thousands of dollars every month, your board will want to award you a medal."

Here's the truth about an objection like this one. The price isn't going to change. It's like an airplane in flight. Sooner or later, it must land. A pivot response like hers, which appeals to the limbic system, doesn't change that fact. It simply makes for a softer landing.

Defer — The final type of response is a deferral. The obvious use-case for a deferral response is when you don't know the answer to a question. You simply ask if you can research (defer) the question and respond later. Deferrals are great use-cases for a personal video that provides a summary of responses to all questions that were deferred.

Obviously, you can't defer too many questions or objections. If that happens, you need to work on your product knowledge. But there are strategic uses of deferrals that should be considered. For example, we had a situation with our video automation platform where someone from marketing was present for the product demo. He asked if we integrated with an unusual marketing automation software platform.

The straight response was: "No, we would have to create a custom interface to accomplish the integration, and that would cost you thousands." The problem with that response is that the marketing rep was only at the meeting as an observer. Such a response would have created a negative undertone to the demonstration for a question that wasn't relevant to their objective to find a sales-motion-specific video automation platform.

Instead, our subject matter expert used a deferral. She verified and clarified the question and finally responded with, "I don't know the answer to your question. Would it be okay if I researched the answer and got back to you directly?" The individual from marketing approved her request, and she moved forward in the demonstration.

On a follow-up call with the sales enablement leader (executive stakeholder), we asked how important that integration was to him. He responded, "Don't worry about it. We don't have a need for the integration. I'll take care of it with marketing."

Because our subject matter expert deferred the question, the demonstration maintained momentum and we were subsequently awarded the business.

In summary, even if you know the answer to a question or objection, a strategic deferral can work in your favor—as can a pivot response and a straight response. Masters understand this and are consciously competent when they decide the type of response they provide.

AUTHENTICITY, TRUST & CONNECTION (ATC)

These three elements are critical to winning over stakeholders during every stakeholder engagement. In your Rule of 24 opportunities, it started when your sales engagement team member's first point of contact effectively communicated with the stakeholders by sending them a personal video in a playlist of content, tailored to what she had understood to be their needs.

The personal video communicated authenticity, enthusiasm, and personal interest in the stakeholder's needs. ATC spread across the stakeholders as that playlist of content was shared among everyone. ATC grew during traditional discovery (limited as it was) and continued to expand in the virtual meeting that led up to the in-person engagement.

In-person events will always be the pinnacle opportunity for ATC. The way that's done is by a human connection, which starts with authenticity. As we've described earlier, a lot of that has to do with your sales engagement team's ability to perform discovery on-the-fly and immediately apply what they learned through responsive demonstrating and presenting. This creates a strong connection with your audience.

At the end of the day, you have to be able to deliver. You have to be able to demo the product, service, or solution, and show how it is connected to what you learned in your various forms of discovery and the subsequent value statements you make. Otherwise, you're a good guy, and they'd like you as a friend, but you don't really provide any value.

When you go into one of these engagements, they often have one or two other products, services, or solutions that they're considering besides yours. You don't have any control over this. If you're the incumbent and they already have a negative opinion of your company, that's the wind in your face—you don't have any control over it at all. You'd be the easiest decision, but they're not overwhelmingly happy with their experience with you. That's just reality; it happens. Your sales engagement team's ability to humbly perform discovery on-the-fly, reflect what they've heard, and responsively present is your opportunity to move the wind to your back.

Then again, you may have the wind at your back—maybe you're the incumbent and they really like you, or you have a reputation for being the hot product or having the best services.

If you're in this position, it's easy to be perceived as condescending or over-confident, and completely miss a critical opportunity to authentically connect. That deeply erodes trust. This connection that you're building must always have empathy within it, and a lot of people don't think of empathy when they think of salespeople. But it's absolutely essential.

Additionally, when you come into a demo with a very strong opinion about how your product is adopted, sometimes you must be willing to have some humility and pivot.

Listen and seek to understand your audience's perspective. That's all part of being responsive. Ultimately, if you're trying to engage in quality interaction, a level of empathy and a level of humility come with seeking the truth.

If you are truly trying to serve the stakeholder, there will be obvious integrity behind that. You can't be authentic if you know deep down that your product isn't really the best fit for them, and you're just going to try to gloss over that fact.

A way to show that type of humility and connectedness is a simple process of reflecting what you're hearing, to show that you're listening. If you're performing discovery on-the-fly and they explain some things to you, go ahead and take a moment to reflect what you just heard: "Well, let me just reflect what I just heard you say. Would that be okay?" They'll say, "Absolutely." Then you reflect, paraphrase, or extend what you heard. This forces you to listen. You can't get ahead of what they're talking about and have your mind multitasking. You have to be focused on what they're saying.

OTHER RESPONSIVE DEMONSTRATING & PRESENTING TACTICS

SALES ENGAGEMENT TEAM MEMBER INTRODUCTIONS

It has been our experience that very few sales engagement teams plan their introductions ahead of the client engagement. Don't fall prey to impromptu introductions. Formalize them and put them in the hands of the executive or sponsor stakeholder. Always seek the help of the executive stakeholder first.

If this individual introduces each member of your team, there is instant implied credibility due to his or her position or authority. We can only think of one instance when we could not get an executive or a sponsor to introduce us, and that was due to an unreasonable consultant overstepping their authority (at least in our opinion).

On separate index cards for each member of your team, clearly write three facts about that member. The first fact should address their role in the organization and in this engagement. The second fact should build their credibility by describing how their experience is of value to everyone in the room. The final fact should be something about that individual's everyday life. The final fact can be the most interesting one. We've seen some people describe how they have climbed mountains on multiple continents. Others go more conservative and discuss the makeup of their family. What appears as the third fact will be culturally and professionally adjusted.

TRANSFER OF OWNERSHIP

This tactic applies to any style of demo or presentation. It's a simple concept of using "you phrasing" to subtly transfer ownership of your product to the stakeholders in the room. It's a way to prime them into thinking subconsciously that this is their product, and they're using it.

This is an interesting challenge for a lot of demonstrators, even highly experienced ones. Frequently, a member of your sales engagement team will say something like: "Next, I'm going to show you how I can do this." If you want to transfer ownership to somebody, you need to replace "I" phrasing with "you" phrasing. For example, it might sound more like this: "Now I'll cover how when *you're* using the software, you can..." We are priming them with language that gives them ownership of the software.

It takes some time practicing new types of phrasing so that it becomes second nature. There is always going to be a learning curve; any behavioral change is difficult. For a behavioral change, the best way you can adjust is to have somebody who's willing to be there to help you as a coach talk to you about it afterward. They can watch to make sure you're transferring ownership as you demo or present.

As you are transferring ownership, people unconsciously imagine themselves using it because now they're actively involved. They can see themselves doing it. That gets them more on board, and then they're more likely to convince others. Their enthusiasm is heightened.

It isn't obvious, though, it's unconscious—they won't necessarily notice that transfer of ownership. It's not just language, either; it's all the different things you do to try and get them on board.

For example, one of the ways we are going to get them on board was discussed earlier with the Today and Tomorrow technique. "Here's how you're doing it today. Here's how you'll do it going forward." People appreciate that; it gives them a sense that you're providing some advice here, some consulting, and that you understand them.

A lot of demos only talk about the future. "You can do this, and here's the benefit." Meanwhile, some members of the audience are thinking, "Okay, but how do I do that today?" They're doing this in their head, but you'll hear it through interruptions. They'll stop you. When that happens, you're not providing enough context of how they do things today to bring them forward to what they could do in the future. There's a chasm of the unknown.

If you create a bridge by continually linking today and the future, they can cross the chasm and not feel so uncertain or fatigued. This is an element of transferring ownership.

Now, this becomes not just a direct delivery of the product demo itself, but rather a conversation. You're giving the stakeholder a journey. You involve them. You're talking to them directly. You're empathizing with their needs and their desires.

When you demo or present using every means of transferring ownership, even if there are audience members who are struggling with the change, you can leverage other stakeholders in the room who are on board to bring them into resonance. These stakeholders actually help you sell your product; they'll start to chime in and talk about it. They'll assist in the demo or presentation. They'll start to explain how they see your product service or solution working and how it would help. That's the amazing result of a demo or presentation done well.

PLANNING AHEAD – NEXT STEPS

As you come into the meeting, have a plan for what you want the stakeholders to do next. Do you want them to download the trial? Buy it right now? Contact an existing customer? What's the call to action? Part of what the sales engagement team needs to agree upon before a key event begins is what you are driving toward.

During the demo or presentation, those next steps can shift. You learn things in the event and you realize, for example, "we don't need to take them to a customer—we need to move on to a contract." This is shifting ground, and you need to adapt.

CRIMES TO AVOID

THE DATA DUMP!

Now it's time to show the product. Take a stance. Your product may be very configurable. It has a lot of options. "When we set up this demo for you, we can set it up five different ways."

Don't demo that way. Don't data dump!

Even though training may involve showing them *everything*, this isn't training. This is a demo. So go ahead and take a stance and make a single choice, even if there are five ways you could configure it.

Data dumping is being a trainer, not a master demonstrator or presenter. People respect the fact that you're taking a stance; since they're already feeling trust for you, you're established as even more of an authority. A lot of people want to learn best practices, and how to get the most out of it (as long as it isn't too difficult). They don't necessarily want to know all the options, just what's going to help their business. They want that opinion from you—so go ahead and take a stance. That's another part of the bridge (from Chapter 4) that's spanning the chasm of the unknown.

WE'LL FOLLOW UP

One of the demo crimes we frequently see is assuming that the next step is always going to be "schedule a follow-up meeting." Why do we do this? As soon as they run into something challenging, they're going to schedule a follow-up meeting.

Sometimes there's good reason to do that: they need more clarification, or they need to work on some back channels to prepare for what you plan to deliver, or you really don't know the answer to the question, or you need different audience members to be present when you deliver a certain message.

Or, it could just be a crutch. It's easy to just say, "Well, let's just schedule a follow-up meeting." Follow-up meetings can delay a deal. Whenever deals are delayed, that creates an opportunity for a competitor to come in. It creates an opportunity for business factors to change what their budget is.

There are other ways to follow up if you really feel like you need to. For example, leverage video automation. If you didn't have the answers to some key questions that require clarification, rather than scheduling a follow-up meeting, create a personal video that covers all the follow-up items. Send it to every stakeholder in the audience, and they can watch it on their own schedule. You will absolutely collapse follow-up time in comparison to trying to schedule a follow-up meeting with the stakeholders.

CUTTING OFF A QUESTION

This is a crime experienced demonstrators often commit. Somebody who's really experienced, who really understands the industry, is often tempted to do this. They've heard just about every question there is that could be asked. As somebody starts asking a question, they'll cut them off: "Yeah, I know what you're asking there. Here's the answer." That completely erodes trust; plus, when you cut off a question, you may be answering the wrong question. You may not understand their question completely.

The right approach is, obviously, to let the stakeholder finish. When they're finished, make sure you pause—because some people pause in the middle of questions. It'll drive you crazy, but they do it. If it's a more complex question, reflect, paraphrase, or extend what you heard, even though you think you know the answer. Now, your expertise will come across to them as valuable, and your trust and credibility will strengthen.

LAY IN THE WEEDS

This one requires a bit of explanation. Bass is a species of freshwater fish. Imagine the still waters of a crystal clear freshwater lake. In the shallows are weeds that have grown from the bottom of the lake and broken the surface of the water. Female bass create nests for their eggs within those weeds and guard their nests by hovering atop the eggs. If a predator to their eggs happens to make the mistake of swimming too close to the nest, the female bass will explode off the nest and swallow the predator whole. Bass don't even have teeth—they just eat their meals whole!

Sometimes, in presentations, you feel like there are certain stakeholders whose goal in life is to eat you whole. Stump the presenter! Stump the expert! They take pride in it. It's the role they relish. They'll ask a question that, on the surface, seems straightforward and innocent. It might sound something like this: "So, if I understand what you just demonstrated correctly, anybody in a building will be able to adjust the temperature in a zone without having to bother building maintenance, is that right?" Well, the obvious positive answer is, "Yes, absolutely!" With your response, you're trying to resonate with this stakeholder's enthusiasm—even though you know the solution can be configured in a number of ways.

But they're laying a trap for you. They'll say "That will never work for us! Can you imagine what would happen with our energy bills if every person was able to move the temperature in a zone up or down at their whim? This will never work for us." Congratulations! This bass just ate you whole!

Now you get to spend the next five minutes talking about how you can configure it otherwise, but it's too late. The damage is done. It's a little bit like being in court: the prosecuting asks an objectionable, damaging leading question. The defense attorney objects, and the judge agrees and tells the jury to ignore what they just heard.

If somebody like that is in your audience, don't get defensive. Don't start getting competitive with them. Don't be prey to this bass. Just accept them for what they are. As soon as you recognize them, adjust your strategy.

The next time a difficult person asks a question, don't answer the question they asked. Instead, ask a question back, reflection style. "Well, that's a good question, let me make sure I understood you correctly. What I heard you say is, going forward, you'd actually like every individual in the building to be able to adjust the temperature anytime they want in a zone. Is that right?"

Now they have to answer "yes" or "no". "No, actually, we wouldn't want that." "Well, good news, here's exactly how we'd recommend setting it up for you." The beauty of that response is this stakeholder actually respects you for professionalism. You weren't defensive, you just asked for clarification. Everybody else in the room loves how you just handled this bass because they hate them too! This stakeholder does the same thing to each of them during internal meetings.

SUMMARY

Rule of 24 demands new, creative approaches to in-person demos and presentations. eDiscovery skills and the application of the information learned must improve. You must accept the fact that, like it or not, you'll find yourself leading one of these meetings with under-known information in a room full of demanding stakeholders.

Agile discovery on-the-fly combined with effective responsive demonstrating is the way of the future. You'll quickly find that you can once again feel in control of these critical events. Commit yourself to the behavioral changes necessary to succeed in these events, and you'll find yourself on the top of the leaderboard within your sales organization.

ELEVEN
COACHING

Coaching starts with an understanding of where you're at as a manager. Perform a self-assessment to determine your Rule of 24 readiness. From there, you'll want to define your goals. Areas to concentrate on include planning and preparation, being remembered, selling value, adaptability, and connection. These categories are applicable whether you and your team are creating content, performing a virtual demo or presentation, or participating in an in-person event.

Assessments should be adapted for each area of the Rule of 24. For example, the illustration below is used for individuals who perform product demos. Adjusting this assessment for video content creation requires that you add skill areas such as scripting. You'll then use the appropriate assessment to evaluate each member of your team. Below is an example of a team assessment with a concentration area of "Planning and Preparation" and the skill of "Discovery."

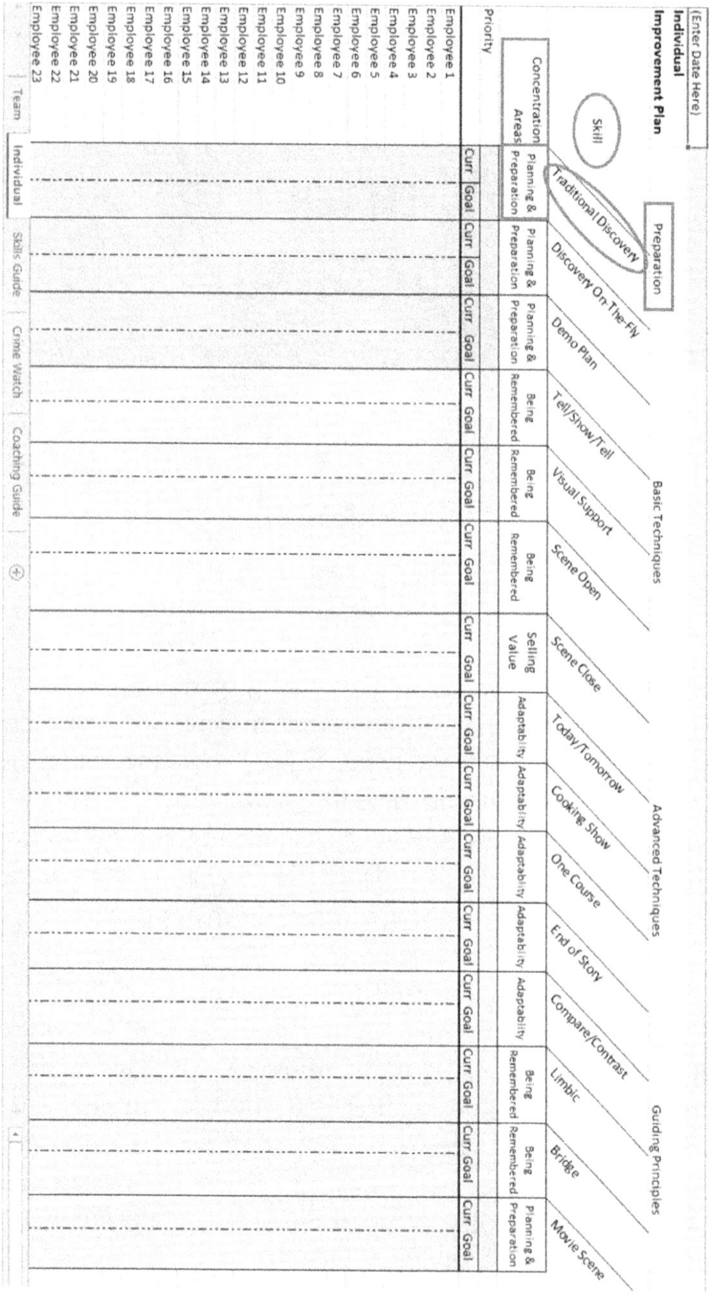

Illustration 11.1 — Assessment and Improvement Plan for Demonstrations

PLANNING AND PREPARATION

This concentration area is the foundation for all great video content, virtual demos and presentations, and in-person engagements. Some might suggest that with Rule of 24 opportunities there is little time for planning and preparation. They would be wrong.

Your team's ability to effectively react in Rule of 24 situations has everything to do with their planning and preparation. For example, if one of your team members is on a virtual presentation and the stakeholder challenges her with a requirement she had not anticipated, she must be prepared to perform discovery on-the-fly and responsively demo or present. This requires mental preparation and practice with those skills. As you assess your team members, the illustration below provides guidance on scoring a team member on their traditional discovery skills.

Assessment Scoring	
Guiding Principles	Discovery
Level 1	Not ready or able to participate in discovery exercises
Level 2	Can prepare for discovery, but uncomfortable in interviews
Level 3	Comfortable in preparing & conducting, but information is incomplete or not conveyed well
Level 4	Fully capable of working alone and in teams in all aspects of discovery, including C-level
Level 5	Creates discovery strategies, conducts full discoveries, prepares full information flow, and teaches others on discovery techniques

Coaching Guide	
Technique or Skill	Discovery
Negative Impact if Missing	Preparation Discovery leads to demo that is generic and doesn't connect w/prospect. Will wind up doing discovery on-the-fly during the demo. Can result in any number of crimes being committed.
Improvement Tips	1. Build a strong process and set of tools to make discovery easier and more automatic. 2. Practice by setting up prospect case studies and having people interview each other.

Illustration 11.2 — Assessment Scoring & Coaching Guide for Discovery

ADDITIONAL SKILLS FOR PLANNING & PREPARATION

The Assessment and Improvement Plan for Demonstrations as shown in Illustration 11.1 isn't intended to be a comprehensive list of skills that require assessment.

For example, if your team is responsible for content creation of demo videos, you will want to enhance the planning and preparation skills to include scripting, clarity of message, and other key skills as described in Chapter 6. Because you will likely need to personalize the improvement guide for your team, we offer this tool in a "soft" format.

As shown in illustration 11.1, the additional skill areas for the planning and preparation concentration areas include the following.

DISCOVERY ON-THE-FLY

As described in Chapter 9, a presenter in a virtual or in- person setting should strive to naturally and conversationally perform ad hoc discovery on-the-fly. This includes the use of leading open-ended questions that funnel the stakeholder to a single subject area. A team member who has mastered this skill is able to draw out of the stakeholder their current situation, their desired state, the impact of moving from current to desired, and potentially how they would measure the improvement.

DEMO PLAN

Team members who master this skill are in the habit of planning the 20 percent of the presentation that will have the greatest impact on the prospect. They also plan the teamwork aspects of the engagement to account for unplanned situations as they arise.

MOVIE VIEW

For live stakeholder engagements, this team member makes movie view seem effortless and invisible to the stakeholders. They always build their movie view from each stakeholder's perspective, and consistently deliver a strong open and close to the event. Their presentation contains well thought out sub-scenes.

BEING REMEMBERED

This concentration area starts with securing and maintaining a client's attention. That's accomplished with good limbic techniques and extends into other areas as shown in Illustration 11.1. As you assess your team members, the illustration below provides guidance on how to score their limbic skills and what you should do to coach them to new levels of proficiency:

Assessment Scoring	
Guiding Principles	Limbic Techniques
Level 1	Does not use limbic techniques. May not be comfortable with the idea.
Level 2	Tends to focus in on one limbic technique and use repeatedly. Not aware of "bad limbic" in the demo. Often not relevant.
Level 3	Fully understands both good and bad limbic. Has a standard variety of techniques. Not always directly relevant.
Level 4	Full variety and understanding of limbic, including on the fly current events and illustrations. Always mixes it up in the demo. Always relevant.
Level 5	Master at creating new limbic techniques that are directly related to the company, the prospect, and the software. Helps others in creating. Comfortable with props.

Coaching Guide	
Technique or Skill	Limbic Techniques
Negative Impact if Missing	Without limbic, there is not attention. With no attention, there is no memory. Without memory, your software will not stand out in the prospect's mind. At best, it makes the process analytical. At worst, it gives the edge to the competition.

Improvement Tips	1. Find non-threatening environments to practice limbic techniques. Technical people have to build a comfort with these techniques. 2. Remember the behavior types - controls emotion / displays emotion. Find limbic examples (numbers, facts) that can work for people that control emotions. 3. Teamwork is great here. Team up strong and weak limbic players and have them build techniques together

Illustration 11.3—Assessment Scoring & Coaching Guide – Limbic Techniques

Whether your team members are creating video content are performing a demo or a presentation, it is critical that they present the information so the stakeholders are engaged and your information is remembered. The most basic assessment addresses the following skills in the Being Remembered concentration area for demos and presentations:

LIMBIC

Masters of limbic are always seeking and implementing new techniques in recorded videos and live events that are directly related to the prospect and the stakeholders.

BRIDGING

Level 5 team members are constantly bridging stakeholders in recorded video and live events from their existing products, services, or solutions to yours. They may even help others in learning and applying bridging techniques. They never leave any stakeholder "stranded" on the bridge. They always work from a stakeholder's perspective.

TELL-SHOW-TELL

This team member can spot and correct tell-show-tell mistakes in videos and live events and helps others correct them. They incorporate advanced techniques and introductory techniques to keep tell-show-tell fresh and invisible to the audience.

VISUAL SUPPORT OF TELL-SHOW-TELLS

Makes extensive use of visuals in both basic and advanced techniques. Spends as much time with visuals as with the product and can help others in creation and use of visuals.

SCENE OPENING (AND IMPACT VIDEOS)

Use a variety of scene opening styles (illustrative analogy, case study, etc.) as dictated by their plan and executive stakeholder needs and interests. Your "being remembered" assessments may vary based on your sales organization and the products you represent. The implementation of specific, measurable assessments is your best tool for team improvement regardless of the areas you want to implement.

ADAPTABILITY

Rule of 24 requires constant adaptability on the part of your team members. Illustration 11.1 lists a number of advanced techniques that we teach in our "Masters" workshop. These skills are simply alternative choices for the "show" portion of the sub-scene. Below is an example of the Assessment Scoring and Coaching Guide for the "Cooking Show" technique.

Assessment Scoring	
Guiding Principles	Cooking Show
Level 1	Does not use. Walks through complex pieces step by step.
Level 2	Can demo a scripted cooking show set up by someone else. Understands the need and use of the technique.
Level 3	Plans for CS based on the subject matter. Usually successful and smooth in implementation.
Level 4	Can anticipate the need for CS and smoothly perform it repeatedly. Uses "gift" from prospect to increase CS usage through the demo.
Level 5	Can switch easily between basic and CS technique, has CS already "at hand" wherever it might be needed. Tends to get "gift" early and often.

Coaching Guide	
Negative Impact if Missing	The prospect may see the product, service or solution as very complex due to the work needed to get to a particular result.
Improve-ment Tips	1. Work with the team to identify all areas that this might be a problem or has been a problem in the past. 2. Create fully prepared data and processes that easily allow for the stakeholder to see results quickly like the final product on a cooking show. 3. Practice transitions from "making the cake" to "showing the cake", focusing on how much is too much in the "making" phase.

Illustration 11.4 — Limbic Assessment Scoring & Coaching Guide – Cooking Show

As you adopt Rule of 24 across your sales engagement team, you will most certainly want to add adaptability skills to your assessment and coaching guide. For example, the skills required for responsive demonstrating or presenting a sub-scene are crucial to your team's success, so add that to your assessment.

SELLING VALUE

You may recall that we advocate completing every sub-scene you record on video, demo, or present with what the *result* is going to be. In other words, with all the features you just showed, *what's the key benefit?* What's the thing your team members want the stakeholders to remember? You want these delivered every two to five minutes.

Once again, we refer to these as operational benefits. Expressing an operational benefit is usually something along the lines of: "You can see how easy that was!" How easy, or how fast, or how accurate, or how you won't have mistakes anymore. Now, twenty to forty minutes later, your team members completed X number of these sub-scenes where they delivered a lot of operational benefits. At the end of that sequence, your team members have earned the right and the trust to be able to present a value benefit.

When you're training your team, pay attention to this. Explain where they have an opportunity to put an exclamation point on the value your solutions provide.

If it's a video they're creating, move the operational benefits to their opening tell of the sub-scene. Then add context by telling the viewer *why* what they're about to watch is important. The stakeholder watches, and then your team member reemphasizes the benefit at the end of the video. Stakeholders need to hear the benefit early—or you risk them dropping off. They need to know why this is going to be important before they watch it. Make sure you assess your team members on that structure and those skills.

ENSURING CONNECTION

There are a lot of ways sales engagement team members can lose their connection with their audience. One of the most common, which we touched on earlier, is when they use your company's terminology instead of the prospect's. Remember, during discovery you want your team members to listen for and record the terminology their prospect uses. Then, when presenting or demonstrating in either a planned or responsive manner, make sure they use the customer's terminology.

Use the names of their processes, their acronyms, and their data. Have each scene represent processes, tasks, roles, or projects that are common in your prospect's business. Don't be "me-centric." We call this "talk the talk." We believe it is important enough to warrant assessing your team members on this skill.

DRIVING TEAM IMPROVEMENT

Driving team improvement begins with an understanding of each individual team member's strengths and weaknesses. All too often in B2B sales organizations, individual assessments are almost entirely subjective. This leads to inconsistencies and non-measurable results.

Earlier in this chapter, we provided you with a platform for transitioning team assessments and improvement plans from subjective to objective. As a reminder, objective assessments are fact-based, measurable, and observable. It is for that reason that we advocate a "level-based" scoring system for each skill a team member needs to succeed in their role.

Guiding Principles	Level 1	Level 2	Level 3	Level 4	Level 5
Limbic Techniques	Does not use limbic techniques. May not be comfortable with the idea	Tends to focus in on one limbic technique and use repeatedly. Not aware of "bad limbic" in the demo. Often not relevant	Fully understands both good and bad limbic. Has a standard variety of the techniques. Not always directly relevant.	Full variety and understanding of limbic, including on the fly current events and illustrations. Always mixes it up in the demo. Always relevant.	Master at creating new limbic techniques that are directly related to the company, the prospect, and the software. Helps others in creating. Comfortable with props.
Bridge Demonstrating	Not aware of or does not understand how to implement the concept.	Understands the concept, but often fails to implement. Demo's from the perspective of the product, not the prospect. Uses terminology and descriptions that are not prospect centric.	Good understanding and execution. Good at making sure audience is moving with him/her at all times. Usually uses terminology & descriptions familiar to the prospect.	Full understanding. Ability to bring different personalities across the bridge. Can motivate and guide. Distinguishes from competition. Stays prospect centric at all times.	Designs bridging techniques for the overall demo plan. Helps others in learning and applying bridge demonstrating. Never leaves any personality type "stranded" on the bridge. Always works from prospect's perspective.
Movie View	Tends to not set up demo scene. Works well in a scene, but not proficient at designing scenes. Sometimes fails to standard flow. Does not break into subscenes.	Follows script or implement subscene technique	Understands and builds scenes with open/close and subscenes. Sometimes fails to open/close.	Builds movie view into every demo plan. Implements 80/20 and has strong open/close. Sometimes too "scripted" in use.	Makes MV seem effortless and invisible to prospect. Always builds from prospect's perspective, always delivers strong open and close. Well thought out subscenes.

Illustration 11.5 — Objective, Level-Based Skills Guide

With an objective, level-based assessment and skills guide, your goal is simple: increase each team member's skill level with specific actionable feedback. In the absence of an objective assessment, you can still improve team members' skills; however, it will be challenging if not impossible to objectively determine if an individual is improving in each skill area.

THE COACHING FEEDBACK LOOP

Successful coaching, regardless of whether it's for improving their skills or something else, starts with a feedback loop that allows the individual to talk first about what they thought was positive, before the coach provides any feedback. Studies have shown that you should have a three-to-one ratio of positive to constructive feedback. It has also been proven that it is much easier to improve someone's strengths than it is to correct somebody's weaknesses. The coaching feedback process we've developed has been tested and proven across the world through hundreds of thousands of hours with clients.

The process follows a positive loop of feedback to an individual before transitioning to a constructive loop of feedback:

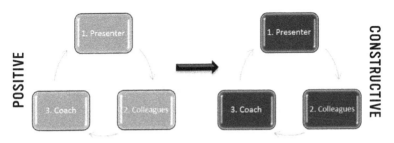

Illustration 11.6 — Positive-Constructive Feedback Loop

POSITIVE FEEDBACK LOOP

The feedback process starts by asking the person being coached, "What are some things you just did that you think worked well, and that you believe you would want to do again?" And you wait for him, and only him, even if he has peers around the table, to respond.

If he tries to redirect and discuss negatives with a comment like this, "Honestly, I don't know that it really went all that well. In fact, I think what I'd change is this," you need to stop him and redirect to the positive aspects of what he just did in the meeting. You might say something like, "You can share things that you feel you need to improve on in a few minutes, but surely there were some things you did that you think were positive. I know I saw a number of things that went well."

After you take our recommended approach, he will accept your direction and comment on some positive aspects of his performance. Then, continue to lead him through additional positive aspects of his performance. Next, you can invite peers to provide positive feedback—but if you do that, there's something you've got to watch out for.

Frequently, peers start to say something positive, and then they'll say, "...but one thing I didn't like is..." As the saying goes, *Nothing good in my life ever happened after the word "but" or "however."* This poor feedback practice will initiate defense mechanisms in the individual being coached.

Additionally, the individual being coached will mentally throw away every positive comment made as their reptilian brain takes over their emotions. Do not let this happen. Instead, the instant you hear a peer use the words "but" or "however," stop him or her immediately. Remind the peer that he or she is currently to focus exclusively on the positive aspects of this individual's performance. Stay very strong in this guidance.

To prevent this problem, ask the peers to comment on the positive aspects of what they saw using this approach. To do this, turn to the peers in the room and this question: "*What did you like about what he just did? Think of it this way—what would you steal from his presentation?*"

During the positive feedback loop we encourage managers to support all positive feedback they agree with, and provide additional comments as necessary and appropriate. As the manager, you will be the last individual to comment during the positive feedback loop. Complete the feedback by challenging the individual to continue to execute on the positive aspects of the feedback. You might even consider asking this individual to mentor others on their positive skills.

After you complete your positive feedback, it's time to move to the constructive loop.

CONSTRUCTIVE FEEDBACK LOOP

We purposely left out the word "criticism" between the words "constructive" and "feedback" because the purpose of this portion of feedback is to build up the person and their skills, not criticize.

During this loop you will once again ask your team member to comment first. The question sounds like this, "Mark, it's time to turn your attention to areas that you would like to do differently the next time you do this presentation. What, if anything, would you change or do differently?"

What you will find amazing as he comments on what he would change, is how perceptive he will be toward areas that you spotted as well. However, the fact that he brings them up first and articulates them to the room (assuming there's a group of peers) will significantly improve the likelihood that he will implement changes in future. We often find that the individual we're coaching knows what they did wrong, but doesn't necessarily know how to correct the problem. That is where your expertise as a leader becomes invaluable.

As he discusses what he would change, do not let his peers in the room pile on to his observations. You control the room and you control the discussion. Doing so avoids a flood of suggestions—which results in no changes in behavior. Feel free, however, to ask him what he thinks he should do differently next time, and then comment on his thoughts.

Next, solicit feedback from the peers in the room. Let them know they need to be specific in their observations. After a peer makes an observation, take control as to whether you agree, and if so, ask the presenter what they might do differently. If they don't know, you can offer some suggestions. No more than two constructive observations from the peers. Any more than that won't be actionable, as an individual can only change a limited number of behaviors at any one time.

As in the positive feedback loop, you will complete the comments in the constructive loop. Follow the same methodology with your personal comments as you did with the peers. When you're finished, asked the presenter to summarize from the positive loop what they will continue doing, and how they might expand on that in the next engagement they have with a stakeholder. Then ask them what they plan to change with the next stakeholder engagement.

This final summary reinforces their commitment to acting on the feedback and provide you an opportunity to note in their assessment what level they are at in each skill, and to highlight areas they plan to work on. Now you have objective goals you can review with each member of your team as part of your quarterly reviews.

MASTERS OF THEIR MEDIUM

Most of the content in this chapter has addressed demos and presentations. Please don't take this as an indication that assessments, feedback loops, and improvement plans are not prudent in all areas of Rule of 24. For example, consider demo video content creation. As you learned in earlier chapters, this medium within the Rule of 24 is valuable across the entire sales process. You may recall that there are stark differences between the creation, effectiveness, and use of personal videos, and that of library content such as demo videos. Each requires its own skills for assessment and improvement. Each also requires different timing for when you provide feedback.

A personal video feedback loop is performed after your sales engagement team member sends you a copy of the video that they sent to stakeholders or, preferably, before they send it to the stakeholders. After you perform your feedback loops with your team member, you will want them to re-record that personal video and have them send you the enhanced version. Because personal videos are so quick and easy to do, a re-creation of the video shouldn't be met with much resistance.

Library content, such as a demo video, requires feedback as the asset is flowing through the production process. Providing team members feedback after one of these videos has gone through an *entire production process* is incredibly frustrating to everyone involved in the project. Going back through the production cycle requires a significant amount of time and work, so help them get the piece right the first time.

For example, have them send you the script before they enter deeper phases of pre-production with the talent, such as the production-level edit. You may recall from Chapter 8 that during the production-level edit, the talent reads the script aloud in front of the production team so the script fits the natural spoken language of the talent. Cues for vocal emphasis, pauses, gesturing, etc. are inserted in the script. Imagine how frustrating it is for the production team to fine tune the production-level edit only to learn that you have a number of changes to the base script. Not only will they need to change the base script, but the production-level edit process will need to be completely repeated.

Discovery, discovery on-the-fly, and responsive demonstrating and presenting all deserve attention in your assessments, as do the key elements of the virtual demonstrating and presenting that help your team members differentiate themselves from the competition (e.g., engagement skills, virtual teamwork, production, etc.).

MISTAKES TO AVOID

THE RUBBER BAND CRIME

The first mistake to avoid goes back to the use of the words "but" and "however" during feedback loops. Remember when, as a child, you had that annoying classmate or sibling who would wrap a rubber band around their hand, slowly draw it back, and aim it at you? They didn't even have to shoot it— they just had to pull it back—to make you flinch.

Illustration 11.7 — Rubber Band Crime

It's universal—everybody flinches. I think even a U.S. Navy SEAL would probably flinch.

The same thing happens when we hear the word "but." As soon as we hear the word, we flinch, waiting for a bunch of negative feedback. Your team members during feedback are thinking "Oh, here we go. I'm about to be destroyed!" Get the words "but" and "however" out of all coaching and feedback sessions. They simply don't belong.

VAGUE BUT TRUE

Vague but true is when you provide feedback for somebody without any specifics. It's true, but it's so vague that truth becomes useless. "You know, your demo was pretty good. In fact, it was real good. But, generally speaking, your opening tell needs some work." The first thing I'm going to say is, "Okay, can you give me an example?" But the individual providing feedback can't think of an example. It's just sort of a feeling— but feelings don't help anybody. I won't have any idea from that how to improve. We need specifics; vague doesn't work.

This usually happens because they didn't have the discipline to write down a note of exactly where something happened and the specifics about why it happened. So if you're running the meeting, and you notice someone's not really taking notes, talk to them about it later. If you're the one being coached, feel empowered to respond, "Do me a favor in the future—make sure you take a note of exactly where I do that. Because I really value your feedback, and I want more of it."

TWELVE
TEAMWORK

There are a variety of challenges when working with multiple people in a selling event. First, if the team doesn't have a coordinated strategy, including the desired outcome for each client engagement, different people could be working toward different goals. The team needs to be on the same page.

When *everybody* wants to get their opinions heard, it can be detrimental. Coordinated interactions between teammates are viewed by stakeholders as indicative of what their long-term relationship will be with the vendor; but if they're not handled properly, they can be disastrous.

We've seen deals won and lost based on the client *feeling* like the company worked really well together. Your people and your teamwork speak volumes. They say a lot about your culture, your communication, and your future customer service. Like it or not, you're forecasting what the client's experience will be like after they sign the contract, and clients are reading that.

Working in a team with two or more people means you will be able to provide expertise and answers to many of the client's questions. Many stakeholders appreciate the fact that an executive is present and participating in an opportunity; they believe it says a lot for a possible vendor's commitment.

When certain services are complex, you may need subject matter experts for every key area, as you need to go in-depth in those areas. For example, if a big accounting firm is competing for consulting, tax specialization, and auditing services, there's probably going to be a partner from every area in the room. With so much at stake, rising to the challenge with multiple partners in attendance is worth it.

Technologyevaluation.com did a study comparing how clients select among multiple vendors, and how their solution and their functionality to each other related to that. In this study, they examined how the vendors demonstrated their software solutions. Each vendor had multiple subject matter experts participating in the client engagement.

One of the conclusions of the study was that prospects do, in fact, project their satisfaction in the future implementation and support based on how well the participants from each vendor worked together as a team. Many of you reading this won't want to believe such a conclusion. But remember that Rule of 24 stakeholders are selecting organizations based on the experience of the process as well as the solution.

BLURRING THE LINES

The lines blur when the team is preparing and working so well together that the stakeholders in a major demo experience superior flow from the team during the event. In fact, they feel they are being addressed by one cohesive team, rather than several individuals who each have a specific, separate part to play in the presentation and, perhaps, separate agendas. To accomplish this, your sales engagement team must embrace peer-to-peer coaching. In Chapter 10, we provided you with a proven method for peer-to-peer coaching—the positive and constructive feedback loops. Everybody must agree on what their contribution is going to be in the meeting, how they're going to communicate, and during preparation before the meeting, be open to healthy coaching to make sure every team member is working toward the same strategy. The team must successfully interact to accomplish your goals.

For the remainder of this chapter, we will elaborate on how teammates coordinate and communicate during a customer-facing event. Coaching happens before or after the event. There should be no coaching taking place during an event; it's just teamwork at that point. The same happens in soccer (or football, for everyone outside of North America): in the British Premier League football, there's always a coach on the side of the "pitch" (field), but the coaching really happens before the game. Very little coaching takes place during the game and at the break. There are not a lot of substitutions like there are in many other sports. There aren't timeouts, like there are in basketball, during which a coach has the opportunity to coach.

MAJOR OPPORTUNITIES INVOLVE MULTIPLE TEAM MEMBERS

Major opportunities often involve multiple team members; the bigger the opportunity, the more people you should have on your team. You might have a salesperson, one or multiple subject matter experts (solution consultants, sales engineers, product managers, practice managers, implementation leaders, etc.), and one or multiple managers and executives—and it starts to add up. If it's a highly technical product, you could actually have the engineer who created the product, or the software developers, in the room. There might be some specific technical questions, so you should have all the right people ready to respond—even managers or executives.

Managers and executives are the hardest people to coach in a major opportunity, because no one really feels empowered to tell them to put their phone down, or quit reading, or quit walking out of the room and making phone calls. But having them excluded from the coaching process can be extremely detrimental to the engagement. If your executive comes to the meeting, they need to be committed to the meeting. If you're going to show up, then show up. Their impact is so crucial, and the shadow they cast is so large, that you want to make sure their contribution is exactly what you want it to be. They need to be onboard, they need to read the room, and they need to know when to interject—and when not to.

IN-PERSON TEAMWORK

For in-person events, you still have some lead time. Be sure to put processes and expectations in place so the necessary teamwork becomes second nature for everyone involved. The processes should resemble templates, and the people on the team must understand their roles within that template when the baton is passed to them.

In larger sales organizations, sales engagement teams frequently prepare for major events by leveraging their formalized sales process. That's a great business practice to employ. To succeed in Rule of 24, a sales process should be second nature due to the accelerated characteristics of opportunities. Many sales processes need to be enhanced to address the needs of the more realistic aspects of today's opportunities. Here are some considerations to keep in mind:

The leader of the sales engagement team, usually the salesperson, should start the preparation process by reviewing the desired outcome of his or her opportunity—best case versus worst case scenario. For the best case, what is he or she hoping for if this event is to be a success? What's the call to action he or she is hoping the prospect will respond to?

By comparison, the worst case for any salesperson in any sales organization is that they are being used as "column fodder." In other words, the prospect has a mandate to look at a minimum of three organizations. Two of them are their preferred companies, and your organization's just column fodder. Your team is being included because the prospect has to have a third option. No one wants to be in the column fodder position.

If the salesperson really believed they were column fodder, in theory he or she wouldn't have assembled a team and asked all these people to reserve their schedules. They wouldn't have brought all these people together to go to a prospect to give this major presentation. The problem is, we're all biased—toward ourselves. Salespeople have a number to hit, and they're trying to get as many chances at winning deals as possible. So, of course, it can be very difficult for them to be unbiased in their view of whether or not they're column fodder. This means any team member should voice their opinion on disqualifying out of an opportunity, and the salesperson's manager should make the final call.

For the best case, if you get the sale and the dominoes are all falling the way you wanted them to, then as a salesperson you want everybody on the team to know what you're driving toward. That includes specifics: what are your company's sales process requirements? Every sales organization has a process. That process is going to have certain items that need to be checked off in terms of qualification. Do you have an executive contact? Who are your friends in this opportunity? Who are your potential enemies? Who's neutral, and you need to win them over? All these details need to be addressed.

Then, the salesperson needs to provide the names, images, and biographies of everyone who's going to be in the meeting: executives, staff, management, everyone. He or she can conduct the research and prepare it for the rest of the team, so that when you head into the meeting you're not worried about remembering names or figuring out roles. You'll know all that already.

Following a strategy discussion and a final qualification decision, the team needs to decide how they are going to open the presentation. Specifically, what is the strategic initiative the team is there to support, and how are they going to incorporate that in the opening? Secondly, what are the key impact areas? The key impact areas become the scenes of the presentation, and those are all from the prospect's perspective—their point of view. What are the key areas of this demo or presentation that the team is expected to address?

In Rule of 24 opportunities, the prospect may have provided detailed requirements of what they want to discuss; organize their requirements as key impact areas from the prospect's perspective. Those are the twenty- to forty-minute scenes that make up the movie of your presentation. While the salesperson is responsible for most of the preparation, it won't normally be the salesperson who is defining the scenes. In fact, in key impact areas, that's probably a discussion between the subject matter experts or the sales engineers.

Similarly, in the planned sub-scenes, the subject matter experts are going to have the most influence. They're the ones who are going to know what and how they will address stakeholder requirements during the event. The sub-scene is especially essential for planning and incorporating competitive differentiators.

If the team anticipates a lengthy presentation, it would never be realistic for the subject matter experts to plan every single sub-scene. There are just too many of them. If it's a four-hour-long or three-day-long demo, they're not going to sit down and create an outline of every opening tell, each moment of context, and every benefit statement. Rule of 24 opportunities don't allow that amount of time for planning.

However, key competitive differentiators should always be planned. There's nothing worse than leaving a presentation realizing you have forgotten to present a key differentiator. Imagine the strongest pillars that hold up the roof of a building, and how strategically they're placed. In the same way, strategically plan the sub-scenes that will showcase your key differentiators.

The movie view of your engagement is then organized based on a team discussion for what you know up to this point: discovery (at whatever level performed), opportunity review, stakeholders' biographies, requirements from the prospect, identified competitive differentiators, etc. The limbic opening for the meeting will connect the executive's strategic initiative to an illustrative analogy, customer case study, your discovery, or an industry expert. Next, is what the team decided to use for the James Bond demo or presentation opening.

The movie view can also help you plan additional demo or presentation strategies. For example, where will you strategically integrate priming and anchoring? Earlier in the book, we talked about the power of priming and anchoring. Those strategies are great inclusions at the opening and closing of scenes of the demo or presentation.

The movie view can also help you plan where you need to be careful. Your products might have differentiators in one area, but are considered weaker than your competition in other areas. So what is your plan for addressing that? Don't just hope it doesn't come up. Plan on it happening, and plan on a response and who will respond. There are always going to be cautionary areas.

THE DRY RUN (REHEARSALS)

When we facilitate a complete demo or presentation workshop, we always provide the participants with opportunities to perform their presentation. It's fascinating to see the difference between the first presentation and the second. The improvement in the second presentation is usually an order of magnitude better than the first. At the conclusion of the workshop, we will often suggest that everyone in the room (in person or virtual) should be performing team dry runs before every key client engagement. Here's what we hear back:

› "We would—if we just had the time."
› "We would—if we weren't all in different locations."
› "We can't—because we always arrive from different cities the night before the event."
› "You are right—we should."

If you're interpreting what workshop participants are saying as excuses, you'd be right. The excuses are valid, but they can be overcome by strong leadership. It is for that reason that we work with our clients' senior management to convince them of the value of enforcing team dry runs.

For significant opportunities, the time allotted for dry runs needs to be part of the team plan. If team members are in multiple locations and you won't have enough time ahead of the event, use your virtual presentation platform to perform your dry run. Live or online—practice it. You don't need to rehearse the entire event. What you need to rehearse is your opening, your scene openings and closings, the James Bond opening, your key differentiators, and any specific requirements from the prospect. These are the roman numerals of your outline, and that's what you need to go over—not all the other supporting points.

Use Pareto's Law as a guiding principle: 20 percent of what you present and show in the meeting is going to make up 80 percent of the client's decision. So that 20 percent would include the items mentioned above. You're not going to guess the 20 percent perfectly; no one does. But you *should* have enough knowledge of the prospect at this point, and enough insight into your competition, to have a pretty good idea of what that 20 percent might be. And if you're going to do a dry run, that's the 20 percent you need to be rehearsing.

What we see happening way too often across the globe is that rehearsals are a walkthrough and a discussion of what somebody's *planning* on showing, rather than live rehearsing. A key aspect of a dry run is that team members go into the role and present as if they're in front of the stakeholders—they're just in front of the rest of the team instead.

But, in a positive organization, this is your opportunity to take risks and improve what will be presented to the stakeholders. If you're going to make a mistake, make it during a dry run, when it doesn't cost anybody anything. This is a perfect opportunity for manager and peer-to-peer coaching.

Is there a lot of risk involved in that? Yes and no. Yes, in the sense that you're in front of your peers and your managers, and that always feels pressure-packed!

This is also the time to discuss team member roles. Determine who's opening and closing the demo or presentation, who's opening and closing which scenes, and who takes what type of questions or objections. For example, if a team member is in front of the stakeholders doing a presentation on a solution area, and somebody asks a question that has to do with price, the prospect is naturally going to ask whoever's in front of the room. That team member may not be the right person to answer that question. So make sure you've discussed ahead of time who is assigned to answer different categories of questions or objections.

BORING BUT IMPORTANT STUFF

This might seem boring, but it's important: have a checklist for prep. This should include a list of equipment, the right adapters, network or internet access (if needed), etc. It should also include questions to ask: what is the Wi-Fi situation? Are we going to have to deal with a firewall? What's our backup situation if that goes down? Whose phone are we going to pair with if that happens? Will you need sound if you plan on playing videos? Is there a white board in the room? Is there a projector in the room? Create a checklist for your own needs, and triple check *everything*.

PREPARING THE PROSPECT

We find it helpful to send the prospect pre-demo presentation videos that provide service overviews and key value propositions. You might also consider sending a company overview video. This helps introduce your company and what you'll be demonstrating, in a video that never has a bad day. It provides star power for the people who are on the videos, which builds credibility.

Send these videos to your sponsor. Ask the sponsor if they could have the executive send it to all the stakeholders. The executive sends it out and says something like, "We're investing a lot in these meetings and demos coming up. Vendor X has asked that we send this out ahead of time. Please watch this ahead of the demo."

If your sponsor convinces the executive to send out the playlist of videos with a note like the one above, you're tactically piggybacking on that executive's authority. Ultimately, this establishes differentiation before your team even shows up in the room. Again, the videos you send are probably going to be more overview-oriented, so you won't have to cover the same content at the opening of your presentation. You don't have to spend fifteen or twenty minutes going over your company and through the overview portions of your solution. Depending on the opportunity, you might even send a video of the James Bond portion of your presentation ahead of time. One of the biggest challenges for key, in-person events is running out of time. This practice creates time!

THE STAND UP, SIT DOWN TECHNIQUE

Jennifer, the product expert, is in front of the room demonstrating the company's software to a group of stakeholders. The demo is going great! She is demonstrating a point of sale retail system and has been setting the stage to show how the flexible pricing formulas in the software eliminate costly errors.

This is all-important to several of the stakeholders. She has the audience's full attention and is steadily moving them toward her objective of convincing the prospect that their value proposition is supported by the software. Suddenly, Robert, the account executive (and Jennifer's teammate), interrupts from the back of the room. "Jennifer, I think this would be a great time to show how the information you're working with impacts analytics and is immediately available for social analysis purposes."

Everybody shifts their attention from Jennifer and the all-important pricing flexibility to Robert and the equally important sales analysis functionality. Unfortunately, Jennifer hadn't planned on demonstrating social networking analytics because the prospect was, prior to this interruption, more interested in other areas of the software. Not anymore! In an instant, the momentum Jennifer has been building stops.

And so it goes with teammate interruptions during many demonstrations. It's as if we're wrestling for the attention of our audience among ourselves, which has a negative impact on your prospect, your message, your professionalism, and the prospect's experience. In this situation, Jennifer has a right to be frustrated. She worked hard to prepare, plan, and orchestrate her demo, only to be derailed at an epic point. Now she has to shift gears, even though she was so close to wrapping up the pricing with a powerful scene closing. Worse yet, she appears unprepared to the prospect because the sales person couldn't resist interrupting.

Is Robert to blame? Not entirely. After all, he's the account executive and has ultimate responsibility for the deal. Jennifer has some responsibility as she should have made it clear to Robert prior to the event that her demo plan did not include social analytics. If you assume discussed and planned on social analytics, there's a better way for team communication.

A BETTER WAY

Jennifer and Robert need an agreed upon procedure for teammate communication and coordination during their demonstration. Creating one can be surprisingly easy. Consider the following illustrative analogy: Improvisation has always been a mainstay of live performances for rock bands. If the lead guitarist is "on fire" and the band wants her to "take it," they have a simple hand signal that every musician knows. The band lead simply points at her with the signal to improvise a solo. If she wants to "shake off" the solo, she simply signals back by inconspicuously shaking her head. The "big hit" signal is used when a song is about to end. This is done by the lead guitarist raising the neck of his guitar or the drummer raising their sticks high. The final chord in the song comes when the guitar neck or the sticks come down.

Teamwork during a demonstration should work much the same way. Robert, the salesperson's, first task is to signal Jennifer that he has something to say. Then he must wait patiently for Jennifer to reach a logical transition point, at which time she can give him the solo.

TEAMWORK ROOM POSITIONING

Your first consideration for managing your room as a team is the seating position of your team members. If Jennifer is in the front of the room presenting, Robert must be positioned toward the back so he has a view of all the stakeholders. Robert should be constantly scanning the stakeholders for expressions that suggest confusion, disagreement, or enthusiasm. These visual cues provide Robert the information he needs to determine if he should act on what he is seeing.

Illustration 12.1 – Teamwork Room Positioning

SIGNAL

Assume for a moment that you are a salesperson observing a demo. The best way to signal your teammate during a larger demonstration is to simply stand up (as if you are stretching your legs) and wait for your teammate to make eye contact, acknowledging they know you have a comment to make.

Illustration 12.2 – Standing Signal

Some people advocate a small wave of the hand, but there are two reasons that doesn't work very well. First, it's much easier for your teammate to notice a big motion, like someone rising out of a chair, as opposed to a small motion like a hand waving. Second, if you start making obvious gestures, your audience will notice and immediately shift their attention away from the presenter.

Sometimes your teammate will be so intent on what they're doing that they won't notice you stood up. Assuming you're seated toward the back of the room (hint, hint), create some motion to make it easier for them to see you. Slowly move from one position in the room to another. If that doesn't get their attention, you can do a small hand wave—and the audience isn't likely to see it, because you're in the back of the room.

This technique means members of your demonstration team can't congregate in the back of the room, because the presenter won't be able to distinguish between when a teammate has a comment to make and when someone is just stretching their legs. Also, it's distracting to both the audience and the presenter when people stand in the back of the room. You can't control if your prospect does this, but your demonstration team never should.

WAIT

When your teammate (the presenter) makes eye contact with you, that's your signal that they recognize you have a comment to make. However, they're still in control. The band is in the middle of a measure, so the soloist would wait for the turnaround heading for the chorus or the bridge. The same holds true in a presentation. You must respect that. Remain standing and wait for them to finish the sub-scene or scene. This is important for a couple reasons:

1. They're probably setting the stage to show something important. Until they have closed the sub-scene or scene, interrupting them is going to be counterproductive.
2. Most presenters have transition points in their material to keep themselves organized. By signaling and waiting to make your comment, you're helping them remain organized and professional in the delivery of their material.

PASS THE LEAD

When the presenter finishes their thought process, they'll pass the lead to you. Two things need to take place to do that:

1. The presenter must make a "transition statement," which informs the audience that you're taking control. In our Jennifer/Robert example, this could be as simple as saying, "Robert, would you like to make a comment?" When this happens, your audience will naturally shift their attention from the presenter to Robert (you).

2. If you are going to speak for a while, the primary presenter needs to sit down or move off to the side. This ensures that the audience's attention doesn't shift back to that individual until you finish your comments. In other words, you have the solo until you pass it back.

To return control to the primary presenter, the signal can be completely silent. You simply move back to your chair and sit down. Alternatively, you can make a transition statement ("Jennifer, what's the next thing you have for us?") as you are sitting down. This passes control back to the presenter.

OBSERVATIONS

As we've watched colleagues use this technique, there are a couple of observations we found particularly interesting. First, it's very easy for an audience to focus their attention when only one person is standing. It's difficult for them when two or more are standing. Don't confuse your audience by putting the burden on them to figure out whom to pay attention to. If you have the lead, stand. If you don't have the lead, sit down.

Second, it's surprising how many times I've seen somebody stand up to signal they have a comment, only to sit down before the lead is passed to them. Why? Because the person about to interrupt realized that they no longer needed to say anything. Sitting down before being recognized by a teammate is its own signal. When this happens, the presentation continues on a smooth and uninterrupted path.

OTHER USES

The Stand Up, Sit Down technique will prove effective at other times during demonstrations, presentations, or key client meetings. Here are a couple examples:

A QUESTION OR CONCERN FROM STAKEHOLDERS

If you're participating in a client engagement, but aren't actively presenting, one of your responsibilities is to observe the audience for questions or concerns. Confused looks, frowns, or an exchange of glances are all signs that someone has a question or concern, but for whatever reason is not sharing it (shy, doesn't want to look foolish, etc.). It's your job to bring the question to the attention of the presenter. How? Use the Stand Up, Sit Down technique using these three steps:

1. Stand up to get the attention of the presenter.
2. When they pass you the lead, make a transition statement that brings the question to their attention ("Jennifer, I believe Andy had a question about the price matrix.")
3. As soon as Jennifer addresses Andy, sit back down so the question is directed to the presenter, not you.

This is important. Because the question probably relates to the material they're covering, the presenter is more than likely the best person to address the question. Most importantly, if you start answering too many questions, you'll undermine your teammate's credibility. This is particularly true if you are more experienced than the presenter. Unless you want to take over the presentation, have the question directed to the presenter. If they don't know the answer and want your help, there are ways of asking for it (see below).

DON'T PUT A TEAMMATE ON THE SPOT

Here's the scenario: You are Jennifer. You're demonstrating your pricing formulas. Somebody asks you a question about rebates, and you have no idea how to answer their question. Luckily, Judy (a senior product manager) is in the room because she's next up on the agenda. You look at her and ask, "Judy do you know the answer to this question?" Unfortunately, Judy relies on one of her subject matter experts for rebate expertise—and that person isn't in the room. She can't answer the question.

Good thing you brought in the "expert," right? You look unprepared, and momentum is lost. Here's a more effective way to handle the question:

First, make eye contact with Judy. This signals her that you don't know the answer to the question and you need her help. (Adding a bit of a pained look can sometimes be helpful!) If she stands up, that signals she can answer the question. Without saying a word, sit down and let Judy answer the question. If Judy doesn't stand, you know she can't answer the question. Don't make the situation worse by putting her on the spot.

Instead, restate the question and get as much information as you can. Then acknowledge that you aren't prepared to answer the question right now. Indicate that during a break, you'll do some research, set up some data to show the capability, whatever is needed. Then, have the salesperson (not Judy) write down the question so the person who asked it can see the question is being noted. (You don't want to direct the room's attention to Judy when she doesn't know the answer.) This will assure the stakeholders you'll get back to their question, allowing them to move on.

WHAT ABOUT THE "PARKING LOT"?

Often, "parking lots" are promoted as a giant white board Robert will get up and walk over to, and write all the questions that couldn't be answered. Consultants love this. We hate it! The last thing you want is a large list of questions sitting in front of the stakeholders throughout your entire presentation (and long after you leave). It's a billboard announcing everything you *don't* know!

Instead, have Robert write the stakeholders' questions on a notepad in front of him, and make sure the audience knows he has the "parking lot." When the presenter says, "Robert, would you please make a note of that question?" the stakeholders will glance back to Robert. Then they can mentally release the question, because they know he wrote it down.

AN ACTION PLAN

It's simple, isn't it? Stand up when you have something to say. Wait for your teammate to pass you the lead (transition statement). Sit down when you're not addressing the audience. The key is making sure your teammates understand how to use the technique. Here are some suggestions to help make that happen:

1. Call a fifteen-minute meeting of your entire demonstration team prior to the demo. Don't forget to include specialists who are often called on to address unique situations, even though they don't participate in many demonstrations. Examples include support, implementation, or other technical personnel you bring in to answer functionality questions.
2. Explain the Stand Up, Sit Down procedure. Have copies of this overview available for all to read.
3. Include the three situations discussed above (a teammate who wants to make a comment, somebody in the audience who has a question, and the proper way to get a teammate's help in answering a question) in your dry run.

4. Remind everybody that congregating in the back of the room is not allowed. If they're going to be in the room, they have to be sitting down when they're not addressing the audience.

SMALLER AUDIENCES

Some presentation venues don't lend themselves to a teammate standing up in the room. This can be caused by a smaller room, smaller audience, or unusual room configuration. Don't worry—this technique stills works with minor modifications. You simply need to replace standing up with another signal.

For example, assume our sales representative, Jennifer, is presenting at the front of a conference table, and Robert the sales representative is seated toward the back. If Robert has something to say, he simply takes his pen out of his pocket and places it toward the center of the table directly in front of him. That movement in a smaller setting is almost as effective as Robert standing up, but not nearly as disruptive. If Robert decides not to say something after all, he simply retrieves his pen and Jennifer never calls on him. Alternatively, Robert simply pushes himself six to twelve inches back from the conference table.

VIRTUAL PRESENTATIONS

Most virtual presentation platforms have a private chat capability. This private chat can work well for signaling a teammate that you want to take lead or that a stakeholder has a question or concern (assuming you're in the room with the stakeholder). We are not fans of using the private chat option. Too many times, we've seen a salesperson think they are sending a private chat when, in fact, the chat is going to everyone. This can be incredibly embarrassing.

A better alternative is to use instant messaging in another application or with your mobile device. The key is the presenter must pay attention to the second application or their mobile device. This means you are now relying on your presenter multitasking. As you learned earlier in the book, multitasking is a myth and made even more difficult in this type of high-pressure situation.

The best option is to use your webcams. In our example, if Robert has a comment he'd like to make, he turns on his webcam. This is Jennifer's signal that Robert has something to say. Jennifer then simply completes her sub-scene or scene and passes Robert the lead. Once Robert takes the lead, Jennifer goes off camera and puts Robert in full-screen mode. When Robert is done, he simply turns off his webcam and Jennifer takes back the lead.

TECHNICAL PROBLEMS

They happen! When there's a technical problem, you want to have a plan ready.

Establish with the salesperson several subjects they could talk about while the lead presenter recovers from the technical problem. Everyone has a role and a plan for these incidents, so you're not dealing with interpersonal confusion on top of your technical issues.

It's rare that you can't recover at all from a technical problem, but have a backup plan just in case. Plan some screenshots or a video that you can pull up separately. Or, worst case scenario, allow for a break. Just ask everyone to grab some coffee and return in fifteen minutes; most people understand when things like this happen, and there aren't many situations you can't take care of in fifteen minutes.

MISTAKES TO AVOID: CRIME FILES

Remember our two characters: Robert the salesperson and Jennifer the demonstrator. In the middle of the demo, Robert properly attracts the attention of Jennifer using the teamwork methods mentioned earlier in this chapter. He says, "Hey, Jennifer, why don't you show them..."

Jennifer hasn't talked about this with him ahead of time. This isn't a planned interjection. This is just something Robert saw last week, and he wants Jennifer to show it.

Lead presenters and demonstrators hate this. They hate, hate, *hate* it! Their mind is not on that solo right now. Now Jennifer has to think, "Well, how do I show that?" More often than not, Jennifer is not ready to show it. Her product isn't configured to show that right now, she's not set up to show it, or she doesn't know how to show it. This happens all the time. When we train on teamwork we often roleplay this with the audience and, tongue-in-cheek, tell the demonstrators in the audience to answer, "Robert, that's a great idea! Why don't you come up here and show that to everybody? I'm just kidding. Robert, do me a favor. . ."

The simple answer to this is for Robert to write down his idea and approach Jennifer during the break. Jennifer can then evaluate whether she has the capability to address his suggestion. The role of the team is to provide value, not to cue Jennifer.

Even if a salesperson thinks Jennifer should show something, he shouldn't interject without communicating the need away from the audience's eyes and ears. Jennifer's focused on presenting the solution, making sure it works right, and expressing the benefits in the best way possible.

Don't ever ask a question of anyone on your team unless you know they know the answer. Don't surprise anybody on your team while they're presenting.

PILING ON

Piling on is a common crime, and it comes from a good place. Picture the Football World Cup: Costa Rica scores a goal on Mexico. What happens? The person who made the goal does the knee slide and the team all piles on, right?

If Costa Rica has an 8-1 lead and score, they don't pile on. It doesn't mean they're not proud of their teammate; it means they know when to stop celebrating.

In a demo, teammates may sometimes feel like every time a really good point is made by a team member, they have to pile on. They have to add on to it. They have to say something on top of what the person just said. This habit is incredibly annoying to the audience. Robert makes a really good interjection, and then Jennifer says, "That's a good point, Robert. I'll add to that..." Then the manager goes, "Yeah, that's a great point, team. You know what else?" Everybody's got something to say.

THIRTEEN
SERIOUSLY

Hey, we're in sales! Do you really think we are going to publish the unlucky number 13?

FOURTEEN
AN ILLUSTRATION OF A MODERN RULE OF 24 STORY

A MASTER OF 24 THROUGHOUT THE SALES PROCESS

Imagine a B2B sales opportunity being run by a sales engagement team where every member is a Master of 24. Masters who anticipate modern stakeholders' wants and needs. Witness how your masters could do just that at every step in the B2B sales process.

Illustration 14.1 — Sales Process

Day 1, 8:42 AM — Lead: The efforts of your digital marketing team were rewarded with a "marketing qualified lead." That is someone who has responded to a marketing campaign or website inquiry by providing your firm with their "real" contact information. The business development representative (Aaron) on your sales engagement team examined the lead and recorded a quick, personal video that identified this individual by name, responded on video to their requests, and included two videos from your library that provided more details per the stakeholder's request.

Day 1, 9:18 AM — Lead Response: The moment the stakeholder began watching the videos, Aaron was notified and timed their telephone follow up within five minutes of the notification. He reached the lead's voicemail and left a message to please look for an email request for a meeting. The request included a live link to the business development rep's calendar. The stakeholder clicked on the link, was immediately presented with Aaron's calendar, and secured a fifteen-minute initial meeting. The meeting was scheduled as an online event, and the stakeholder's calendar included a link to the virtual meeting.

Day 1, 10:47 AM — Qualification (eDiscovery): Before the meeting, Aaron performed eDiscovery and examined the stakeholder's LinkedIn page, company website, and other public sources as a basis for foundational information that he could use in the meeting. He learned that this individual was an individual contributor, located in Chicago, Illinois.

Day 1, 11:00 AM — Qualification: At the agreed upon meeting time, the stakeholder and Aaron clicked on the meeting link and were immediately connected. Aaron was on camera with a virtual background that included the stakeholder's logo. The stakeholder immediately recognized Aaron as the same person in the personal video, and the rep immediately engaged her in a discussion of her needs and budget, and probed for other stakeholders. The stakeholder shared what she knew and asked Aaron if he could schedule a demo of the solution at one o'clock that afternoon with her and her boss. Aaron agreed, and they ended the web meeting. Aaron sent her a new meeting request with a new link.

Day 1, 11:46 AM — Qualification (continued): Aaron received notification of another viewing of the videos he sent to the stakeholder. He clicked on the link and noted that the entire personal video was viewed along with 80 percent of the second video. The third video wasn't watched. Upon further examination of the viewing analytics, he saw that this viewer was in San Jose, California.

Day 1, 1:00 PM — Qualification (continued): Aaron started the web meeting on camera with the same background and was pleased to see the original stakeholder and her manager on camera as well. He focused his questions on the likely needs of the manager based on her position on the Value Pyramid. These questions went beyond product and service needs.

He asked questions that uncovered what the solution would do for their productivity, and how they were planning on measuring it. After each question, the rep performed a short, responsive demo in conjunction with what he had learned during the questioning. He then asked the managing stakeholder financial qualification questions. Aaron concluded the discovery and responsive demo by explaining that he would be getting other sales engagement team members immediately involved.

The virtual meeting concluded with Aaron suggesting next steps, and the manager transparently stated that there would probably be five to seven people involved in the evaluation and selection. The manager agreed to get Aaron a list of their needs and the individuals involved by close of the next day's business as they were on a "tight timeframe."

Day 1, 1:30 PM — Qualification Follow-up: Upon concluding the virtual meeting, Aaron forwarded this qualified lead to Tonya, a strategic account representative. Next, Aaron made a personal video for the prospect that introduced their stakeholders to Tonya, summarized his understanding of the prospect's needs, and outlined the next steps in the process. He also included product and impact videos in a playlist and sent a link to those videos to the stakeholders who had attended the virtual meeting. He encouraged both stakeholders to share the link with the other stakeholders who would be involved in the decision.

He summarized his notes in the company's CRM system. All stakeholder video viewing history was automatically recorded in the CRM. Within thirty minutes of sending the video link, Aaron, Tonya, and the CRM system received multiple notifications of video viewing activity from the additional stakeholders.

Day 1, 2:30 PM — Prospect Handoff Meeting: Aaron, the business development rep, led an internal virtual meeting with Tonya. A virtual meeting was necessary, as the two of them were geographically dispersed. During the meeting, Aaron reviewed the brief history of the prospect along with their video viewing analytics. At that point, Tonya began organizing the team of people she would need to involve with the prospect and the team's steps going forward.

Day 2, 8:48 AM — Solution Definition: Tonya, along with Sharon, her direct manager, had a virtual meeting with Karen, the solution consulting manager, to determine the appropriate solution consultant for this opportunity. Karen determined that Mark was the best fit. Tonya and Karen then added Mark to their virtual meeting to review the history of the opportunity, which included CRM notes, eDiscovery, and video viewing analytics. Tonya then shared her recommended strategy. The three of them refined the strategy. At the conclusion of the internal meeting, Tonya created a personal video that introduced next steps to the prospect's stakeholders and offered a link that they could click to schedule a group meeting between Tonya's team and the stakeholders.

Day 2, 11:14 AM: The majority of stakeholders watched Tonya's personal video and clicked on the scheduling link. The next meeting was set for the same day at 3:15 PM.

Day 2, 3:15 PM — Solution Definition/Presentation: As the sales engagement team (Tonya, Sharon, and Mark) awaited the arrival of all the stakeholders to the virtual meeting, Mark (the solution consultant) engaged everyone by asking them, as they joined, to chat about what they were hoping to learn from the session. All the stakeholders responded, and Mark, based on their responses, had an immediate picture of who the staff level members were versus managers versus executives. In other words, at the beginning of the meeting, Mark completed his Value Pyramid.

As Tonya introduced each member of the sales engagement team, they appeared on camera. They understood that today's B2B stakeholders want information quickly, but they also want a personalized approach. Appearing on camera made each team member appear authentic, and it created a personal connection.

Immediately following introductions, Tonya took control and asked the executive stakeholder if they were prepared to make a decision today based on the information they would receive at this meeting. Tonya, Sharon, and Mark discussed and debated ahead of the meeting what to float to the executive for next steps in the sales process. They made a unanimous decision to ask the executive stakeholder for decision as a next step.

The executive stakeholder responded that they still had one more solution to review, after which they would invite the vendor of choice to make a final presentation at the corporate headquarters. Tonya acknowledged the executive stakeholder's plan and began her formal opening to the meeting. The team decided to use discovery for their limbic opening, so Tonya began by reflecting a brief summary of her understanding of what her team had already learned.

At strategic points in that reflection, Tonya called stakeholders by their names based on where they were in the Value Pyramid to validate her understanding. Sometimes a stakeholder provided clarification to what Tonya reflected. At the conclusion of each element of discovery, she summarized it on the electronic white board, using the touch screen on her laptop. Mark noted all their clarifications, as he would be addressing their needs in a moment.

Upon completing her summarization, Tonya said, "I want to turn the first few minutes of our meeting over to Mark. He's going to show you what we believe to be one of the most impactful areas of our solution based on our brief understanding of your needs." Mark came on camera, Tonya went off camera, and Mark began delivering his James Bond sub-scene. Upon completing the opening tell, Mark moved immediately into the "show" portion of the sub-scene by going off camera, which automatically displayed the solution in full-screen mode. This portion of the demo was specifically directed at the executive stakeholder who was on the call, and Mark's closing tell drove the benefit up the Value Pyramid to an executive-style benefit.

After completing his James Bond sub-scene, Mark began exploring the additional pains, needs, and wants of the stakeholders. Rather than spilling out ten minutes of "here's what we understand," he explored each item individually and responsively demoed that area of interest.

For each item he explored, he sought verification of his understanding. When they disagreed with one of his assumptions, he asked leading, funneling, open-ended questions about the topic and engaged the stakeholder seeking clarification. But he didn't stop there. For each leading, open-ended question, he also asked about the impact of resolving their need, pain, or desire and how they might measure the success.

After each series of questions, Mark appeared on camera and discussed the solution. He would then go full screen and off camera to present the solution using the tell-show-tell technique. Mark's demo was highly responsive to what he had just validated or clarified in his discovery on-the-fly that preceded the demo sub-scene. Each demo sub-scene included operational benefits for the staff, and he directed those benefits by calling staff members by their names, while delivering benefits.

He then delivered management benefits by first using the manager's name—ensuring that, if they were multitasking, they would switch tasks and focus on what he had to say. Finally, when the timing was suitable, he delivered executive-style benefits to the executive stakeholder.

This agile approach to discovery on-the-fly, responsive demonstrating, continued for forty-five minutes. Throughout the meeting, Tonya, Sharon, and Mark worked flawlessly as a team by communicating with each other through back channels and turning on their camera during interactions with the stakeholders.

When the sales engagement team saw that there were ten minutes left in the meeting, Tonya turned on her camera. This was her signal to Mark that it was time to summarize the meeting and establish next steps. Tonya's summarization included a return to their discovery findings and then a slide that highlighted a case study of a customer similar to the prospect. It contained compelling before-and-after productivity improvements.

While delivering the improvements, Tonya engaged Monique, the executive stakeholder, by using her name. Tonya asked her, "Monique, which of these metrics do you find most compelling?" Monique replied, "Probably their year-over-year growth, although I don't know how realistic that is for us." Tonya acknowledged Monique's interest and observation, but knew at this point she had created anchoring with her year-over-year metric.

The meeting concluded with Mark summarizing action items that required further research. He committed to having a response to them by the end of the day.

Day 2, 4:15 PM: After the stakeholders left the virtual meeting, Tonya, Sharon, and Mark stayed in the virtual meeting for their regular feedback and coaching session. Sharon led the discussion by asking Tonya for positive feedback on what went well during her portions of the meeting. Sharon and Mark both commented on what they thought Tonya did well. Sharon then asked Tonya what she'd do differently, after which Sharon and Mark made one suggestion. They repeated this same coaching process for Mark.

Day 2, 5:15 PM: Mark, after brief research, found answers to the stakeholders' questions. During the research, he found a document that supported one of his follow-up items. The other follow-up item required a brief screen recording. Mark created the screen recording using the tell-show-tell technique and uploaded that recording to their video automation platform.

He then recorded a personal video that addressed the open items and directed their attention at the conclusion of the personal video to watch the follow-up video of the screen recording he had created. He also told them to read the document he attached. He used a video automation platform to send the videos and documents to each of the stakeholders, while copying Sharon and Tonya on the communication.

Day 3, 10:33 AM: Throughout the evening of Day 2 and the morning of Day 3, the video automation platform delivered notifications and analytics of each stakeholder's consumption of the follow-up items. Tonya predicted, before she heard back from the client, that they would have been selected as the finalist, simply based on the heavy consumption of Mark's follow-up by all but one stakeholder.

Day 3, 1:49 PM — Customer Commit: Tonya was elated to receive the news that her prediction was correct. The sponsor stakeholder notified her that they had been selected as the vendor of choice, but there was work to be done. The sponsor went on to explain that the stakeholders would be compiling a final list of questions and requirements for her and her team to address in person, in three days' time. He went on to explain that all the stakeholders were going to be at corporate headquarters on that day for their annual planning meeting. He was confident that Tonya and her team could work out the logistics.

Tonya deliverd the good news to Sharon and Mark, along with the challenging news that she and Mark would need to travel to the prospect's offices. But with the initial value of the contract being high and the automatic renewals being significant, she believes it is a justified the expense. Sharon agreed, but made the decision that Tonya and Mark would effectively run the meeting and land the contract.

Tonya responded to the sponsor that she and Mark would be able to meet on that date, but asked that the list of requirements and questions be delivered by the end of the following business day. Tonya also asked that the proposal and agreements be reviewed by the appropriate individuals before the meeting. The sponsor replied to Tonya's email immediately and confirmed that Tonya's requests would be met.

Day 4, 2:32 PM: Tonya received notification from the sponsor that the executive stakeholder would be prepared to address the proposal during their visit and that their legal team had no issues with the agreement. Tonya was thankful that her organization simplified their legal agreements! The sponsor also included the list of questions and requirements submitted by the stakeholders as an attachment to his email. Tonya immediately forwarded this email to Sharon and Mark.

Mark and Tonya met to go over the two-and-a-half-page list of questions and requirements. There was a total of 24 items on the list. Mark needed clarification on eleven of the items and requested such from the sponsor in the hopes that he would receive that clarification before their on-site engagement. Mark began preparing for all twenty-four items, placing priority on those that did not require further clarification. He then prepared for the items that did require clarification, knowing that if he did not receive a response from the stakeholders, he would need to perform discovery on-the-fly and responsive demonstrating or white boarding during the meeting.

Day 5, 11:00 AM — Dry Run: A rehearsal turns a great presentation into an excellent presentation. Tonya and Mark knew this, so the evening before their meeting they met in the lobby of the hotel for a dry run of key elements of the presentation. Tonya decided that for her limbic opening she would use an illustrative analogy, comparing a farm-to-kitchen meal delivery service to the strategic initiative of the executive stakeholder.

She presented her opening to Mark, and it was excellent. Mark rehearsed the demo of his James Bond opening sub-scene, and three challenging requirements the stakeholders had requested, using the tell-show-tell technique with visually supported benefits. Mark and Tonya both agreed that the "show" portion of the follow-up sub-scenes covered multiple topics, so they worked on simplifying those sub-scenes.

Day 6, 9:00 AM: (On-site at prospect's location) As feared, Mark didn't receive clarification on any of the eleven items. He had prepared as completely as he could with under-known information. As he addressed the items needing clarification, he would need to pause the solution presentation, perform discovery on-the-fly, and be responsive and agile.

Upon arrival at the prospect location, Tonya and Mark were led to the conference room that contained everything they needed for their discussion and solution presentation. Like all master presenters, they brought their own projector and supplies, including fresh white-board markers, just in case the room fell short of any of those items. Ahead of the meeting, they had sent the sponsor a checklist of items they would need for the presentation, and he had assured them everything would be in place.

As the stakeholders entered the room, Tonya and Mark greeted them. Many of the stakeholders commented on how they felt like they already knew them, based on the videos they sent and the virtual meeting they had led.

The sponsor opened the meeting by formally introducing Tonya and Mark. Tonya had the foresight to provide the sponsor with an index card that contained key information about Mark and herself, which she wanted the sponsor to convey. Tonya knew this helped reaffirm their credibility; and because the introduction contained a personal element about each of them, the sponsor was also able to create a sense of individuality and authenticity for both of them.

Tonya started the presentation with a picture of a beautifully prepared meal of fresh ingredients. She briefly told the story of her kitchen, which she had remodeled even though she didn't like to cook. For a working professional, shopping, assembling recipes, and all the ingredient preparation wasn't compatible with her lifestyle.

Within sixty seconds of starting the story, Tonya connected the story to what her prospect was trying to accomplish. She used the phrase, "It reminds me of. . ." to make a natural connection. The stakeholders loved the analogy, and it was a great launching point for Mark to step up and introduce how the day's session was much like Tonya's challenge. Tonya took a seat toward the back corner of the room so she could watch the room's reaction throughout Mark's presentation.

Mark took the front of the room and stood while presenting. He began using the James Bond technique and demonstrated the one item on the list the executive stakeholder would most care about. When he finished, he built the benefits up to the impact this capability would have on the managers.

At this point, Tonya inconspicuously rose from her chair, which caught Mark's eye. This was their silent signal that Tonya had something she wanted to say. Mark turned to Tonya and said, "Tonya, did you have something you wanted to say?" to which Tonya replied, "Yes, thank you, Mark. Monique (the executive stakeholder), what Mark just showed you will help you maintain complete visibility of your business, ensuring you achieve your strategic initiative of double-digit, year-over-year revenue growth. From what you've seen, are you comfortable with this solution's ability to deliver that information to you at a moment's notice?" Monique replied, "I'm comfortable—as long as everyone in the room does their part to ensure the information that produces this dashboard is accurate and timely."

At this point, Tonya thanked Monique, and then turned to the room and said, "For the remainder of our time, Mark will show you how you'll be comfortable inputting information, which will provide Monique the accurate and timely information she needs. Sound good?" To which everyone provided an affirmative nod. After they responded she simply sat down, and Mark seamlessly took over the presentation and moved on to his first item.

The third item was the first one Mark needed further clarification for. He blacked out the screen, stepped away from his portable, table-top podium and said, "For this next item, I have a few questions to ask before presenting the solution. Who in the room requested clarification on this item?" Two people raised their hand. Mark then engaged the two people in discovery on-the-fly.

He learned more about their current situation and what they desired. He also learned the business impact of solving the challenge this item caused, as well as the impacted business metric. He made a note of terminology they were using that was unique to their organization.

Once he had gathered the information he sought, Mark went to the white board and performed a responsive tell-show-tell illustration and explanation of the solution, using the prospect's terminology, and he confirmed that the solution was viable and that the impact was achievable and measurable.

The solution presentation, discovery on-the-fly, and responsive demonstrating continued for another thirty minutes. At the conclusion, Mark turned the presentation over to Tonya. Tonya addressed the room with a slide that contained two pictures. One was of her remodeled kitchen with her holding up a completed meal.

Below it was a headline that contained the name of the prospect dated one year in the future and read: "XYZ achieves double-digit YOY growth." She explained that while she was able to accomplish something she wasn't that thrilled about (cooking), she'd come to enjoy it after making the changes in her kitchen. She then compared it to the prospect's situation: "Change is hard. And while your goals are challenging, they are achievable. Let us be your farm-to-table partner and help you achieve your goals—and enjoy the work along the way!" Tonya then turned to Monique, who'd never left the room, and asked if she and Mark should step out of the room while the team made their final decision. Monique said, "Yes, I'd appreciate that. Once we are finished, I'll meet you outside my office."

Tonya and Mark went to Monique's office and told her executive assistant, "Monique asked us to wait here for her. She said she'd only be a few minutes." The EA offered them coffee or water, and they took a seat.

Ten minutes later, Monique appeared and asked them to join her in her office. The three of them sat at her small conference table, and Monique gave them the news that, pending negotiations, they would be moving forward. Monique asked for a substantial discount to do something immediately; otherwise, they would need to wait until the end-of-the-quarter results.

Tonya explained that waiting on quarter-end results would mean delaying the project, and doing so would have a cascading effect on their ability to leverage the solution to achieve double-digit growth. She said, "I know from experience that trying to catch up on a goal is one of the hardest things there is to achieve in business. It puts extra pressure on everyone and negatively impacts morale. It sounds like we have an opportunity to help you and your team get ahead of the goal versus working from behind."

Tonya sought and received Monique's agreement, and then offered a reasonable concession. With Monique's approval in hand, Tonya made an adjustment to the financial elements of the contract on her mobile device, and the agreements were instantly re-delivered to Monique, who then electronically signed them.

Tonya and Mark thanked her, left the building, and initiated a virtual meeting from Tonya's mobile device in front of the prospect's headquarters. They included Aaron the business development representative, Karen the solution consulting manager, and Sharon, the sales manager, and delivered the good news. Everyone was on camera smiling and shouting. Sharon ended the meeting with a confident, "Nice work, everyone! It's going to be a great year!"

FIFTEEN
ORGANIZATIONAL EXECUTION

The new battlefront across companies is the fight for the best customer experience—bringing the B2C experience to B2B, and meeting the new reality of client expectations, this is the Rule of 24. We have a saying at our firm: "The landscape is evolving; if buyers are waiting for you, you're losing!"

Integrating all aspects of this trend in your sales organization will help you rush ahead of the competition, stay more relevant with stakeholders who demand a B2C experience, accelerate your sales cycle, and differentiate your team from the status quo.

That's why you're reading this book, after all. Now it's time to link all that to organizational execution. In this chapter, we will help you understand what it takes to execute Rule of 24 in organizations of every size.

ORGANIZATIONAL CHARACTERISTICS

Generalizations can be dangerous, but the simplification they offer can be extremely helpful. When it comes to organizational execution, we categorized sales engagement teams into five types of sales organizations, based on the number of sales engagement team professionals and geographic markets served:

1. **Enterprise** — 1,000 or more globally deployed sales professionals
2. **Mid-Market** — 100 to 999 sales professionals deployed globally and on a single continent
3. **Small** — 6 to 99 sales professionals deployed globally and on a single continent
4. **Startup** — 1 to 5 sales professionals in a single country.
5. **Resellers** — Various-sized organizations that are owned and operated independently of your company

Many of you reading this may find that your sales organization includes characteristics from multiple sales organizations described above. For example, many of our mid-market style clients service major markets with the direct sales organization, and developing markets with resellers. If you believe your sales organization adopts the characteristics of multiple categories from above, read each section that applies to you and execute accordingly.

One fact is consistent across all entities—the dynamics of the Rule of 24 aren't just a future prediction, they are today's reality. In fact, even in the time between the conceptualization of this book and its final print, we saw clients embracing a need for this change at an accelerating rate. Regardless of what size organization you lead, you need to secure budget, arrange resources, and begin training for the reality of today's B2B stakeholder. You need to own, execute, and fund these elements as part of your client engagement model.

Be aware that marketing may press you on your Rule of 24 initiative, as they are responsible for brand consistency and typically responsible for video content development and video automation tools. Take the example of a demo video content—your sales engagement team needs authentic content that is rapidly and efficiently developed by subject matter experts at a low cost. Remember the description of a demo video from Chapter 6:

> *"Unlike an impact video that relies on graphics, imagery, and keywords for its primary visual support, demo videos rely on the actual products, services, or solutions. A stakeholder watches a demo video to get a sense of using the product, service, or solution."*

Marketing lacks the core expertise to rapidly and efficiently produce a video that gives a stakeholder a true sense of using your product. Their creative team will likely argue for sophisticated graphics and imagery to produce this style of video. They will also need to solicit members of your team as the talent for the video production because your team members have the tribal knowledge of how your products, services, or solutions are authentically demonstrated or presented in the "real world." Additionally, marketing will likely go outside your organization and hire a video production firm to produce each demo video. Do you see the problem? Blown budget, long production times, and slick videos that don't pass the authenticity requirements of stakeholders. It is the antithesis of "scalable."

Solving this challenge within your sales team may seem overwhelming to you, as it was for many of our clients. The sales leadership of one of our enterprise clients recognized the need for owning the responsibility of their Rule of 24 initiative. They began the project with impact and demo video production with our assistance. After training them on our content development strategies and techniques, they were soon producing demo videos from concept to completion in four hours. That is the type of speed and scalability you need in your organization.

In this chapter, we offer Rule of 24 considerations that are consistent across all categories of sales organizations. We will describe how your sales team (large or small) can apply Rule of 24 tools and techniques as an opportunity progresses through a typical B2B sales process. Finally, we will provide suggestions that are specific to each type of sales organization from the list above.

CLIENT ENGAGEMENT MODEL CONSIDERATIONS

Start by looking at your current client expectations. Today's prospects aren't patient. They are researched and experienced, so once they engage with one of your sales engagement team members, they expect to move at their pace. Are you meeting the clients where they are? How would you assess your sales engagement team's speed to the client? How about the quality of those engagements? Speed and quality should be defined by what the client wants and expects, not necessarily by your measurements.

For example, if you get to a client within 2.4 seconds and they want to see the product, is your team member prepared to make that interaction effective? Are your salespeople demonstrating your services? If so, have you equipped your salespeople with the training and tools they need to make their demonstrations successful? What is your sales and subject matter expert structure? Are you structured to take advantage of the Rule of 24 in every step of your sales process? The answers to these questions are the first steps toward understanding your ideal client-engagement model.

Are you a new company or division that wants to think about your ideal model? Perhaps you are a mature company in an industry that is evolving, and you need to transition over time to a Rule of 24 organization.

From a tools perspective, what tools do you already have? What tools are you using to engage with clients? Are they helping you differentiate from your competition? Do your tools help drive efficiency and speed in sales cycles? While it is commonplace for sales organizations to leverage tools like CRM and marketing automation, most are ignoring the power of video.

Are you leveraging demo videos today? Do the videos adhere to the practices we described in this book? Are your demo videos too long? You would be shocked to find out how many companies use thirty- to sixty-minute-long webinars as demo videos. While that may be effective for a stakeholder who needs education, it will not work for stakeholders who want quick information. Studies by YouTube and others show that after four minutes of viewing, the drop off rate is substantial. Not the result you desire with digital engagement!

Consider your personnel. You may have excellent tools and video content, but if your personnel are not properly trained, they might accelerate your sales cycles off a cliff due to poor practices.

Reflect on your team's client interactions. Do you believe they have a quality that embodies Rule of 24 techniques? Do you have a small number of "A" players and inconsistency with the remainder of the team?

To help you answer all those questions and simplify the enablement of the Rule of 24, we produced this summarized list of considerations for all B2B sales organization sizes and types:

›   **Personal video training** — Every member of your sales engagement team should take advantage of personal video to set the context for the information they include in their communication with stakeholders. Personal video should be used throughout your sales process and in multiple client engagement opportunities. Refer to Chapter 7 for more information. Educate your team on the simple production and execution of impactful personal videos.

› **Demo style videos** — These are videos that focus primarily on your product, service, or solution for visual support. These should be single sub-scene videos of two to four minutes in length. If your subject matter experts begin demos with a brief product overview, create those demo videos first. Next, consider the areas of your product that have the highest impact or generate the most questions, and create your impact-style videos. The benefit statements in impact-style videos are from the bottom of the Value Pyramid. Refer to Chapter 6 for more information.

› **Impact style videos** — Assign your subject matter experts the task of determining the value your services offer to stakeholder managers. These are the benefit statements for the middle of the Value Pyramid (managers). Refer to Chapter 6 for more information.

› **Explainer style videos** — Designed for the very top of the Value Pyramid. They provide executive-style benefits and value for your products, services, or solutions. Marketing will lead in the creation of these videos. Production quality should be high. The benefits these videos provide help an executive achieve their strategic initiatives. Refer to Chapter 6 for more information.

› **Video automation platform and training** — Proper dissemination of videos of all types requires a sales-specific video automation platform. Your marketing organization may already have a video automation platform, but it is likely optimized for marketing motions, rather than sales motions.

You will not want to use a marketing-optimized video automation platform any more than marketing would want to use your CRM system for managing their marketing campaigns. Find a video automation platform and company that suits the specific needs of your sales organization. Make sure your video automation platform provider offers services that help create sales-specific video content and training, and that ensures effective interactions during each sales motion. At 2Win, our video automation platform isn't differentiated by technology but, rather by our expertise.

If you want to bring content creation in-house, choose a provider that is willing to teach your team their Rule of 24 content creation methodologies. Refer to Chapter 5 for more information.

› **eDiscovery tools & procedures** — eDiscovery is an essential element of a successful Rule of 24 sales organization. You should formalize the tools and procedures you want your sales engagement team to leverage in each step of the sales process. Refer to Chapter 10 for more information.

› **Virtual presentation and demo/presentation training** We dedicated an entire (meaty) chapter to this medium because of the criticality of improving your team's skill with this essential Rule of 24 tool. Don't fall victim to assuming your team knows how to drive stakeholder engagement with your virtual presentation tool. Commit to an honest appraisal of your team's ability to be effective in this medium, and train your team accordingly. Refer to Chapter 9 for more information.

› **Discovery on-the-fly training** — You will find that if your team becomes experts at discovery on-the-fly, their effectiveness in demos and presentations with all styles of stakeholders will reach new heights. Discovery on-the-fly is the new reality in a Rule of 24 world. Embrace this fact, and train your team to be masters at this crucial skill. Business development reps, client success specialists, salespeople, subject matter experts, and leaders will all benefit by improving this skill. Refer to Chapter 10 for more information.

› **In-person demonstrating/presenting training** — Similar in importance to discovery on-the-fly training is the ability for every member of your sales engagement team to perform a planned and responsive demonstration or presentation using the techniques we described in Chapter 9.

These include strategically planned events that are structured using a movie view of a demo or presentation. During the client engagement, your team must also be able to responsively demo or present with discovery on-the-fly information. Refer to Chapter 10 for more information.

› **Coaching** — Commit to having your sales leaders formalize Rule of 24 assessments for every member of their team. Different roles require different assessments, which are crucial to successful improvement plans. Train your leaders on our coaching methodology found in Chapter 10, as this will help you rapidly improve your sales engagement team. Refer to Chapter 11 for more information.

› **Teamwork execution** — In team-based events, you always want the whole to be greater than the sum of its parts. Teamwork is essential in accomplishing that goal. Have your sales leaders assess how effective your sales engagement team members work together in every style of client engagement. Improvement in this area requires a commitment by every team member to agree to practice and execute the strategies we described in Chapter 12.

APPLICATION OF TOOLS AND TECHNIQUES THROUGHOUT A TYPICAL SALES PROCESS

Below is a summarization of the application of Rule of 24 tools and techniques in each stage.

Illustration 15.1 – Typical Sales Process

BUSINESS DEVELOPMENT

This step in the sales process consists of lead generating activities that originate from a combination of marketing activities (e.g., marketing campaigns, click through ads, etc.) and direct activities by your business development representatives or salespeople.

As a sales leader, your primary focus should be on effective responsiveness. For example, if a stakeholder clicks on a chat button, is your team prepared to effectively respond to a request for a demo of your product, service, or solution? Below is a summary of content, tools, and sales enablement activities to consider in the business development stage of the sales process:

› **Discovery on-the-fly** — Crucial to understanding a stakeholder's interests and needs. The same techniques are used for performing prospect qualification.
› **eDiscovery tools & procedures** — If you have dedicated business development reps performing outbound activities, the formalization of your eDiscovery tools and procedures results in higher quality leads.

› **Virtual presentation and demo/presentation** — Business development reps should be prepared and effective at initiating a virtual session with a stakeholder if the opportunity presents itself. They will, of course, be limited in what they can demonstrate or present. Make them masters of this medium (i.e., use of the camera, driving engagement, etc.).

› **Responsive demonstration or presentation training** — Depending on your organization, you may allow business development reps to demo or present responsively after performing discovery on-the-fly. They should be trained in these skills.

› **Video automation platform** — Business development reps should always have the video automation platform open in a window. They need to be ready to send a playlist of videos to a stakeholder as the opportunity is qualified. Remember, a recorded demo or presentation never has a bad day. Your business development reps should be highly proficient in the strategic use of your sales-optimized video automation platform. Creative business development reps also use the platform for sending a personal video after the initial contact. The platform is also used for disseminating personal, explainer, impact, or demo videos to stakeholders.

› **Explainer videos** — Needed if the stakeholder is a senior executive or wants to share the benefits of your products, services, or solutions with a senior executive.

› **Impact style videos** — Needed if the stakeholder is a manager or wants to share the benefits of your products, services, or solutions with their manager.

› **Demo style videos** — Needed if the stakeholder wants to view videos to get a sense of using your product, service, or solution.

> **Personal video** — When a business development rep completes a call with a qualified stakeholder, their follow-up activity should include a personal video to the stakeholder, which sets the context for the additional videos and/or materials included with the communication. The personal video is assembled into a playlist with the additional content in the video automation platform. If your business development rep performs discovery and a demo during their initial interaction with the client, personal video can precede those activities to establish rapport before the activity and set expectations. The rep can also summarize the next steps in your process.

SOLUTION DEFINITION

In this stage, a more complete picture of the solution is defined through formal discovery with stakeholders. You may recall that our research indicates fewer stakeholders are accessible for discovery, which leads to "under-known" information. In less complex, shorter sales cycle opportunities, where the prospect has performed significant research and decided what they need to see in a demo or presentation, the solution definition step can be difficult to secure.

When this step can be secured, we find that most of our clients involve subject matter experts at this stage to perform the discovery. Below are the elements of the Rule of 24 that should be considered during this stage:

> **Discovery on-the-fly** — These are crucial skills needed during this step. Your team may have a framework for formal discoveries, but your team needs to be prepared to gather additional information using this discovery methodology.

› **eDiscovery tools & procedures** — Necessary for researching stakeholder roles, strategic initiatives, and financial size and viability.

› **Video automation platform** — In this step, the platform can be used by your team member to send a personal introduction and set the expectations for the discovery. This video can be shared with everyone scheduled for discovery. Post discovery, a summary of understandings can be provided in written or video form and sent to the stakeholders.

› **Explainer videos** — These videos can be shared with the executive stakeholders during this step to reinforce the value of your products, services, or solutions.

› **Impact style videos** — Post-discovery, these can be valuable for "pre-suasion" (see Chapter 10) of the manager stakeholders.

› **Demo style videos** — Needed if a stakeholder requires a more complete understanding of how the products, services, or solutions operate before they see a demo or presentation.

› **Personal video** — Perfect for reflecting a summary of what your sales engagement team member learned in their discovery, and sets the context for other assets being sent in follow-up to discovery.

SOLUTION PRESENTATION

In Rule of 24 opportunities, this critical stage of a B2B sales process can happen at the same time as the first four steps. However, for most B2B opportunities, solution presentations are usually a formal stage. Virtually every strategy and technique we've discussed in this book applies during this stage, as is evident by the list below:

- › **Video automation platform** — This tool plays a key role as you enter and exit this stage of the sales process. This is an opportunity for your subject matter experts to create a halo effect for the live event (virtual or in-person). This effect is created by a trained and strategic subject matter expert who takes the time to perform pre-suasion by using the video automation platform to disseminate a personal video that sets the context for the demo or presentation.

- › **Explainer videos** — Needed if a senior executive is planning to attend the demo or presentation. The explainer video is included in a playlist of videos. The playlist also contains a personal video that reflects the salesperson's understanding of the strategic initiative your products, services, or solutions will support. The personal video precedes the explainer video and is sent most frequently to the sponsor stakeholder, who then forwards it to the executive.

- › **Impact style videos** — These videos are intended for the stakeholder managers and preceded by a personal video that, like the explainer video, sets the context for the manager stakeholder value that will be presented during the demo or presentation.

- › **Demo style videos** — These videos are intended for stakeholder managers and staff and preceded by a personal video that sets the context for the live event. We've seen great success with clients that send demo style videos ahead of the solution presentation.

- › **Personal video** — These short, crisp, personal videos set the context for other assets being shared with stakeholders. Additionally, a personal video in the minutes or hours following the solution presentation is an impactful follow-up for addressing open questions and responding to additional requests made during the event. Doing this is a great way to shorten sales cycles, because no follow-up meeting is required and stakeholders can consume this critical content on their own schedule.

› **eDiscovery tools & procedures** — Your subject matter experts will leverage what's been learned in all prior stages.

› **Discovery on-the-fly** — Execution of discovery on-the-fly is a pillar to a successful solution presentation in Rule of 24 opportunities. Your sales and subject matter experts must be trained and proficient in this key skill to successfully navigate demanding stakeholders.

› **Virtual presentation skills** — Many Rule of 24 opportunities move so quickly that your team's only option is to perform the solution presentation virtually. Therefore, they must be trained and highly proficient at driving engagement as described in Chapter 8.

› **Responsive demonstration or presentation skills** — It is crucial that your team excels at using the movie view structure (see Chapter 4) for the planned portions of their demo or presentation. However, they need to be agile enough to leverage what they will learn during the event for unplanned areas of the presentation using discovery on-the-fly and responsive demonstrating and presenting.

› **Teamwork** — You will likely need a team of people to address all the stakeholders' needs in larger opportunities or complex demos and presentations. Whenever more than one person is involved in an event, your sales engagement team members must have flawless teamwork skills. Anything less than that risks a disjointed appearance and a negative customer experience. The team should also be performing dry runs for key opportunities to ensure an effective event.

CUSTOMER COMMIT

Convincing the customer to select you as their vendor of choice in Rule of 24 opportunities is an essential step toward securing the client. Ideally, your salespeople are attempting to secure the customer commitment at every stage in your sales process. However, if the executive stakeholder isn't present and the selection team is still evaluating other options, the executive stakeholder will delay a commitment. If a delay takes place, there are many tools, skills, and strategies your sales engagement team can leverage that help secure a customer commitment:

› **Video automation platform** — In the solution presentation stage, we discussed the use of the video automation platform as a follow-up mechanism for your subject matter expert. Your team should also leverage the video automation platform in the commit stage. The videos your subject matter experts send through your video automation platform will differ in both audience and content from what a salesperson will send in the commit stage. The primary use of the video automation platform in this stage is to secure executive approval of your products, services, or solutions.

› **Personal video** — In this personal video, your salesperson, sales manager, or senior executive will provide a targeted message that reflects the executive stakeholder's strategic initiative, as well as how your products, services, or solutions will help them achieve that initiative. The CEO of one of our clients has made this a regular practice. She sends her personal video directly to the prospect's CEO and finds that the prospect CEO shares it with the entire executive team. As an executive in your organization, this is your opportunity to demonstrate Rule of 24 leadership across your entire team.

> **Impact videos** — If you have impact videos that align with the needs of the manager stakeholders, your salesperson or subject matter expert can send those as value reinforcement to the managers along with a personal video that sets the context for the impact videos.

> **Demo videos** — In the commit stage, demo videos should only be sent if the stakeholders make a specific request. Demo videos at this stage are more likely to confuse the stakeholders, slow the deal down or—even worse—create a "no" decision. Make sure your sales engagement teams understand this to prevent stalled or lost business.

> **Virtual presentation skills** — Don't be misled by the title. It's unlikely that the members of your sales engagement team will perform a presentation at this stage. However, you or they may use your virtual platform to connect with the executive stakeholder in an attempt to secure the commitment. If the executive stakeholder requests an executive summary presentation, make sure the presentation is only three or four slides.

Your team should be prepared to be nonlinear in their presentation, as executive stakeholders often interrupt presenters and want their questions answered immediately. The web camera is very important here, as executives continue to place value on a sense of relationship. Your team should be proficient in the use of the virtual white board for impromptu illustrations or an interactive ROI discussion.

CONTRACT

At this stage of the sales process, Rule of 24 tools, skills, and strategies continue to apply. It has been our experience that issues with agreements fall into two categories: business issues and legal issues. Witness how your team can continue its momentum by leveraging the following:

› **Virtual presentation skills** — Your virtual presentation platform can share a screen or an application. If you are prospect's legal representation has redlined your contract, share that redline in the virtual meeting. You will find this improves the efficiency and clarity of contract negotiations, as everyone is reviewing the same information at the same time. Also, plan on using webcams as part of your teamwork. For example, if your legal representation is discussing a business issue—and you want to address that business issue—you simply turn on your camera, which is the signal to your legal representation that you have something to say.

› **Teamwork** — Good teamwork at this stage can significantly collapse the time between commit and contract. Your legal manages the legal issues, and your executive leadership manages the business issues. Your organization may have a different approach. Regardless of your approach, teamwork between legal and business should be planned ahead of the virtual meeting with the prospect.

› **Discovery on-the-fly** — These skills apply to contract negotiations. In the contract stage, discovery on-the-fly serves the purpose of deriving a full understanding of a contract issue and creating a sense of active listening. These skills are the basis for good negotiations.

› **Responsive demonstrating and presenting** — Like discovery on-the-fly, the skills we discussed in responsive demonstrating and presenting apply to contract negotiations. No, your team won't be performing a demonstration or presentation during this stage. However, the skill of taking what you just learned during discovery on-the-fly and applying that to how you respond to a contract issue will accelerate the completion of the agreement.

CLIENT SUCCESS

The vast majority of B2B organizations recognize the value of client success for retaining customers, renewing recurring revenue, and increasing the footprint of their products, services, and solutions. Witness how Rule of 24 tools, skills, and strategies will improve the performance of your client success team:

› **Video automation platform** — Client success should utilize the video automation platform to share personal, explainer, impact, and demo videos to existing clients.

› **Tutorial videos** — These videos are short pieces that focus on common tasks and use cases for your products, services, and solutions. These videos provide existing clients with value by helping them expand the use of your products, services, or solutions.

› **Explainer videos** — Needed when client success needs to reestablish the value of the solution to secure a renewal. These videos are also useful when the client has changed senior management, as they will reestablish the value of your products, services, or solutions.

› **Impact style videos** — If client success is trying to expand the use of your products, services, or solutions to additional divisions, departments, or users, these videos help the stakeholder managers understand the value.

› **Demo style videos** — In some organizations, client success is measured by product utilization. Demo style videos can help increase product utilization by expanding the use cases of the product and the benefits associated with the expansion. These videos can also be used in conjunction with impact videos when client success is trying to expand the footprint of the products, services, or solutions into other divisions or departments.

› **Personal video** — As in a normal sales process, client success uses personal video to set the context of their communication.

› **Virtual presentation skills** — Client success will make extensive use of your virtual meeting platform and, as such, should be highly proficient at the skills described in Chapter 9. This team must learn how to drive engagement while operating in the platform to drive a high level of customer experience.

› **eDiscovery tools & procedures** — Your client success team should be skilled at researching information on clients through internal and external sources.

› **Discovery on-the-fly** — This skill should permeate across your client success team as part of their client communications. Understanding the needs and motivations of clients is central to motivating them to expand the use of your products, services, or solutions.

› **Responsive demonstration or presentation skills** — This team should be able to perform quick demos and presentations as determined by their discovery on-the-fly. The cost/benefit of improving their skills versus always relying on someone from your subject matter expert team or services team to perform the demos and presentations is tremendous. Additionally, their self-sufficiency leads to faster decisions and shorter sales cycles.

EXECUTION BY ENTITY TYPE

For the purposes of simplicity and brevity, we will provide execution recommendations in this section as if your entire organization fits a single enterprise type. If you believe your organization has a mixture of enterprise types due to acquisition, structure, or strategy, consider applying our suggestions to each type.

LARGE COMPANIES

At the large enterprise level, it's highly likely that you already have various types of video assets. Most were probably created by marketing. Larger organizations often professionally produce video content through a combination of in-house resources and outside contractors. But remember, there's a big difference between marketing videos and videos created specifically for use in sales motions. Marketing videos are intended for interest generation in marketing campaigns, in conjunction with marketing automation tools like Marketo, HubSpot, and Pardot. They're often considered "top of funnel" content. Videos intended for sales motions are designed to move prospects through the sales funnel. They are much more subject-specific and intentional.

As an enterprise company working to drive efficiency, execution of Rule of 24 might be an examination of how you can be more innovative with tools, people, or processes. Building efficiency is exactly what we've been talking about in this book! Seek to understand where you can you connect the Rule of 24 into your current systems and/or processes. For example, we have enterprise clients who successfully interact with marketing, and frankly, marketing's helped fund some of the demo and impact videos, in cooperation with the subject matter experts from the sales organization. At the risk of overstating our opinion, the sales organization and their subject matter experts need to own their video content—such as personal, impact, and demo videos.

As a large enterprise, you might think you don't have room in your kitchen for any more tools. When it comes to kitchens, it would be a beautiful thing if you had a single appliance that could do it all. Let go of that dream. There are times when you need a juicer, not a blender. If you're planning on getting healthy by using a blender to make your cold-pressed juice, you'll be disappointed. As a result, you might give up on eating "healthy."

Don't create a problem for your sales organization by trying to "get by" with tools that aren't designed for sales motions. Your sales engagement team will give up on their Rule of 24 health kick.

If you want to be an organization that's agile, that adapts to customers' current desires for styles of communication, you'll need certain tools to accomplish that goal. These tools are investments. The tool we see missing the most from enterprise style organizations is a video automation platform. The tool we see most underutilized is the virtual presentation platform.

To simplify your planning and budgeting, we've developed checklists for every style of organization. Here's the enterprise checklist:

Tool, Skill, or Process	Budget Considerations
Rule of 24 Rapid Response: As an enterprise company, you probably have a global presence. Consider having subject matter experts available for all time zones. If a stakeholder clicks on the chat box on your website, a business development team member either performs the demo or hands it off to the subject matter expert.	You only need a slice of each subject matter expert's time every week to make this a reality. No additional cost to you, with potentially great return.

eDiscovery: Determine what information is most valuable for opportunity planning. Consider tools that uncover stakeholder, company, and strategy information.	Free tools only get you so far. eDiscovery tools that provide 360 degree views of stakeholders and companies have broken into the market. Look beyond LinkedIn and publically traded-based information sources like Hoovers, to the startup community.
Virtual Meeting Platform: You've probably been using the same platform for years. You may even think the decision to change platforms is out of your control. It's time for you to resist. Find the platform that embodies the features (chat, white board, camera, virtual background, etc.) we've presented that will help your team embrace Rule of 24.	Skype For Business may be included in your Microsoft Office licensing, but is it what you really need? New tools have hit the market and they are reliable, modern, and help your team drive engagement. Pricing is usually flexible and competitive with legacy products.
Virtual Meeting, Demo and Presentation Training: To improve the prospect experience, it is imperative that you focus attention on improving the existing quality of virtual demos and presentations. Hire a firm that combines an understanding of the needs of B2B demos and presentations, with expertise in driving interaction and engagement in a virtual setting.	Costs can be reduced if the training firm offers a "flip-the-classroom" approach to this training. This approach provides your team members with self-paced training, combined with virtual-meeting.

Video Automation Platform: YouTube is chaotic, and marketing-oriented platforms don't provide what your team needs for sales motions. You'll likely need to have content developed, so choose a partner who is an expert in video content for sales motions.	A single, Rule of 24 opportunity that avoids the cost of travel for a post-solution presentation follow-up meeting pays for the platform for 10 sales engagement team members. The cry for more sales tools is never-ending, but this one is pivotal to a successful Rule of 24 sales team.
Video Content Development: Inventory and categorize your video content as Explainer, Impact, or Demo. Determine the subject matter experts who should be the writers and talent on the videos. For your first set of videos, partner with a content developer for assistance.	Your first sets of videos will be more expensive due to the use of contracted services. Pick a provider that will teach you their methods. Make sure the videos are built using our methodology for maximum effectiveness. Over time, bring these services into your team by allocating existing subject matter expert resources to building videos. You won't need any additional budget, but you'll receive immense multipliers.
Personal Video Training: You'll be surprised at how reluctant a salesperson will be to creating personal videos. Remove their reservations by training them on the right method from the start. Your video automation platform provider should offer these services. Make sure they train according to what we've described in Chapter 7.	This project provides maximum benefit for minimal cost. Absolutely essential for an effective Rule of 24 rollout.

Video Automation Use Case Education: Our experience in working with enterprise clients is they tend to use video automation for a single use case such as business development. Resist that tendency. Over time expand contextually relevant use cases (e.g. send a pre-demo overview, post-demo follow up, etc.) on an internal basis through the use of the platform.	Miminal budget consideration. Have your subject matter experts assigned to video content creation produce a use case example for every 3 videos produced.
In-Person Masters & Teamwork: Have your salespeople and subject matter experts trained on discovery on-the-fly and responsive demonstrating and presenting. Include objection and question handling in this training.	Your team members need training for this new reality. High-demanding stakeholders force the best talent into bad habits such as data dumping the features of your products, services, or solutions versus following our methodology. Reduce your expense by making this training initially available to your top performers.
Coaching: Drive consistency and steady improvement through team assessments and coaching. Invest in your managers so you can receive a multiplier across all team members. This will also help you weed out low performers and low potential.	This training must include Rule of 24 assessments and coaching training with real world scenarios. Travel and time out of the field can be mitigated by virtual follow up for coaching practice sessions.

Client Success: These teams have become large and global. Determine which members drive revenue, and train according to Rule of 24 elements that are most applicable.	Your client success leadership team can minimize expenses by prioritizing team members who have the greatest impact on recurring and account expansion revenue.

Illustration 15.2 — Rule of 24 Execution Checklist – Large Enterprise

MID-MARKET ENTERPRISES

If you're a mid-market enterprise, your focus is probably high-growth and scale. Many mid-market companies have multiple product lines, vertical markets, and a global reach. In this size organization, it's essential to determine which tools, strategies, and processes you will use to engage with clients quickly, to deliver the information the way they want it.

For companies that are trying to determine how to scale and become an enterprise-sized organization, your strategic initiative is likely to be to grow quickly and profitably.

As your company grows, you may be establishing or growing positions in sales enablement and sales operations. Their role is to determine how to help the sales model become more efficient and effective, so you can achieve your strategic initiatives—whether that's with processes and people, or technology and tools. Collaborate with them to establish your Rule of 24 execution priorities. You're their customer; tell them what you need!

For example, we have a U.S.-based client worth more than $150 million. They're in high-growth mode, with a goal to be at $300 million within the next five years. But how? One of their initiatives was to reassign their top subject matter expert, to create an optimal Rule of 24 client experience through multipliers, like video content creation and video automation.

If you have a similar resource, you might consider a similar initiative. This doesn't mean adding headcount, it means rearranging priorities and responsibilities. Consider shifting one of your subject matter experts to the creation of video content and the video automation initiative. In this way, you'll receive a true multiplier of her talents.

Here's your mid-market checklist:

Tool, Skill or Process	Budget Considerations
Rule of 24 Rapid Response: As a mid-market company you probably have a global presence, but leverage partners in much of the world. Consider having subject matter experts available for your major markets. Perhaps start with North America and EMEA. If a stakeholder clicks on the chat box on your website, a business development team member either performs the demo or hands it off to the subject matter expert.	You only need a slice of each subject matter expert's time every week to make this a reality. No additional cost to you, with potentially great return.
eDiscovery: Determine what information is most valuable for opportunity planning. Consider tools that uncover stakeholder, company, and strategy information.	Free tools only get you so far. eDiscovery tools that provide 360 degree views of stakeholders and companies have broken into the market. Look beyond LinkedIn and publically traded-based information sources like Hoovers, to the startup community.

Virtual Meeting Platform: Consider re-evaluating your current platform. Find the platform that embodies the features (chat, white board, camera, virtual background, etc.) we've presented that will help your team embrace Rule of 24.	Skype For Business may be included in your Microsoft Office licensing, but is it what you really need? New tools have hit the market and they are reliable, modern, and help your team drive engagement. Pricing is usually flexible and competitive with legacy products.
Virtual Meeting, Demo and Presentation Training: To improve the prospect experience, it is imperative that you focus attention on improving the existing quality of virtual demos and presentations. Hire a firm that combines an understanding of the needs of B2B demos and presentations, with expertise in driving interaction and engagement in a virtual setting.	Costs can be reduced if the training firm offers a "flip-the-classroom" approach to this training. This approach provides your team members with self-paced training, combined with virtual-meeting live coaching.
Video Automation Platform: YouTube is chaotic, and marketing-oriented platforms don't provide what your team needs for sales motions. You'll likely need to have content developed, so choose a partner who is an expert in video content for sales motions.	A single, Rule of 24 opportunity that avoids the cost of travel for a post-solution presentation follow-up meeting pays for the platform for 10 sales engagement team members. The cry for more sales tools is never ending, but this one is pivotal to a successful Rule of 24 sales team.

Video Content Development: Inventory and categorize your video content as Explainer, Impact, or Demo. Determine the subject matter experts who should be the writers and talent on the videos. For your first set of videos, partner with a content developer for assistance.	Your first sets of videos will be more expensive due to the use of contracted services. Pick a provider that will teach you their methods. Make sure the videos are built using our methodology for maximum effectiveness. Over time, bring these services into your team by allocating existing subject matter expert resources to building videos. You won't need any additional budget, but you'll receive immense multipliers.
Personal Video Training: You'll be surprised at how reluctant a salesperson will be to creating personal videos. Remove their reservations by training them on the right method from the start. Your video automation platform provider should offer these services. Make sure they train according to what we've described in Chapter 7.	This project provides maximum benefit for minimal cost. Absolutely essential for an effective Rule of 24 rollout.

Video Automation Use Case Education: Our experience in working with mid-market clients is they tend to use video automation for a single use case such as business development. Resist that tendency. Over time expand contextually relevant use cases (e.g. send a pre-demo overview, post-demo follow up, etc.) on an internal basis through the use of the platform.	Miminal budget consideration. Have your subject matter experts assigned to video content creation produce a use case example for every 3 videos produced.
In-Person Masters & Teamwork: Have your salespeople and subject matter experts trained on discovery on-the-fly and responsive demonstrating and presenting. Include objection and question handling in this training.	Your team members need training for this new reality. High-demanding stakeholders force the best talent into bad habits such as data dumping the features of your products, services, or solutions versus following our methodology. Training your sales engagement team is expensive, but for mid-market companies, the cost outweighs the benefits gained.
Coaching: Drive consistency and steady improvement through team assessments and coaching. Invest in your managers so you can receive a multiplier across all team members. This will also help you weed out low performers and low potential.	This training must include Rule of 24 assessments and coaching training with real world scenarios. Travel and time out of the field can be mitigated by virtual follow up for coaching practice sessions.

Client Success: These teams have become large and global. Determine which members drive revenue, and train according to Rule of 24 elements that are most applicable.	Your client success leadership team can minimize expenses by prioritizing team members who have the greatest impact on recurring and account expansion revenue.

Illustration 15.3 — Rule of 24 Execution Checklist - Mid-Market Enterprise

SMALL ENTERPRISES

Small, stable enterprises that have carved out their market niche will have their own set of needs to adapt to Rule of 24. In a small organization, talent must be multi-faceted. Each team member often blends roles and contributes in a variety of ways. Why is this important? Because small organizations don't have the luxury of specialization.

For example, your salespeople may not have demo specialists to lean upon. In that case, they need to own the demo or presentation and have the skills and tools to make it highly effective. Tools like a video automation platform, and Rule of 24 skills across multiple roles, creates multipliers. Ultimately, every opportunity counts. Each one can mean the difference between hitting your targets or missing payroll.

Strategic initiatives for this size organization range widely from building the business for an exit strategy to improving profit distributions to the owners. The priority you place on each potential Rule of 24 tool, skill, and strategy are determined by the strategic initiative you plan to achieve.

If improving your profit distributions is your strategic initiative, place emphasis on Rule of 24 elements that decrease your cost of sale or improve your top line revenue. If that is too large, narrow your scope to those that you believe will be the largest contributors to your goals. The following illustration is an example of a simple exercise the ownership and leadership team of a small enterprise can perform on a large white board to help determine your execution priorities:

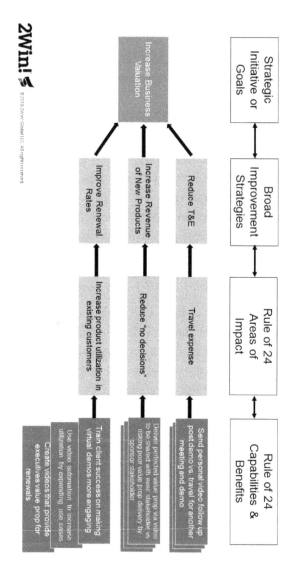

Illustration 15.4 – Small Enterprise Strategic Initiative Map

For our company, we're constantly trying to uncover what we're missing. What's a better way to do something? What will help us deliver a better experience to our clients and do it in a way that's profitable? What will improve profit distributions?

Below is your small enterprise checklist:

Tool, Skill or Process	Budget Considerations
Rule of 24 Rapid Response: Very difficult for small organizations. Consider putting your efforts into video content development and a video automation platform. Train your team members on other elements below.	High cost for small organizations. Probably not worth the expense.
eDiscovery: Determine what information is most valuable for opportunity planning. Consider tools that uncover stakeholder, company, and strategy information.	Free tools only get you so far. Focus on smaller startups that offer a 360-degree view of prospects vs. legacy services such as Hoovers.
Virtual Meeting Platform: For small companies, a quick evaluation of the best new solutions is prudent. You need to drive a great customer experience with a great tool. This is a perfect place to start.	New tools have hit the market, and they are reliable, modern, and help your team drive engagement. Pricing is usually flexible and competitive with legacy products.

Virtual Meeting, Demo and Presentation Training: To improve the prospect experience, it is imperative that you focus attention on improving the existing quality of virtual demos and presentations. Have the team attend training with a firm that combines an understanding of the needs of B2B demos and presentations, with expertise in driving interaction and engagement in a virtual setting.	Have your team attend an "open workshop," 2 to 3 people at a time. This spreads the expense and lets you see results before committing your team to one approach.
Video Automation Platform: Product expertise in small companies tends to be concentrated with a few individuals. Remove some of that concentration by sending video content featuring your best performers through a sales optimized video automation platform. You'll likely need to have content developed, so choose a partner who is an expert in video content for sales motions.	The cost is offset by the increase in productivity and your team's ability to deliver a customer experience that today's stakeholders really want. Your team will move more business through the sales funnel quicker.
Video Content Development: Inventory and categorize your video content as Explainer, Impact, or Demo. Determine the subject matter experts who should be the writers and talent on the videos. For your first set of videos, partner with a content developer for assistance.	If you already have video production talent in-house, get your first set of videos produced by a firm that has experience with our methods, and produce your own videos afterward. If you don't have that expertise, plan on contracting for these services to avoid additional personnel costs.

Personal Video Training: You'll be surprised at how reluctant a salesperson will be to creating personal videos. Remove their reservations by training them on the right method from the start. Your video automation platform provider should offer these services. Make sure they train according to what we've described in Chapter 7.	This project provides maximum benefit for minimal cost. Absolutely essential for an effective Rule of 24 rollout. This training can all be done remotely at minimal expense.
Video Automation Use Case Education: Our experience in working with small clients is they are constantly seeking new use cases for video. Take advantage of your video automation platform's client success team to help you in expanding the use and success of this tool.	Miminal budget consideration. Your vendor's client success team will assist you for free. They probably offer videos that provide use case examples for dissemination to your team.
In-Person Masters & Teamwork: Have your salespeople and subject matter experts trained on discovery on-the-fly and responsive demonstrating and presenting. Include objection and question handling in this training.	Your team members need training for this new reality. Reduce your expense by initially training only your top demonstrators and presenters at an open workshop.
Coaching: Drive consistency and steady improvement through team assessments and coaching. Invest in your managers so you can receive a multiplier across all team members. This will also help you weed out low performers and low potential.	This training must include Rule of 24 assessments and coaching training with real world scenarios. Assessments are available from us. Enroll in an open enrollment course to reduce expenses.

Client Success: Determine which members drive revenue, and train according to Rule of 24 elements that are most applicable.	Start with video automation platform and personal video training, and then move to in-person masters training to minimize expenses.

Illustration 15.5 — Rule of 24 Execution Checklist – Small Enterprise

STARTUP ENTERPRISES

Strategic initiatives for startups often involve a successful launch that builds immediate momentum or achievement of goals established by your funding sources. Unless your startup is a unicorn, your financial and personnel resources are limited. If you're a startup, you've got a changing environment, changing technology, changing consumer behaviors—you name it.

Many founders are passionate evangelists for their company and solutions. One of a founder's many challenges is the concentration of their knowledge and passion for themselves. This is where execution of certain key elements of the Rule of 24 is extremely valuable. For example, a video content production house, skilled in the development of impact and demo videos, can extract a founder's knowledge and passion for use by everyone in the organization. Add in a video automation platform that supports personal video, and you've created a scalable organization for significantly less than adding one full-time employee.

Embracing video as a part of your go-to-market strategy might also help you go viral. Companies like Dollar Shave Club and Squatty Potty used low-budget, simple videos that went viral—and helped their businesses explode. It didn't take much—a little equipment, a homemade studio, and a focus on videos. And it created their greatest opportunity. This also means leveraging social media, from LinkedIn to Twitter, Instagram, Facebook, and Snapchat.

You may still consider yourself a startup, but you have the resources to staff subject matter experts. In such a situation, we recommend enhancing your video initiatives with Rule of 24 skills training such as virtual engagement, discovery on-the-fly, and responsive demonstrating. As the skills become part of the DNA of the organization, you will differentiate the client experience you deliver with automation and skillful interactions.

Below is your execution checklist for startups:

Tool, Skill or Process	Budget Considerations
Rule of 24 Rapid Response: Not practical for most startups to have a team available 24 hours a day.	Too expensive to contract or staff for this level of service.
eDiscovery: Determine what information is most valuable for opportunity planning. Consider tools that uncover stakeholder, company, and strategy information.	Combine free tools with products like LinkedIn Sales Navigator.
Virtual Meeting Platform: For startups, look for a solution that is extremely easy to use for both you and your prospects. A quick evaluation of the best new solutions is prudent. You need to drive a great customer experience and with a great tool. This is a perfect place to start.	New tools have hit the market, and they are reliable, modern, and help your team drive engagement. Pricing is usually flexible and competitive with legacy products.

Virtual Meeting, Demo and Presentation Training: To improve the prospect experience, it is imperative that you focus attention on improving the existing quality of virtual demos and presentations. The founder or person responsible for sales should attend training with a firm that combines an understanding of the needs of B2B demos and presentations, with expertise in driving interaction and engagement in a virtual setting.	Attend an "open workshop." This is an excellent way to establish your firm's foundational practices for this venue.
Video Automation Platform: Product expertise in startups is almost always concentrated with a few individuals. Remove some of that concentration by sending video content featuring your best performers through a sales-optimized video automation platform. You'll likely need to have content developed, so choose a partner who is an expert in video content for sales motions.	The cost is offset by your ability to scale by reducing your concentration of talent. Video automation will allow multiple individuals in the startup to address the requests of investors, prospects, and customers.
Video Content Development: You probably have an explainer video. You likely need impact and demo videos. For your first set of videos, partner with a content developer to assist.	Plan on contracting for these services to get your key founder messaging into the market as quickly as possible. Only work with agile contractors that can provide good video content for minimal expense.

Personal Video Training: Have your video automation platform partner send you examples of effective personal videos. Practice replicating their approach. Send them examples for their feedback.	Leverage your video automation partner for minimal, if any, expense.
Video Automation Use Case Education: Take advantage of your video automation platform's client success team to help you in expanding the use and success of this tool.	Miminal budget consideration. Your vendor's client success team will assist you for free. They probably offer videos that provide use case examples for dissemination to your team.
In-Person Masters & Teamwork: Your founder or go-to demonstrator/presenter should enroll in an open workshop course to hone these key skills.	Start your business off on a positive path by training for this new reality. Reduce your expenses by attending an open workshop.
Coaching: As you add new members to your startup, coach them from the outset based on criteria set in your assessments.	This training must include Rule of 24 assessments and coaching training with real world scenarios. Assessments are available from us. Enroll in an open enrollment course to reduce expenses.
Client Success: Determine which members secure renewals, and train according to Rule of 24 elements that are most applicable.	Start with video automation platform and personal video training, and then move to in-person masters training to minimize expenses.

Illustration 15.6 — Rule of 24 Execution Checklist – Startups

VALUE-ADDED RESELLERS

The Rule of 24 needs of small enterprises and value-added resellers are very similar. Strategic initiatives, like increasing profit distributions, are common. Broad improvement strategies that positively impact profit distributions, such as improving top-line revenue, increasing renewal rates, and reducing expenses, are also shared. What's different is that a value-added reseller can leverage digital assets, such as impact and demo videos, from their primary supplier—whereas startups must create each of those assets. Depending on the supplier, this can save significant time and expense.

If you are an OEM selling through value-added resellers, it is imperative that you begin producing video content for their benefit and, ultimately, yours. Doing so will minimize variability of messaging across salespeople, and value-added resellers can help your organization achieve multiple improvement strategies.

The content strategy of a value-added reseller shouldn't end with what your supplier provides. What is your value-add? Who in the company is the best at articulating it? Do you have your own products or services that you can capture on video?

Many of the other elements of the Rule of 24 apply, such as your team's ability to be highly effective at virtual events, in-person events, discovery on-the-fly, and responsive demonstrating. In many cases, value-added resellers also have client success that needs Rule of 24 methods.

Here's your execution checklist for value-added resellers:

Tool, Skill or Process	Budget Considerations
Rule of 24 Rapid Response: Very difficult for small organizations. Consider putting your efforts into video content development and a video automation platform. Train your team members on other elements below.	High cost for small organizations. Probably not worth the expense.
eDiscovery: Determine what information is most valuable for opportunity planning. Consider tools that uncover stakeholder, company, and strategy information.	Your supplier may offer tools in this area. Combine free tools with products like LinkedIn Sales Navigator.
Virtual Meeting Platform: For small companies a quick evaluation of the best new solutions is prudent. You need to drive a great customer experience with a great tool. This is a perfect place to start.	New tools have hit the market, and they are reliable, modern, and help your team drive engagement. Pricing is usually flexible and competitive with legacy products.
Virtual Meeting, Demo and Presentation Training: To improve the prospect experience, it is imperative that you focus attention on improving the existing quality of virtual demos and presentations. Have the team attend training with a firm that combines an understanding of the needs of B2B demos and presentations, with expertise in driving interaction and engagement in a virtual setting.	Have your team attend an "open workshop," 2 to 3 people at a time. This spreads the expense and lets you see results before committing your team to one approach.

Video Automation Platform: Product expertise in small companies tends to be concentrated with a few individuals. Remove some of that concentration by sending video content featuring your best performers through a sales-optimized video automation platform. You'll likely need to have content developed, so choose a partner who is an expert in video content for sales motions.	The cost is offset by the increase in productivity and your team's ability to deliver a customer experience that today's stakeholders really want. Your team will move more business through the sales funnel quicker.
Video Content Development: Inventory and categorize your video content as Explainer, Impact, or Demo. Determine the subject matter experts who should be the writers and talent on the videos. For your first set of videos, partner with a content developer for assistance.	If you already have video content from your primary supplier, consider enhancing it with your own video content. Have your first set of videos produced by a firm that has experience with our methods.
Personal Video Training: You'll be surprised at how reluctant a salesperson will be to creating personal videos. Remove their reservations by training them on the right method from the start. Your video automation platform provider should offer these services. Make sure they train according to what we've described in Chapter 7.	This project provides maximum benefit for minimal cost. Absolutely essential for an effective Rule of 24 rollout. This training can all be done remotely at minimal expense.

Video Automation Use Case Education: Our experience in working with small clients is they are constantly seeking new use cases for video. Take advantage of your video automation platform's client success team to help you in expanding the use and success of this tool.	Miminal budget consideration. Your vendor's client success team will assist you for free. They probably offer videos that provide use case examples for dissemination to your team.
In-Person Masters & Teamwork: Have your salespeople and subject matter experts trained on discovery on-the-fly and responsive demonstrating and presenting. Include objection and question handling in this training.	Your team members need training for this new reality. Reduce your expenses by initially training only your top demonstrators and presenters at an open workshop.
Coaching: Drive consistency and steady improvement through team assessments and coaching. Invest in your managers so you can receive a multiplier across all team members. This will also help you weed out low performers and low potential.	This training must include Rule of 24 assessments and coaching training with real world scenarios. Assessments are available from us. Enroll in an open enrollment course to reduce expenses.
Client Success: Determine which members drive revenue, and train according to Rule of 24 elements that are most applicable.	Start with video automation platform and personal video training, and then move to in-person masters training to minimize expenses.

Illustration 15.7 — Rule of 24 Execution Checklist – Value-Added Resellers

ONE MORE TIME! YOUR SUBJECT MATTER EXPERTS OWN VIDEO CONTENT CREATION!

As described throughout this book, your subject matter experts need to drive your video content strategy. Sales leadership and, if in their own department, subject matter experts need to look at the where and the why—where does it make sense to create video content, and why? How will that content be used within the sales process, and who is ultimately going to send the video assets to prospects?

Your salespeople and subject matter experts are the people closest to the conversation. They're right in the middle of it every day. They live and breathe these challenges, these stakeholder demands, these experiences. Through all this, they've learned how to succeed in a variety of different scenarios, including virtual and in-person interactions. They're also closest to the solution. Subject matter experts know the products better than anybody (other than the founder). They live and breathe your products, services, or solutions.

Someone from marketing, engineering, or services delivery hasn't experienced what it's like to live in that style of stakeholder conversation on a daily basis. It really is an ecosystem that you live and grow in, and you learn through it. They have incredible product knowledge, and a fantastic understanding of customer challenges. What are the clients trying to get done? Why are they buying the new solution? Why is a staff stakeholder pressing them on that feature? What are they constantly bringing back to product management and development about what clients are saying they wish they had? Subject matter experts are in the center of every one of those conversations; these are the people who should own your video content for sales motions. With professional assistance and training, they are the talent you need to produce highly effective video content.

RETHINK YOUR SALES MOTIONS

If you are an organization that has not defined a sales process, consider creating one around Rule of 24. This takes some thought and courage. We are asking you to take sales processes that were invented forty years ago, break them, and reassemble them. Take some time to sit down with your executives or team leads and determine how the Rule of 24 changes the typical sales process steps with new or re-engineered sales motions.

For example, when you look at the solution presentation stage (or whatever you call it) in your sales process, you might currently have eight steps a salesperson needs to complete to move from this stage to the next. Rule of 24 may make three of those steps obsolete and introduce a new one. An example of a new sales motion at this stage could be requiring the subject matter expert to send a personal video and demo overview videos ahead of the solution presentation to all stakeholders.

THE ELEPHANT'S IN THE ROOM AND HE'S SITTING ON YOUR COUCH!

Throughout this book, we've provided evidence of the shift in the B2B stakeholder expectations and solutions to the challenges of demanding prospects. We've provided solutions to this new selling landscape that solve many of the issues your sales engagement and client success teams face today. But know that we aren't deaf to the concerns of many executives contemplating these new approaches to modern client demands.

ELEPHANT #1
"What if video automation reduces my sales engagement team's opportunity to have valuable interactions with the stakeholders?"

A big objection we hear about expanding the use of video is that it will supplant valuable conversations and interactions they have with stakeholders. These conversations provide sales engagement teams the ability to, among other things, establish relationships and learn where their differentiators are going to apply.

Video automation, combined with the proper content strategy, will drive *more* conversations with stakeholders. Like it or not, B2B stakeholders simply don't want to talk to anyone until they're done researching. If they're talking to your people, it's because they're really close to buying or because your people uncovered or created an opportunity. Remember the 67 percent of prospects who do the research before you ever have a conversation with them? If your people don't proactively provide them with the content they want and demand, they'll find it on their own (YouTube—the wild west), or worse, they'll give up on you and find what they want through your competitor.

Make sure your team is trained to send videos that guide the process and limit the free thought on the part of 68 percent of stakeholders that leads to no decision. Remember this quote from Gartner/CEB research, *"The biggest challenge for buying groups is not in selecting a supplier, but simply agreeing on a problem and course of action."* Don't let your team leave stakeholders to the whims of their individual interests and the chaos of the internet.

From the moment they contact a member of your team, or your team uncovers the opportunity, the most current and strategic videos that guide stakeholders can be sent. Now your team is managing stakeholder research rather than reacting to poor, dated, uncontrolled content on YouTube. Additionally, your team will receive analytics of exactly what the stakeholder's watched, for how long, and what they shared. Try getting that from YouTube!

When the stakeholders view the curated playlist of videos, your team receives immediate notification of their viewing history. This moment is a great opportunity for your team to contact the stakeholder and engage in a discussion of what they saw and what they'd like to learn more about.

To a stakeholder, the asynchronous nature of receiving videos is exactly what they prefer. No interruptions taking a telephone call. No lengthy emails to scour through or, worse, immediately delete. No meeting to fit into their busy schedule. They consume it when it works for them, and they really appreciate that experience. To a stakeholder, a personal video is better than a telephone call or planned meeting; plus, they get a sense of relationship because of the nature of the personal video.

ELEPHANT #2
There is nothing to prevent a stakeholder from sharing our videos with our competitors.

That is absolutely correct. That is a risk. It is the same risk you have with a stakeholder sharing your proposal, literature, and other information. However, if a sales engagement team member sends videos to a stakeholder using a video automation platform, and the stakeholder shares the video, you can track their shares. With other information you send, it's very difficult to track if they forwarded one of your attachments.

When the team member receives notification of viewing or sharing, they should immediately contact the stakeholder and engage them. The team member should ask them who else is involved in the evaluation and decision, along with the names of the stakeholders she shared the video with.

Have you looked on YouTube lately? Our clients find that much of their so-called private information has been posted to YouTube from all types of sources. Your video automation platform makes it extremely difficult for someone to download your videos and post them on public sites.

The real question to ask is can you afford to frustrate stakeholders, slow down your sales cycles, and risk a competitor offering a better buying experience by not meeting their expectations?

ELEPHANT #3

The sales team has been operating the same way for years. They'll never adopt all this change.

Once again, you are **absolutely correct!** If you try to implement the Rule of 24 en mass, the initiative will crash like the Hindenburg. That's why your leadership team needs to create a strategic map of your current initiatives, prioritize the highest Rule of 24 impact areas, and implement over a timeframe of twelve to twenty-four months.

The success of each stage of the project is predicated on finding thought leadership in a cross-functional group of sales engagement team members. That strategy ensures buy-in from your team members. They need to be interested and believe this approach is going to produce personal results and personal wins. For example, say Sandra is subject matter expert. You assign her to start the initiative by creating four demo videos to replace product overviews in live interactions. The videos are excellent, and with your approval, they are uploaded to the video platform. They're accessible for sales to use, but guess what happens?

The salespeople don't actually use them.

Sandra can't sell the initiative alone. She needs thought leaders like you to get internal stakeholder buy-in by leading Rule of

24 discussions about the sales motions Sandra's videos would benefit from.

Make sure you make the right investments in these initiatives, including assigning the proper number and type of personnel. But don't try to boil the ocean. Nothing will happen. Instead:

› Set a clear strategy
› Identify key sales motions
› Train on tools
› Train on soft skills
› Inspire on the outcomes
› Inspect and hold accountable

FINDING YOUR ROCK STARS

Whether you promote or reassign team members to lead this project, it's a great opportunity to inspire them as agents for change. These team members need to be your evangelists. They need to be solid communicators. They need to have strong communication skills, and they need to be educated on best practice Rule of 24 approaches that meet the current and future needs of your organization.

At the outset, these team members should be seen by their peers as cursors, demonstrating Rule of 24 through leadership to the broader sales engagement team: "Look, this is what we can do with these tools. Look at what this prospect said after they watched my video playlist ahead of a presentation!" Eventually, they become rock stars with their peers. They are the strong face of your organization's new and amazing client experience. It becomes a great way for them to contribute to the organization they're working for and be a part of helping it grow.

INVEST IN COACHING

Coaching is also essential for scaling your team, regardless of whether you're a startup or a large enterprise. But coaching against (or for) what? We encourage you to re-read Chapter 11 on coaching, and pay particular attention to the discussion on assessments. As you iterate Rule of 24 into your organization, have your sales engagement team managers establish simple but effective assessments as a foundation for coaching using the objective methods we describe. If necessary, seek out Rule of 24 experts who can assist you in this critical element of your success.

HOW MUCH TO BUDGET: QUALITY VS. QUANTITY

With an initiative this significant, where does the funding come from? In some areas of the Rule of 24, you're looking for funding for initiatives that have never been funded before. For example, traditional marketing videos are often funded with the marketing budget. The need for impact and demo videos never existed before now. You can try to squeeze some money out of marketing, but don't expect a windfall. You'll probably need to push for funding these projects from your own budgets.

This is new ground. The money for this type of project probably isn't in your current budget, but there are a few ways to get past that challenge. First, consider shifting funds from tired projects, sales meetings, or travel budgets to these initiatives.

Secondly, if you're an organization with a sales enablement department, is there money within sales enablement that you can lobby that leader to prioritize for Rule of 24 initiatives?

Finally, look to marketing for funding certain aspects of the Rule of 24 (e.g., impact video and demo video content development).

Always remember Pareto's principle when it comes to execution. For example, decide to build content for the 20 percent of your products, services, or solutions that generate 80 percent of your revenue. Alternatively, start small and fund the high potential, underperforming products; but don't fund content creation for the 80 percent of remaining products until you drive results for the high priority items.

It's time to change the existing sales paradigm. It's time to acknowledge that stakeholders are now doing their own research. Your sales engagement team needs to modernize the tools, content, and skills that enable stakeholders to discover you as an organization that delivers an amazing client experience.

Give your prospects a brush and a canvas, and they'll paint you a masterpiece. Every opportunity, every interaction you have with them, they're going to paint their own impression of their customer experience.

What do you want that painting to be? If you think about every touch point with your client as an opportunity for them to paint a stroke on the canvas, a Rule of 24 experience will look like van Gough's "The Starry Night." Sticking with dated sales methodologies, strategies, and tactics will look like a bad paint-by-numbers picture.

Today's demanding B2B stakeholder are judging their long-term partnership with your organization by their experiences as they progress through their buying process. Begin executing on Rule of 24 initiatives now, or you risk falling inescapably behind competitors that are inferior in every way—except delivering on the experience.

CONCLUSION

"You never change things by fighting the existing reality. To change something, build a new model that makes the existing model obsolete."
— BUCKMINSTER FULLER

Old world versus new world. Existing paradigm versus new paradigm. The quotes, the lessons from the past, the clever sayings that describe the future are always there to scare you into change. Maybe we're right about the direction in which B2B commerce is headed. The evidence is compelling, and the shift in buyer expectations is real. One thing we know for sure is, B2B buyers are not going to go in the other direction. They won't want their experience to degrade. They won't want to do things slower. Their B2C experiences will continue to infiltrate their B2B expectations.

Denial is not a strategy. But you know that.

Thriving in a Rule of 24 world means embracing this new reality. Innovators will use some or all the tools, strategies, and skills we've described to enhance the client experience. Survivors will only seek training to patch holes in areas like virtual presentations or discovery on-the-fly when they feel real pain. Laggards will embrace denial and slowly fade.

INNOVATORS

The simple recognition that we are replaceable if we don't meet these new client expectations is the attitude of an innovator. These leaders will embrace the challenge of effective, rapid response in Rule of 24 opportunities. They are also realists. They recognize that there will continue to be prospects who seek out new products, services, and solutions using age-old methods. We don't believe for a moment that all opportunities will transition to Rule of 24 in the next five years. But five years is a very long time. Can you afford to wait?

Innovators will seek and implement a video automation platform designed for sales engagement teams that provides them the automation they need to meet modern stakeholder expectations. They will invest in video content that addresses the specifics of their products, services, and solutions, and the impact these solutions will have on manager and executive stakeholders. They will embrace personal video as a means of providing context and value for this new style of client engagement and experience. They'll realize the need to drastically improve virtual demonstrations and presentations, such that the client clicks "leave meeting" with a heightened sense of client experience.

Innovators accept the fact that it will become increasingly difficult to perform formalized discovery on Rule of 24 prospects, and will, therefore, embrace the skills needed to perform discovery on-the-fly during the event, and demonstrate and present in an agile, responsive, and effective manner. They plan and demand excellent team communication in every client-facing opportunity, because prospects are judging their teamwork. And finally, they'll do the work needed to create assessments that address these new realities and commit to coaching to new standards of client experience.

WHAT'S YOUR ROLE?

There are many roles within a company, but each one plays a part in transitioning the organization into Rule of 24 innovators.

If you are in client success, embrace this new level of customer expectations with new tools, processes, and skills that will help you achieve your renewal, maintenance, or usability goals.

If you're in content creation, partner with your subject matter experts and build video content that exceeds the expectations of every type of stakeholder.

If you are a subject matter expert, find the energy to learn these new tools, processes, and skills, and bask in the satisfaction you'll experience when you exceed client experience expectations.

If you're a salesperson, be the face of innovation at every opportunity, and lead your team with excellent communication. Embrace personal videos that enhance the experience and value you provide to stakeholders. Perform eDiscovery and deliver your insights to your subject matter experts ahead of a client-facing event. Finally, have a willingness to meet this style of prospect where they are.

If you're in sales enablement or operations, seek out Rule of 24 tools and training, and then measure the return on investment.

If you're in management, assess and coach your people with renewed energy.

If you're in executive leadership, incorporate Rule of 24 processes in your strategic initiatives and fight for budget.

What once was will never be again. Be a Rule of 24 innovator and win the client experience battle.

ABOUT THE AUTHORS

Robert (Bob) Riefstahl is a keynote speaker, consultant, sales expert, author of the global best-selling book "Demonstrating to Win!". Bob has brought his demo expertise to over half of the top 400 technology companies in the world including firms like Microsoft, Google, IBM, Siemens and Dassault.

Dan Conway spent 20 years in the software and technology industry helping companies and agencies grow their business. Most recently holding a senior executive position for a leading international software enterprise prior to joining 2Win!

Bob is the founding partner, and Dan Conway is President and CEO of 2Win! Global, an international training, consulting and software company specializing in complex product demos, presentations and demo video automation.

www.ingramcontent.com/pod-product-compliance
Lightning Source LLC
LaVergne TN
LVHW091942060326
832903LV00050B/294/J